Applied Theatre: Research

The **Applied Theatre** series is a major innovation in applied theatre scholarship, bringing together leading international scholars that engage with and advance the field of applied theatre. Each book presents new ways of seeing and critically reflecting on this dynamic and vibrant field. Volumes offer a theoretical framework and introductory survey of the field addressed, combined with a range of case studies illustrating and critically engaging with practice.

Series Editors

Michael Balfour (Griffith University, Australia)
Sheila Preston (University of East London, UK)

Applied Theatre: Aesthetics
Gareth White
ISBN 978-1-4725-1355-7

Applied Theatre: Development
Tim Prentki
ISBN 978-1-4725-0986-4

Applied Theatre: Resettlement
Drama, Refugees and Resilience
Michael Balfour, Penny Bundy, Bruce Burton,
Julie Dunn and Nina Woodrow
ISBN 978-1-4725-3379-1

Related titles from Bloomsbury Methuen Drama

Performance and Community: Commentary and Case Studies
Edited by Caoimhe McAvinchey
ISBN 978-1-4081-4642-2

Affective Performance and Cognitive Science: Body, Brain and Being
Edited by Nicola Shaughnessy
ISBN 978-1-4081-8577-3

Applied Theatre: Research

Radical Departures

Peter O'Connor and Michael Anderson

Series Editors
Michael Balfour and Sheila Preston

Bloomsbury Methuen Drama
An imprint of Bloomsbury Publishing Plc

B L O O M S B U R Y
LONDON · NEW DELHI · NEW YORK · SYDNEY

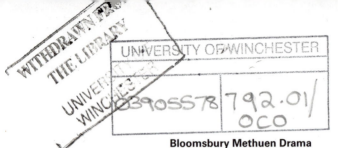
Bloomsbury Methuen Drama

An imprint of Bloomsbury Publishing Plc

50 Bedford Square	1385 Broadway
London	New York
WC1B 3DP	NY 10018
UK	USA

www.bloomsbury.com

**BLOOMSBURY, METHUEN DRAMA and the Diana logo are trademarks of
Bloomsbury Publishing Plc**

First published 2015

British Library Cataloguing-in-Publication Data
A catalogue record for this book is available from the British Library.

ISBN: HB: 978-1-4725-0794-5
PB: 978-1-4725-0961-1
ePDF: 978-1-4725-1385-4
ePub: 978-1-4725-0951-2

Library of Congress Cataloging-in-Publication Data
A catalog record for this book is available from the Library of Congress

Typeset by Deanta Global Publishing Services, Chennai, India
Printed and bound in India

For our friend and mentor,
Professor John Carroll

Contents

List of Figures

Notes on Contributors

Michael Anderson is an associate professor at the University of Sydney, Australia. His research and teaching focus on performance and its application in diverse settings. His recent books include *Partnerships in Education Research: Creating Knowledge that Matters* (with Kelly Freebody, Bloomsbury, 2014), *Masterclass in Drama Education* (Continuum, UK), *Teaching the Screen, Film Education for Generation Next* (with Miranda Jefferson), *Drama with Digital Technology* (with John Carroll and David Cameron, Continuum, 2009) and *Real Players: Drama, Education and Technology* (with John Carroll and David Cameron, 2006).

Esther Fitzpatrick (PhD candidate) is a lecturer in teacher education at the University of Auckland, New Zealand. Her Master's thesis, completed in 2011, used an innovative narrative methodology to gather the 'small stories' of children through a drama experience. She has published on issues of racial-ethnic identity in postcolonial communities, drama as a method of inquiry and ethical issues of arts-based methodologies. Her current research uses a postcritical ethnography where as a bricoleur she draws on a range of arts-based methods to explore her topic of inquiry: Bringing home the Pākehā: a postcritical ethnographic study of what it means to be a Pākehā educator.

Brad Haseman is professor and assistant dean (Academic) for the Creative Industries Faculty at the Queensland University of Technology, Australia. He is widely known as co-author, with John O'Toole, of *Dramawise* and as a workshop leader and speaker. Brad is a leading proponent of practice-led research. His paper 'A Manifesto for Performative Research' is seen as a call-to-arms proposing a non-traditional research methodology for the arts. Currently he is leading a team of artists and educators preparing web-based resource materials to support the implementation of the *Australian National Curriculum: The Arts*.

Jane Luton is currently a student in the final year of a PhD in creative practice in the Critical Research Unit in Applied Theatre with Associate Professor Peter O'Connor and Dr Adrienne Sansom at the University of Auckland, New Zealand. She is the co-author of the *Level 2 NCEA Drama Study Guide* (ESA, NZ, 2013) and *Level 3 NCEA Drama Study Guide* (ESA, NZ, 2014). Her chapter, 'Developing a Method to Explore the Battles, Barricades And Beliefs of Drama Education' is published in *Emerging Critical Scholarship in Education: Navigating the Doctoral Journey* by Jean Rath and Carol Mutch (2014).

Claire MacNeill is an Applied Theatre researcher-practitioner affiliated with the University of Winchester, UK. She is involved in a number of projects working with voiceless, marginalized young people to create media resources and performances about their worlds and issues. As a recent doctoral graduate this is her first key publication beyond smaller publications made in-house for various agencies.

Peter O'Connor is an associate professor at the University of Auckland, New Zealand. He is an internationally recognized expert in applied theatre. His research has focused primarily on using applied theatre as a public education medium to address major social issues including public health, gender equity in schools and the development of inclusive, empathetic and critical school cultures. Recent applied theatre research includes national programmes on preventing family violence and child abuse and parenting programmes in Youth Justice Facilities. His work in Christchurch following the February earthquake has led to UNESCO-funded research and programme development.

Adrian Schoone is a PhD student in the School of Critical Studies in Education, University of Auckland, New Zealand, where he is a member of the Critical Research Unit in Applied Theatre. His phenomenological study uses arts-based methods to explore experiences of alternative education tutors. He writes about his doctoral journey in *Emerging Critical Scholarship in Education: Navigating the Doctoral Journey* (Carol Mutch and Jean Rath, eds, 2014).

Linden Wilkinson is an Australian actor, writer and researcher; she completed her doctorate in generating cross-cultural performance at Sydney University, Australia, in 2014. Recent publications include contributing chapters in R. A. Ewing and A. L. Cole (eds), *Performing Scholartistry* (2014) and J. Ackroyd and J. O'Toole's *Performing Research – Tensions, Triumphs and Trade-offs in Ethnodrama* (2010). Her doctoral verbatim theatre play, *Today We're Alive* (2014), concerning the Myall Creek massacre of 1838 and the memorial erected to commemorate it in 2000 can be previewed at http://www.youtube.com/watch?v=lOlYr1ORUMY&feature=youtu.be.

Acknowledgements

We would like to acknowledge the generosity of Julie and Greg Dunn who allowed us to stay in their place to write and take relaxing pre-dusk swims. We would also like to acknowledge our families who provided support to us during the writing of this book.

Our particular thanks to Caitlin O'Connor who worked as a research assistant on the project.

Some parts of the first section of this book have been adapted from

Anderson, M. and O'Connor, P. (2013). 'Applied theatre as research: Provoking the possibilities'. *Applied Theatre Research* 1(2), 189–202.

Part One

Radical Departures

Research in a Post-Normal World

Peter O'Connor and Michael Anderson

Sitting on a university research grants committee can be a perversely fascinating process. Perhaps there is nowhere easier to see the manner in which research has become a competitive business, one with clear losers and winners. We have both sat on such a committee where we have had the task of first reading research proposals before giving them percentile scores based on rigidly defined criteria. Then, with other senior scholars across our faculties, we have listened to 15-minute presentations, with set questions (and equally set responses) before deciding on who would be lucky enough to get the grants. At times, when we have written such proposals and found ourselves using the snake-charm words needed to open the nearly glued-down wallets, we have felt like second-hand car salesmen. We know the business of finding easy and soft answers to hard questions, and finding ways to sell our particular charms (all of course, without obvious selling). We know our value as scholars, at least in part, is determined by how much worth of external funds we bring in to our universities, how many citations we get for each of the academic journal articles we write. We know too that only certain journals count, and that within the academy we are working endlessly to promote ourselves – merely to stay afloat. Research as business is something everyone involved with universities understands. It is cut-throat, competitive and often self-serving. It is an outcome of a neo-liberal business and market model imposed on universities, one which celebrates the individual at the expense of the collective, with highly attuned accountability measures based often on the likelihood of how the research will benefit both the university and the researcher.

When sitting on the committees discussed above, the key criterion for success is how much the funding would assist the applicant's career prospects. No matter where you look, it is highly unusual to find any criteria on what the research might do for those who are to be the 'subjects' of the research. Instead, it becomes clear listening to the presentations made before these committees that the primary consideration is on how many publications can be secured, what international collaborations might be entered into and how the status of the university might be enhanced by the growing reputation of the applicant scholar.

It's difficult not to be cynical about research when you are embroiled in a process where the competitive nature of universities seems to make it nearly impossible to remember the true value of research, beyond what it might do for an academic's career prospects.

Much of the research undertaken in universities is not merely self-serving. We are not suggesting there is anything intrinsically wrong with traditional research methods, nor with how much university-led research has made significant and important contributions to improving people's lives. Both of us have used traditional quantitative and/or mixed-method approaches in the past, and we hold the highest regard for our colleagues who have expertise in these research strategies. However, we are arguing that the researcher's personal and political motivation, and their understanding and sensitivity, is the starting point for a critical examination of research. This book seeks to be part of a different tradition, one that positions research as a collaborative catalyst for change. It is part of a way of thinking about research, which suggests its value is not dependent on whether it makes it into elite journals, but whether it is vital, and whether it gives back to the communities from which it springs.

Within this first section of the book, we attempt to position research and applied theatre inside wider political, social and methodological contexts to better understand its place within the university and the communities they are supposed to serve. It is necessary to understand the several research traditions and current political tensions which have contributed to the disconnect between research and 'the researched'. In this book we will propose a set of foundational principles we believe are necessary to elevate research beyond the business as usual model, by reconnecting knowledge generation to processes of critical hope and participatory democracy. We will advocate for research that deliberately seeks to work alongside the silenced and dispossessed, creating partnerships that build community capacity through aesthetic engagement in theatre.

Research has a long tradition of not only being self-serving, but also being destructive and complicit with agendas, causing considerable harm to the 'recipients' of the research. Perhaps this has been most clearly demonstrated in the complicated history research has had with the processes of colonization.

Linda Tuhiwai Smith argues that research, when it has been presented as a gift to disempowered Indigenous communities, has been part of the process of silencing and destroying cultural knowledge. She argues,

'Those observers of Indigenous peoples whose interest was of a more scientific nature could be regarded as far more dangerous in that they had theories to prove, data to gather and specific languages by which they could classify and describe the Indigenous world'.[1]

Brown and Strega[2] argue, 'Aboriginal peoples have been misrepresented and exploited for countless generations as the subject of academic, "scientific" studies conducted by non-Aboriginals. As a result, Aboriginal communities today are no longer content to be passive objects of "scientific" study, but demand to know who is doing research and for what purposes.'

We suggest that research, whether it wants to be or not, is always part of the wider political process. However, research can align itself to the interests of Indigenous and other marginalized peoples in ways they might begin to heal from the ravages of colonization, neoliberalism, and be enabled to reclaim their histories and identities.

Research within this book is, therefore, considered first and foremost a political activity. It is a process and means of confronting, challenging and disturbing the status quo that marginalizes, dispossesses and imprisons millions to the advantage of the few.

This book is in part a response to the challenge of 'The need for a civic, participatory social science – a critical ethnography that moves back and forth among biography, history, and politics – has never been greater. Such a performative discourse, grounded in the sociological and ethnographic imagination can help individuals to grasp how the fascist structures of the neoliberal world order, the global empire, relate to one another'.[3]

In positioning applied theatre research as part of a liberatory and critical research tradition, we acknowledge that critical research is centrally concerned with critiquing and transforming existing social relations. Brown and Strega argue that

> traditional social science research, whatever its intentions, has silenced and distorted the experiences of those on the margins, taking a deficit-informed approach to explaining their lives and experiences. The histories, experiences, cultures, and languages (the 'ways of knowing') of those on the margins have historically been devalued, misinterpreted, and omitted in the academy, where, as noted, only certain conceptualisations of information are counted as 'valid' (objective and therefore authoritative) knowledge.[4]

We argue for research that engages in processes where the marginalized might be the authors of their own stories, as co-researchers, and equal collaborators. We argue that there is a growing urgency to find research methods that spring from the need for social justice, requiring different kinds of knowledge and more congruent ways of creating that knowledge from marginalized worlds.

We believe that these times we live in demand forms of research that declare themselves to be morally biased. Like Howard Zinn,[5] we argue that indeed, it is impossible to be neutral. In a world already moving in certain directions, where wealth and power are already distributed in certain ways, neutrality means accepting the way things are now. It is a world of clashing interests – war against peace, nationalism against internationalism, equality against greed, and democracy against elitism – and it seems to me both impossible and undesirable to be neutral in those conflicts.

There are multiple risks in taking a stance of non-neutrality in research, not least in the potential response from researchers who still seek objective and measurable truth in the social sciences. We also risk with such a positioning for this book and our research, for as Russell Bishop suggests, 'espousing an emancipatory model of research has not of itself freed researchers from exercising intellectual arrogance or employing evangelical and paternalistic practices'.[6]

We are aware of the dangers of overselling the potential for research, but deny the possibility in overselling the gravity of the disease of neoliberalism and rampant greed that is tearing communities asunder. Resisting, but perhaps failing to avoid an evangelical tone, we recognize that the research we advocate for is, at its best, a form of individual and collective resistance. We will argue that this is not rehearsal for revolution, nor is it merely a reclaiming of voice; it is research as active resistance to the forces of global oppression. We suggest there is a moral urgency to resist because we suggest we are moving into a time, described by Ziauddin Sardar as the post-normal, where resistance at every level will be vital.[7]

Research and the post-normal

Turning and turning in the widening gyre
The falcon cannot hear the falconer;
Things fall apart; the centre cannot hold;
Mere anarchy is loosed upon the world,
The blood-dimmed tide is loosed, and everywhere

The ceremony of innocence is drowned;
The best lack all conviction, while the worst
Are full of passionate intensity.
                              William Butler Yeats[8]

Writing in a different time, Yeats considered the nature of a world gone mad. A time where things have fallen apart, and the centre is no longer able to sustain itself. To understand the particular urgency for the type of research we actively advocate for in this book, we now consider the nature of the madness that infects the body politics of the world in the twenty-first century. In doing so, we hope to contextualize the place and the potential for both applied theatre and applied theatre research.

Life in the early twenty-first century can perhaps best be understood by considering the nature of the post-normal as defined by Ziauddin Sardar. Sardar[9] argues that the first decade of the twenty-first century has been a series of wake-up calls. These are system crises – from security, to climate, to food and water, to energy, to financial markets and more. What is unique about these crises is that they have occurred simultaneously:

> "[w]e have never seen any era when we have been hit by all these multiple crisis at the one time," says UN General Secretary, Ban Ki-moon. "It is not just that things are going wrong; they are going wrong spectacularly, on a global scale, and in multiple and concurrent ways. We thus find ourselves in a situation that is far from normal; and have entered the domain of the post normal."[10]

It is perhaps because of the confluence of these multiple, compounding and complementary crises that we believe that humanity exists in murderously dangerous times, beyond anything we have experienced in the past. Although global capitalism has wreaked havoc environmentally, culturally and economically, wherever it has gone, we argue that the more recent rampant and unchecked greed has fuelled a system that threatens now to destroy itself. Aligned with governments who are either unwilling or unable to create stable systems of governance, to restore checks and balances on rapacious international conglomerates, it has been a recipe for multiple calamities; physical, social, and spiritual. The globalized economy and spectacular rising income inequality throughout many industrialized nations, with obscene levels of wealth captured by a tiny international elite, 'poses serious risks for the stability of governments, future global economic growth, and life on the planet itself'.[11] Natural and human-made disasters proliferate, once in a lifetime storms, floods and other weather events turn homes and communities into rubble within a time frame that is out of kilter with those of the past. Life for many, in the increasingly chaotic, complex and crumbling world of the twenty-first century, begins to feel like a war zone, a world without hope.

We believe there is an argument that we have moved through the optimism of modernism, and through the inertia of postmodernism, into what has been described as the post-normal. The term first emerged as philosophers of science, Silvio Funcowitz and Jerome Ravetz,[12] were searching in 1993 for a way to understand 'unpredictability, incomplete control and a plurality of legitimate perspectives'. While they do not argue that the post-normal paradigm completely replaces the scientific method, they *do* argue, 'we would be misled if we retained the image of a process where true scientific facts simply determine the correct policy conclusions.' This is perhaps what we might recognize as a normal paradigm, where stimulus A creates response B in a completely ordered, logical and uncomplicated way. This is what we could call the normality paradigm. We of course know that the normality paradigm is an inadequate starting point for understanding twenty-first-century life. And yet we know that our worlds are almost universally predicated on assumptions arising from normality – cause and effect, economic growth and industrial prosperity. In his paper, 'Welcome to Post normal Times', Sardar[13] nominates three features of post-normality that are demanding change in our approach to the world. He argues the post-normal age is

> characterised by uncertainty, rapid change, realignment of power, upheaval and chaotic behaviour. We live in an in-between period where old orthodoxies are dying, new ones have yet to be born, and

very few things seem to make sense. Ours is a transitional age, a time without the confidence that we can return to any past we have known and with no confidence in any path to a desirable, attainable or sustainable future.[14]

We need to consider now the mounting evidence that the conditions we are facing are in many ways different from conditions we have always faced, and that our feelings of the times being 'out of joint' are anything but a by-product of us all aging into the shock of the new, or merely a repeat of Yeats' concerns from almost a century ago. Sardar[15] nominates three features of our modern age that qualify these times as being post-normal. They are complexity, chaos and contradictions. We intend to establish the case for the post-normal by examining all of these approaches.

Complexity and the post-normal

One of the more compelling stories about complexity that comes to us through the latest round of geopolitical wars that many of our governments have entangled us in is that of networked global terror and neoliberalism. In what feels like the last days of the West's hegemonic rule, we are being dragged into wars that seem to many even more pointless than those fought in the past. Wars without any seeming end, wars against nouns, where the stated aims for starting the wars get lost in the fog so we end up fighting for a brand of oil nicknamed democracy. Wars where the civilian deaths mount, and where torture and inhumanity become institutionalized and justified on the basis of protecting our 'freedom'. The so-called war on terror, with its theatres in New York, London, Bali, Afghanistan and Iraq, has taken an enormous toll on human life and on human hope. It is a war that was not against a standing army but against a theo-political force of guerrillas who belonged to no nation state but mobilized the West's military industrial force in 'pursuit of freedom'. This remains a complex war that was, and to a certain extent still is, about international esteem, community confidence, energy supply and the place of the United States within international power plays. Politicians have of course attempted to present the war in simple terms: good versus evil, democracy versus the jealous. In the heated emotions of the aftermath of the 2001 terror attacks, the mayor of New York City, Rudy Giuliani,[16] argued for a simple response to the complexities of terrorism.

> Let those who say that we must understand the reasons for terrorism, come with me to the thousands of funerals we're having in New York City – thousands – and explain those insane maniacal reasons to the children who will grow up without fathers and mothers and to the parents who have had their children ripped from them for no reason at all. Instead, I ask each of you to allow me to say at those funerals that your nation stands with America in making a solemn promise and pledge that we will achieve unconditional victory over terrorism and terrorists.

> There's no excuse for mass murder, just as there's no excuse for genocide. Those who practice terrorism, murdering or victimizing innocent civilians, lose any right to have their cause understood by decent people and lawful nations. On this issue, terrorism, the United Nations must draw a line. The era of moral relativism between those who practice or condone terrorism and those nations who stand up against it must end. Moral relativism doesn't have a place in this discussion and debate. There's no moral way to sympathize with grossly immoral actions. And by so doing and by trying to do that, unfortunately, a fertile field has been created in which terrorism has grown.

Of course unconditional victory is impossible, and the desire to return to the safety of a time where moral codes were biblically derived can be understood. However, the continuing denial of the complexities of the situation, and George Bush's simplistic blunder into Iraq and its consequences (including Abu Ghraib) has removed any sense of moral certitude about the events of the past 13 years.

In the complexity of the war against a noun, it is difficult to situate a response that moves beyond the simple binaries. As the millions of protesters were to discover, as they stood in protests in capital cities across the globe in the weeks prior to the invasion of Iraq, the potential to respond is lost when power is still understood in these chillingly simple ideas infamously expressed by one of George Bush's aides:

> We're an empire now, and when we act, we create our own reality. And while you're studying that reality, we'll act again, creating other realities, which you can study too and that's how things will sort out. We're history's actor . . . and you, all of you, will be left to just study what we do.[17]

As anti-terrorist legislation has stripped people's rights to protest, it has curtailed democratic freedom of speech and expression. For example, within the United Kingdom the state authorities are increasingly characterizing political protest as terrorist activities. Anti-terrorism legislation is routinely used to demonize and punish what had for many years, been considered as legitimate democratic activity. Alan Morrison[18] suggests

> protesting students corralled by police with riot shields, kept in their place by batons, arrested under the whispered excuse of anti-terrorism laws. At what point did the imposition of tuition fees become a direct consequence of 9/11? And yet a climate of fear permits the authorities to bend the rules regarding civil disobedience as and when it suits them.

The never-ending nature of the war, centred within the antagonisms and hurts of generations of mistrust and accelerating grievance, presage an age where notions of 'mission accomplished' are mirages. As chemical weapons are deployed in Syria, solutions are impossible to decipher, let alone imagine. The world seems to be too complex for even complex solutions. Instead, a sense of ennui, of paralysing ineptitude and moral indifference, of populations rendered as mere spectators of and on the world, is not some temporary phase rather it is an entropic version of the post-normal world.

Chaos in the post-normal

These complexities collide and contribute to Sardar's next characteristic, Chaos. 'The global warming phenomenon that will see chaotic changes in weather patterns, a rise in food and water conflict and widespread famine is now upon us.'[19] We see the portents of this effect, in the long droughts and the savage weather that seem to prophesy the chaos to come, as politicians disengage with the issue. Chaos has also become more prevalent in our once civil societies. In 2007, *The Guardian*[20] newspaper reported that 'climate change and an increasing population could trigger a global food crisis in the next half century as countries struggle for fertile land to grow crops and rear animals'. This report, which emerged from a UN climate Council in Iceland, stated the aim of halving hunger and extreme poverty by 2015. While global warming and the complexities that go with it contribute to the seeming intractability of this problem, there is an underlying post-normal phenomenon of extreme capitalism that seems to tolerate famine, drought and extreme poverty as a feature of the globalized modern economy. The obscenity of the West's rampant overconsumption is made worse when we consider these levels of poverty, starvation and general misery (for the most part in the Global East) had been caused predominantly by the industrialist practices of big business, and the climate change misery that has been inflicted on the globe. In post-normal times the problems become more complex because the evidence for change is clear, but the ability to respond to that change is confused by the forces arrayed against the common good. We have perhaps already passed the tipping point where there is no going back to seasons, to predictable months of rainfall and sunshine. Our Nero leaders fiddle while Rome burns and drowns . . . again.

Chaos has also become more prevalent in our once civil societies. Within the United Kingdom during 2011, Hackney, Brixton, Chingford, Manchester and Liverpool saw chaotic riots stain the landscape. These riots had the added feature of social media, propelling both the suddenness and the ferocity of the chaos. Riots are of course not new, but in post-normal times they seem to rise in intensity and strike with little warning in multiple sites. Protest has morphed into highly organized, almost site-specific performances for the voracious 24-hour news cycle.

Martin Luther King's[21] comments immediately following the Los Angeles Watts riots in 1966 remind us that riots occur as a result of a complex interaction of social, political and economic factors:

> It is not enough for me to stand before you tonight and condemn riots. It would be morally irresponsible for me to do that without, at the same time, condemning the contingent, intolerable conditions that exist in our society. These conditions are the things that cause individuals to feel that they have no other alternative than to engage in violent rebellions to get attention. And I must say tonight that a riot is the language of the unheard.

In large measure, the ongoing social unrest and disorder as part of the post-normal is caused by the supercharging of capitalism and the triumph of corporate greed, which has exacerbated the gulf between rich and poor in a way which threatens the stability of nearly every nation state on the planet. Wilkinson and Pickett argue that the 'pernicious effects that inequality has on societies: eroding trust, increasing anxiety and illness, (and) encouraging excessive consumption'.[22] They claim that, for each of 11 different health and social problems, physical health, mental health, drug abuse, education, imprisonment, obesity, social mobility, trust and community life, violence, teenage pregnancies and child well-being outcomes are significantly worse in more unequal rich countries.

The neo-liberal plague exemplified by Margaret Thatcher's famous dictum 'it is our job to glory in inequality and to see that talents and abilities are given vent and expression for the benefit to us all'[23] has resulted in financial and political elites around the world exercising their extraordinary talent for picking off the fruits of economic growth, almost entirely for themselves.

The global super wealthy have always gorged themselves at the expense of others, but they have indulged even more spectacularly since the global financial collapse of 2008.[24] In Britain, the average remuneration of chief executives in the FTSE 100 in 2010 reached 4.2 million GBP, or 145 times the median wage. As the *International Herald Tribune* article concludes, about life post the 2008 crash, 'for the 0.001 percent, life proceeds sweetly'.[25]

Wade further argues that 'in many western countries the rich have been transforming themselves from an establishment elite concerned to foster the well being of a whole society to an oligarchic elite, concerned to use public power to redistribute society's resources upwards to themselves. This elite has acquired a vastly disproportionate influence in politics, civil service and media'.[26]

The anti-big government sentiments of neoliberalism dominates the political discourse of many modern Western states including the United Kingdom, the United States, Australia, Canada and New Zealand. Supported by a transcendent global right-wing media conglomerate that triumphs and celebrates the free market, any attempts to reduce income inequality is seen as weakening the moral fibre of individualism and self-reliance. Increasingly, those who fall by the wayside in these worlds are held responsible for their own failure as human beings, in a world where the state has resiled from its moral obligations to care for the weaker members of its nation. Where millions feel increasingly isolated from the geopolitical decisions of their masters, and increasingly marginalized from the financial excesses of multinational corporate greed, among the many complex reasons why individuals take to violent struggle, the language of the riot is not merely of the unheard, but of the deliberately silenced.

Contradictions and the post-normal

Sardar suggests we now live in 'a complex, networked world, with countless competing interests and ideologies, designs and desires, behaving chaotically, can do little more than throw up contradictions. . . . It is the natural product of numerous antagonistic social and cultural networks jostling for dominance'.[27]

Anyone currently working in education knows the truth of this. We know the importance of sustained supported teacher preparation, and we see governments in the United Kingdom, Australia and the United States delivering programmes where in a matter of weeks you are 'ready to teach' and school ready.[28] The weight of evidence argues against the approaches used by the governments to roll these schemes out to get the quick fix, detailing how they ultimately deliver a series of frustrated teachers and students. Based on their research on Teach for America (TFA), Heilig and Jez suggest that

> policymakers interested in improving poor and minority students educational outcomes should think critically about how well TFA supports the goals. Educational change takes time. In the time it takes to design, pass, and implement effective educational reform, another generation of low income minority students will have passed through schools, ill-equipped to compete in a global economy.[29]

We also know from the weight of research that large and frequent testing does not enhance student learning. There is now a substantial body of evidence demonstrating that the increasing drive towards standardization, testing and accountability may actually be counter-productive in the drive for more effective schooling. Allan Luke and Annette Woods' study of the 'No Child Left Behind' policies in the United States confirms other research. They argue:

> . . . the combination of increased testing, standardised programs, increased accountability and incentives/sanctions for schools, districts and states who do not reach targets has not been a success. Surely these are telling lessons for policy makers in Australia; telling lessons for teachers as they consider their place in the current Australian debates.[30]

Yet that is what keeps rolling into schools, ultimately distorting learning and shaping the curriculum to the mould of a test. Fundamentally, contradictory pieces of knowledge become policy and practice. These contradictions are now so prevalent, they have become part of society's furniture; like a seat you can sit on but which stabs you in the leg at the same time.

Perhaps chaos, complexity and contradictions have always been part of human experience but the combination of geopolitical power shifting from the West to the East, the power and pervasiveness of technology, the globalized implications of local actions and the tight interconnection of money, power and influence and their ability to ruin lives has thrust us into post-normality. The 'normalities' of economic efficiency, the free market, good governance, religion, democracy, integrity all seem somehow less reliable in the face of these insoluble and united threats to our world.

And as we move into a post-normal world, the sector of the population at most threat are young people who know of no other time than the post-normal. They are at the greatest risk of harm in, what Henry Giroux describes as an unrelenting war on youth. Giroux describes the way youth are socially constructed and represented especially within the United States. He suggests that

> recent attacks on youth can be linked to systemic attempts by a corporate and financial elite, conservative think tanks, and other right-wing forces to dismantle the social state and undermine opportunities for critical education, civic courage, and actions that make a world more just and democratic. These attacks range from the militarization of schools and the reduction in social services to the ongoing criminalization of a wide range of youth and adult behaviors and an increasing disinvestment in policies that would provide jobs, health care, and a future for young people.[31]

The young and the global financial crisis

Nearly a whole generation of European and American youth were slaughtered on the battlefields of Belgium and France almost a century ago. Today, another generation of European and American youth have been laid to waste as the greatest victims of the global financial collapse, and the triumph of global neoliberalism. Youth make up 40 per cent of the world's unemployed. Nearly 50 per cent of young people in Spain and Greece, approximately a 1/3 of young people in Italy, Portugal and Eire, and 22 per cent of young people in the United Kingdom were unemployed in 2012. The youth jobless rate of 16.1 per cent in the United States is over double the 7.6 per cent rate experienced by all Americans.

In all these states, where banks were bailed out and the rich continue to get even richer, the young are left to pay the price for the collapse of a capitalist system that seems intent on a feeding frenzy in the present, without consideration of the future. A growing cynicism and a sense of helplessness invade youth who see in post-normal times little sense or reason for hope, little belief in personal agency and understanding as the ways ahead appeared to be pre-determined.

We argue that the remarkable conditions of post-normal times urgently require politically and socially committed research. We argue for research that overtly positions itself as part of active resistance, which advocates for the rights of the marginalized, the silenced, and the forgotten. It demands of those of us in the research business a renewal of forms that return a sense of hope, reclaiming democracy for a tired world turning, and turning in the gyre.

Research and hope

The critical departure of this book is in the cry for research grounded in the hope for change. Not to a return to the 'normal', but a way for people to flourish and sustain their lives in the post-normal present. Like Freire, we understand that 'the world needs critical hope as a fish needs unpolluted water'. Freire understood that hope cannot be naive, it must be critically informed. He recognized that critical hope confronts 'the fatalism that pushes us to compromise with the surrounding reality instead of attempting to transform such reality'.[32] This is hope that challenges the seeming fixedness of the future, hope that

> gives meaning to the struggles to change the world. Hope is grounded in concrete performative practices, in struggles and interventions that espouse the sacred values of love, care, community, trust, and well-being. Hope, as a form of pedagogy, confronts and interrogates cynicism, the belief that change is not possible or is too costly. Hope works from rage to love. It articulates a progressive politics that rejects 'conservative, neoliberal postmodernity.[33]

Hope is founded on the critical imagination. It is therefore not enough for research to tell us what the world is. Instead it must provide opportunities for communities to imagine what it *might* be. Imagining the world as it might become is the first and necessary step in creating the possibilities of social justice. Cesar Rossatto suggests 'transformative optimism is an expression of a deep sense of emancipatory hope'.[34] We advocate that such optimism must sit at the heart of research. Transformative optimism as a guiding principle for research inspires a sense of the collective's ability and possibility to overthrow neo-liberal devotion to the individual. It engages research as a tool for hope and resistance.

Research and democracy

John Dewey recognized that at the heart of democracy is talk.[35] The freedom and ability to talk in a way that is not constrained by the powerful, that is open to the possibilities of dissent, and that actively challenges and resists dominant ideologies. We understand that this sort of talk is central to any notion of democratic citizenship. The ability to participate in talk and in action, the ability to see oneself as capable of resistance, of participating in civil life, marks out a society with democratic ideals. As we have noted earlier, research has been culpable in the past of continuing and supporting undemocratic practices, and in particular of perpetuating the colonization of Indigenous and othered groups. Research which silences and further marginalizes disenfranchised communities has been increasingly challenged by a range of more democratic research methodologies attempting to disrupt the traditional rules of the research game towards practices that are more democratic in nature. These research methodologies include community-based participatory research, participatory action research (PAR) and arts-based research.

Community-Based Participatory Research

This approach to research aims to reposition the 'subject' as an 'actor' within the research making decisions about the matter, and the method of that research. The benefit of positioning the 'researched' at the centre of the research's decision-making processes has its roots in PAR[36] (and is being mandated more enthusiastically by bodies such as the World Bank and the National Health Service (United Kingdom).[37] While there are definitional variations of opinion around what participatory research might be, there is consensus around the conditions that make this kind of research possible, namely a 'democratic and social context'.[38] Community-Based Participatory Research (CBPR) is a

> collaborative approach to research, [CBPR] equitably involves all partners in the research process and recognizes the unique strengths that each brings. CBPR begins with a research topic of importance to the community with the aim of combining knowledge and action for social change to improve communit[ies].[39]

This has real implications for the way researchers approach and navigate the research relationship, bringing stakeholders into the conversation as soon as the design of the research begins. According to Israel et al., there are several principles this kind of working must fulfil, including:

1. genuine partnership means co-learning (academic and community partners learning from each other),
2. research efforts include capacity building (in addition to conducting the research, there is a commitment to training community members in research),
3. findings and knowledge should benefit all partners and
4. CBPR involves long-term commitments to effectively reduce disparities.[40]

In post-normal times, participatory research has particular relevance and resonance for us. In a time of growing disparities, when building capacity within impoverished communities is increasingly vital, CBPR is a socially committed and politically motivated form of research with the potential to use its power to make a positive difference in the communities that researchers engage with. More politically charged in its approach to research is CBPR's cousin, PAR.

Participatory Action Research: Seeds of democracy

The origins of PAR can be traced usefully to a desire within the academy and beyond to create an antidote to research methodologies replicating the intellectual colonialism of Western social research into marginalized worlds. It has been driven by a desire to create more democratic forms of research involving disenfranchised people, as researchers seek answers to the challenges of their daily lives.[41] PAR promotes research as a transformative tool, assisting people to imagine and articulate how they wish to see their world put together and run.[42] Building on the Freirean concept of naming the world so as to transform their own lives, PAR is a means for enabling people to see themselves as actors rather than spectators, as people with agency and control.

Core to the philosophy underpinning PAR is the recognition that it provides opportunities for individuals and communities to challenge hegemonic knowledge that does not reflect the struggles and survival of the routinely disenfranchised. This is achieved largely through the reframing of the roles of the researcher and the researched. The scientific model that artificially separate out the two roles are challenged by the creation of research partnerships that strives for an investigative process where both researcher and participants are actively engaged in the designing, interpreting, analysing and representing of data. In much the same way that Applied Theatre actively resists the actor–spectator divide, PAR seeks to equalize the power relationship and transform both parties of the research into actors.

Arts-based research

The search to find more democratic, participatory and critically informed research methodologies has been invigorated by arts-based research, which has emerged and pushed the boundaries of traditional research over the past 30 years. Dixon and Senior, when advocating for arts-based research, suggest 'the arts in general teach us to see, to feel, and indeed to know. What we are proposing is that the means through which the arts function as illuminating vehicles may find expression and utility in research activities as well as in the arts themselves'.[43] Shaun McNiff defines arts-based research 'as the systematic use of the artistic process, the actual making of artistic expressions in all of the different forms of the arts, as a primary way of understanding and examining experience by both researchers and the people that they involve in their studies'.[44] He argues that arts-based research is different to other forms of inquiry, where the arts might merely play the role of data used for investigation within more traditional scientific methods. Arts-based research practices are increasingly used however, as a set of methodological tools by qualitative researchers, not simply in the arts disciplines during all phases of social research, including data generation and collection, analysis, interpretation and representation.

We have argued earlier that in a post-normal world, there is increasing urgency for research that addresses the ravages of global capitalism in providing an antidote to its poison. McNiff argues that arts-based research is particularly useful in bringing 'relief and insight when difficulties in human experience become deeply lodged within individuals and groups, this is usually a sign that we are stuck in our ways of dealing with them.'[45]

The arts also provide us with ways to look at the world in, and through, different lenses. McNiff argues, 'art embraces ordinary things with an eye for their unusual and extraordinary qualities. The artist looks at banal phenomena from a perspective of aesthetic significance and gives them a value that they do not normally have'.[46] Elliot Eisner, one of the founders of arts-based research understood too that it was through the arts capitalizing on the emotions that it was possible to see beyond what had been obscured by the habits of everyday life.[47] For us in applied theatre, we understand this slightly differently. We know theatre makes the familiar strange, and the strange familiar.[48] As a result, the everyday and commonplace are accentuated and given new or fresh life in the theatre. It is through this process that new understandings in theatre are created.

Arts-based research has challenged more traditional researchers to consider the ways research evidence can be generated, represented and presented. Leavy suggests 'Arts-based researchers are not "discovering" new research tools, they are *carving* them. And with the tools they sculpt, so too a space opens within the research community where passion and rigor boldly intersect *out in the open*'.[49] Haseman and Mafe argue that it is important to rephrase artistic methods and tools as research methods.[50] It has provided a platform for understanding that arts create different ways of knowing, understanding and representing the world – ways that can either complement or challenge scientific ways of knowing. J. H. Rolling, writing from within the education research context, argues:

The scientific and institutionalized belief systems that build taxonomic models in education present a monumental and oppressive structure that too easily occludes those educational stories that emerge from the margins – stories that disrupt the central or centring storyline. Edward

Said argues that travelling along this marginality can open up places for 'innovation and experiment rather than the habitual . . . rather than the authoritatively given status quo'.[51]

Further, Rolling argues, arts-based learning can often be labyrinthine, leading to divergent outcomes resisting those that neatly match taxonomical expectations.[52] The borderland space in both teaching and research is a place where one eschews safe and taxonomically ordered assumptions for the possibilities inherent in making ourselves vulnerable to different ideas, thoughts, and ways of being. For Rolling, and for us, arts-based research gives 'significance of the marginalized, invisible, or silenced story . . . as a site of resistance'.[53]

Arts-based research champions the idea that knowledge of the world cannot and should not be reduced into words and numbers alone. That representation through image, sound, movement and colour are equally valid ways of expressing knowledge. We argue that the almost limitless expressive possibilities inherent in the arts can break though the constraint of words and numbers. In a post-normal world, the arts are uniquely positioned to capture the flux and fluidity of a globe teetering on the edge of multiple extinctions. Although the arts-based researcher knows the world in and through different modes, self-reflexivity is important in adding perspective and to gain distance and viewpoints to avoid self-fulfilling and circular practice.[54]

If the world cannot be reduced to numbers or words alone, arts-based research challenges traditional research's demand for validation and verification. It rejects the notion of singular truths or clear answers, instead searching for contrasting nuances, revealing ambiguities and complex multiple truths.

Joseph Conrad also understood how the arts provide a space for knowing and connecting to things beyond the everyday. For him, the arts touch beyond the material world, into the spaces in-between, into the ephemeral and unmeasurable. He acknowledges that the power of the arts is to shift away from the contemplation of the everyday, into a knowing of fundamental and life-affirming truths. He suggests the arts act as a way:

To arrest, for the space of a breath, the hands busy about the work of the earth, and compel men entranced by the sight of distant goals to glance for a moment at the surrounding vision of form and colour, of sunshine and shadows; to make them pause for a look, for a sigh, for a smile – such is the aim, difficult and evanescent, and reserved only for a very few to achieve. But sometimes, by the deserving and the fortunate, even that task is accomplished. And when it is accomplished – behold! – all the truth of life is there; a moment of vision, a sigh, a smile – and the return to an eternal rest.[55]

Central to arts-based research is the use of the sign systems of the different art forms. For example, dance might be used as the central way of generating data and then be used as a way of analysing and representing the findings of the research. In many arts-based research projects, multiple art forms are used. This reflects the manner in which the boundaries between the arts have been dissolved with the development of new technologies, and the desire of many arts researchers to use a variety of art forms as part of their research. Leavy suggests, 'technological advances have assisted with the development of arts-based innovations. Quite simply, new technologies have allowed for the construction, preservation, and dissemination of many new kinds of "texts." Examples of relevant technologies include the internet, Photoshop, digital cameras, digital imaging technology, and sound files'.[56]

The body in research

The separation and then privileging of the mind over the body is an almost ingrained feature of Western academic thought stretching back to at least Descartian dualism. The dualistic model constructs the mind as immaterial and distinct from, but with control over, a recalcitrant body. The famous dictum, 'Cogito ergo Sum', gives such a privileged status to the observing reflexive capacity of the mind over the body that the person is entirely defined without the body. Susan Bordo traces the binary to antecedents including Plato, Aristotle and Hegel and suggests that the body has been constructed as 'animal, as appetite, as deceiver, as prisoner of the soul and confounder of its projects'.[57] The long-standing association of the higher order of the intellect with men, while women have been pejoratively associated with the body and all its weaknesses, has silenced and marginalized women. It is not surprising then that the reclaiming of the body in academia has been occasioned through feminist theorists, foremost among these being Judith Butler who asserts that 'bodies cannot be simplistically understood as mere object of thought, and they indicate a world beyond themselves'.[58] For Elisabeth Grosz the politics of the feminist reclaiming of the body is to dismantle 'the social devaluing of the body that goes hand in hand with the oppression of women'.[59]

As the body almost disappeared within Western academic thought, in the privileging of knowledge that stems from the intellect as opposed to the senses, one can trace the privileging of the sciences over the arts. Cartesian dualism has created other binaries that have been injurious to the arts within the academy. The false binaries of reason versus passion, depth versus surface, form versus matter, reality versus appearance have inevitably situated the arts as distinct from reason and knowing. This has reduced the arts to peripheral and untrustworthy forms of expression rather than ways of knowing.

In more traditional research approaches, nearly everything is mediated through the intellect alone. The body below the neck barely exists in this sort of research. Arts-based research recognizes that we know the world through all our senses, through our bodies, and that we can sometimes better represent that knowledge through our bodies rather than through what comes from our mind alone. The researcher in arts-based research doesn't merely take notes about what she thinks. She responds instinctively, passionately, critically to what she sees, hears, feels, touches, fears, hopes, dreams and recoils from. She moves, she rests, she draws, she paints, she dances and she feels. She responds with her whole body, and through her senses, to what she discovers. She then uses her body to understand and represent that new knowledge. Dixon and Senior argue that the artist is a researcher with her whole organism, inquiring, testing with the body as well as the mind, sensing and seeing, responding and retesting – a multitude of functions performed simultaneously – registering complexity, then sorting, finding a pattern, making meaning.[60] Denzin argues passionately for the body in research, when he suggests its 'truth effects' should judge the validity of research.[61] By this he understood that the validity of the claims in any research should be judged by how they resonate within the body. Eisner suggests, 'there is no test of statistical significance, no measure of construct validity in artistically- rendered research. What one seeks is illumination and penetration. The proof of the pudding is the way in which it shapes our conception of the world or some aspect of it'.[62]

The body, how it performs and how it is performed, is central to the making of theatre. Understanding is created both in and through the body of the actor, but is also understood and felt within the bodies of the audience. The ability of the body to know in ways that are as valid as any other form of knowing is what uniquely positions theatre as a form of research.

Theatre, performance and research

Finding limitations with representing their research through the written word, researchers turned to performance as it:

> allows one to retain, at least somewhat, the human dimensions of the
> life experience qualitative research attempts to study [helping] not
> to lose research participants in the data or not transform them into
> dehumanized stereotypes.[63]

Erving Goffman's contention in *The Presentation of Self in Everyday Life*,[64] was that 'the theatre of performance is in public acts', and ushered in the influential concept of the performative turn that was progressed significantly by Victor Turner and Richard Schechner. The contribution of the notion was that the performative turn would demystify and democratize the way we could understand and apply performance within social contexts. Applied theatre, as illustrated perhaps most clearly in approaches practiced by Augusto Boal, extended this concept and included the every day occurrences within communities as the subject for dramatic presentation, using community members as the actors. This theoretical and practical advance allowed the practices to be applied in communities to support them in managing an understanding of everyday conflicts.

James Thompson usefully defines performance as 'an inclusive term for all those artistic practices that include the participation of groups and individuals as they present themselves to others'.[65] There has been much interest in the manner in which the everyday is performed.

There are a number of methodologies that represent the outcomes of research through performance, but what most share is the use of real peoples' narratives.[66] Performance provides the opportunity to work with narratives in the realm of metaphors and 'embodied analogies'.[67]

Denzin argues that this shift to the performative in research is driven by recognition that 'it is not enough to want to communicate with ordinary people. That is no longer an option. The critical performance ethnographer is committed to producing and performing texts that are grounded and co-constructed in the politically and personally problematic worlds of everyday life'.[68] Denzin, not surprisingly, also understands the political implications of such research, including 'a commitment to participation and performance *with,* not *for,* community members. Working in this participatory, activist performance tradition gives back to the community, creating a legacy of inquiry, a process of change, and material resources to enable transformations in social practices'.[69]

We believe that these performances of people's lives must be more than a celebration of their struggles. They must also reveal the manner in which political power has shaped and misshaped these lives, recognizing that in a post-normal world, such performances 'become a way of critiquing the political, a way of analysing how culture operates pedagogically to produce and reproduce victims'.[70] These performances must also move beyond the present and provide space for hope for the future.

We argue performance research which focuses purely on the forces of oppression, but does not consider the potentiality of hope, is ultimately disempowering for communities. Applied theatre, as a performance of hope and resistance, provides a unique opportunity for an aesthetic research form, one that challenges hegemonic structure and envisions the world as it might be. In this way performance ethnography meets the challenge that Linda Tuawai Smith makes for creative research, that

> enables people to rise above their circumstances, to dream new visions and to hold on to old ones. It fosters inventions and discoveries, facilitates simple improvements to people's lives and uplifts our spirits. . . . Creating is about channelling collective creativity in order to produce solutions to Indigenous problems.[71]

For Rolling, the forms of narratives employed in performance research need to 'displace an oppressive bias against counterstories in favour of the kind of larger institutional grand narratives that are authorized solely to perpetuate the power of entrenched institutional systems to exert a self-sustaining order over their known world'.[72]

Applied theatre as resistance

Ben Okri[73] claims:

> Our old dreams are exhausted. Throughout the world there is a cry for a new way of being, a new freedom for social justice and fairness. One of the most fundamental cries springing from our hearts is that these earth-shaking times are in fact giving us a new chance to re-dream our lives, and we should take it with courage.

Norman Denzin suggests that

> performance is an act of intervention, a method of resistance, a form of criticism, a way of revealing agency. Performance becomes public pedagogy when it uses the aesthetic, the performative, to foreground

the intersection of politics, institutional sites, and embodied experience. In this way performance is a form of agency, a way of bringing culture and the person into play.[74]

Applied theatre, which always exists in the intersection of the aesthetic, the performative and the political can be seen ultimately as an act of resistance. We argue that applied theatre is part of a long tradition of theatre that at its heart contains the possibility of active and participatory citizenship.

From the beginning of theatre as a recognizable art form, and academic discipline in ancient Greece, theatre has served political purposes. In this book we recognize that the central interweave between research and applied theatre is political activity. In the same way as we have described the potential of research, theatre has provided a space for questioning, for challenging and celebrating our lives as individuals and as communities. Aristotle saw theatre as a tool for maintaining state control while others, including Bertholt Brecht, Paolo Freire and Augusto Boal, have recognized its potential as a revolutionary tool. Aware of, but perhaps also confused by, its potential, Plato banned it from the republic. Much mainstream theatre has also operated in many ways to divert and distract people from their everyday world, providing a chance to escape into safer or less troubled worlds. Theatre has become in many of its forms a social opiate in the same way that sport competitions operate. In much Western theatre, actors perform to silenced and invisible spectators. However, over the past 40 years, new forms of theatre which deliberately break down the space between actor and spectator by involving everybody in the making of theatre has signalled a return to the ideal of the theatre creating a space for communal discussion. Motivated by a belief that theatre might make a difference to the social and political lives of individuals and communities applied theatre uses a range of theatrical practices. This new form of theatre, although richly derived from progressive theatre movements predating the form and connected to people's theatre in non-Western traditions, is described with the portmanteau term 'applied theatre'.

Applied theatre refers to theatre not usually made within traditional theatre buildings, but made with and within communities. The term embraces a diversity of theatrical forms including community theatre, theatre in education, museum theatre, prison theatre, theatre in health, theatre for development, reminiscence theatre, participatory performance practices and process drama. In all of these forms, the boundaries between actor and spectator are deliberately blurred as participatory theatre is constructed to address key social issues, or to tell the stories of people who have been routinely dismissed or silenced.

However, Franc Chamberlain suggests that the term was simply 'a good marketing term' used by university theatre departments at a time of strained economic conditions because of its ability to appeal more widely than traditional theatre subjects, and it doesn't have the problematic associations of terms such as 'Theatre for Development'.[75]

Although arising as a response to social conditions that marginalize and silence, applied theatre's ability to make significant or any difference to the lives of its participants has been problematized over recent years. Hero narratives that plagued the early work of practitioners have become increasingly replaced by a questioning of the claims of its most fervent advocates. Walter Pitman suggests that applied theatre is part of the spectrum of hope that allows

> men and women to soldier on in the face of those things that seem to be disintegrating, undermining and eroding all that is best of the past and offering an illusory picture of prosperity for all in the future.[76]

We recognize how too often applied theatre has been positioned as the new Amway, the new medicine man's brand of cure all, the panacea for lifting literacy, numeracy, stopping truancy, enabling the disabled, a magical potion for curing all the ills of the world. Pitman himself with his claims recognizes that they 'will bring a smile to the lips of any observer who has listened for too long to the exaggerated claims and expectations of educational leaders on "state occasions"'.[77] And yet, like Pitman, we believe 'one *might* (emphasis added) translate drama education into a strategy for humans' survival.'[78] That like Maxine

Greene, we have seen theatre 'arouse persons to wide awakeness, to courageous life'.[79]

Michael Balfour argues that instead of conceiving of applied theatre in romantic and grandiose terms, the most we can hope for is a 'theatre of little changes'.[80] Applied theatre can also be naively complicit[81] with an agenda for social change that can all too easily be subverted or used against itself by state or corporate funders. Applied theatre is morally and politically neutral in that its processes can also be used to inculcate messages just as easily, by fascist states, to create compliant and obedient masses, as it can be used to promote issues of social justice. Judith Ackroyd raises the question of how drama, when it deliberately neglects the reflective mode, can be used to promote 'truths' where the ends being sought are contestable. She gives examples of how such exercises might be used: to promote smoking, or to encourage a group to run into mortal combat with vigour. She reminds us of the 'need to ensure that our practice comprises more than simulation exercises and role play, that it is truly reflective and that we debate the purposes of what we are doing'.[82]

The aesthetic in applied theatre

The changing wisdom of successive generations discards ideas, questions facts, demolishes theories. But the artist appeals to that part of our being which is not dependent on wisdom: to that in us which is a gift and not an acquisition – and, therefore, more permanently enduring. He speaks to our capacity for delight and wonder, to the sense of mystery surrounding our lives; to our sense of pity, and beauty, and pain; to the latent feeling of fellowship with all creation – and to the subtle but invincible, conviction of solidarity that knits together the loneliness of innumerable hearts: to the solidarity in dreams, in joy, in sorrow, in aspirations, in illusions, in hope, in fear, which binds men to each other, which binds together all humanity – the dead to the living and the living to the unborn.[83]

Applied theatre is first and foremost a form of theatre. It is therefore, in its own right, an art form, with distinct features and characteristics. Regardless of its progressive radical heritage, it must always possess aesthetic qualities that move and inspire to emotionally engage the audience and performer. The aesthetics of applied theatre have always demanded participatory forms, often with people without formal theatre training, but there is always the pursuit of beauty in the structure of the work. In our own applied theatre work, we chase the political goals of our work as we delight in the creation of theatre. We recognize that often the theatre we create is with people who have little opportunity to express their lives in aesthetic forms, and have very few chances to luxuriate in constructing beauty among the ugliness of their lives. As theatre makers, whether it is in drama classrooms, prisons, retirement villages, or among the rubble of earthquake zones, we work to make theatre that resonates, in and through the body, with its power and its beauty. Applied theatre is no less theatre, no less pure, than commercial theatre inside purpose built buildings. Applied theatre, like commercial theatre, has a number of agendas it seeks to meet. But first and foremost in our minds is the creation of the aesthetic.

James Thompson argues that the real question to consider is not whether applied theatre has effected change but whether applied theatre causes an affective response in the community it exists in. The creation of beauty and joy he argues should be considered ends in themselves.[84] It seems to us, that the creation of beauty and joy in a post-normal world where these qualities have disappeared or been banished is first and foremost a political act. Thompson recognizes too that such theatre 'far from a diversion, acts to make visible a better world'.[85] In citing Scarry 'When we come upon beautiful things they act like small tears in the surface of the world that pulls us through to some vaster space' Thompson aligns his work with a radical politics for applied theatre.[86] For as Joe Winston reminds us, 'the pleasures of beauty can keep alight the spark of hope in young people'.[87] He draws our attention to the philosopher Schiller who understood that 'beauty was the best way for humans to apprehend what a good society would actually feel like'.[88]

The positioning we take, about the potential of applied theatre, is to understand that its role is 'not to resolve, not to point the way, not to improve, but to awaken, to disclose the ordinarily unseen, unheard and unexpected, to discover new possibilities- new ways of achieving freedom in the world'.[89]

In post-normal times, dominated by geopolitical forces creating the unseen, the unheard and the dismissed as whole classes of people, one of the central roles of applied theatre is to disclose the stories, the lives of those who exist within or beyond the margins. It is an active resistance to this form of silencing and stilling of people, to again create a form of theatre that sits at the heart of democracy.

Perhaps we have come far enough in applied theatre that we can finally reject the false binary of aesthetic versus instrumentalism, and recognize that both are totally and completely entwined. They cannot be meaningfully separated. We understand the quality of the aesthetics will determine the success of any instrumental goal affective or effective in bringing about social change.

Applied theatre and democracy

We take our lead on the possibilities of democracy by understanding as John Dewey[90] did that democracy is more than the government structures derived from popular suffrage. Dewey understood that democracy was about the realization of human potential through participation in the acts of citizenship. He argues that 'the key-note of democracy as a way of life may be expressed, it seems to me, as the necessity for the participation of every mature human being in formation of the values that regulate the living of men together: which is necessary from the standpoint of both the general social welfare and the full development of human beings as individuals'.[91]

Applied theatre, when it creates spaces for those regularly denied the opportunities of full citizenship, when it engages in ways which provides opportunities to participate in thinking and talking about the world to those denied these rights, is a force against the anti-democratic practices of global capitalism. Paolo Freire, who has deeply influenced the pedagogical imperatives of applied theatre through the development of critical pedagogy, was primarily concerned with the creation of pedagogical tools that gave citizens the ability to name and remake the world. For Freire, the aim of critical pedagogy is to enable 'peoples control over their lives and their capacity for dealing rationally with decisions by enabling them to identify, understand and act to transform.'[92] Freire argues that the educator, rather than deposit 'superior knowledge' to be passively digested, memorized, and repeated, must engage in a 'genuine dialogue' or 'creative exchange' with the participants.[93]

We argue that the potential of applied theatre lies in its ability to create dialogue and creative exchange in communities where this has been either lost or stolen from citizens. The chances of such theatre creating more than little change is slim, it is unlikely it will transform the worlds in which the marginalized live. However, what it does achieve in its resistance is a humanizing, and a liberating of potential that should never be underestimated politically, socially or culturally.

Applied theatre and research

Applied theatre practitioners and researchers engage in multiple forms of research to elucidate their practice. Common methodologies include reflective practitioner case studies, critical ethnographies, performance ethnography, historical research, action research and arts-based research.

As a form of participatory and democratic theatre making, applied theatre clearly shares many of the same approaches as PAR and CBRD. Each requires:

- a sensitive and self-reflexive response to the environment
- a willingness to improvise and to take risks
- the employment of multiple roles and changing settings
- a willingness to engage with narrative

Furthermore, both engage with:

- tacit knowledge involving affect and intuition
- personal and social realities
- metaphors and symbols to communicate meanings
- ways of knowing which people use in their everyday lives[94]

More specifically, both Helen Cahill[95] and Diane Conrad[96] argue there are many similarities between PAR and applied theatre. Applied theatre, like PAR, often involves a process of inquiry, based on a topic, theme or problem that is relevant to the participants. Cahill observes that both traditions 'are centrally concerned with dialogue, praxis, participatory exploration and transformation' and involve 'collective processes of enquiry, action and reflection. In both processes the relationship between the researcher/practitioner and participants is a collaborative one.'[97]

Beyond using performance as a way of representing and presenting research within communities, applied theatre can be a process of research which informs and shapes every stage of the research process.[98] Reflecting on her experience of using drama to research with urban high school students, Kathleen Gallagher comments: 'Led by art, researchers, teacher, and students moved differently: We created an experiment in research that changed the terms of engagement.'[99] Gallagher also argues that drama gives participants as co-researchers the opportunity for '*self-representation*', whereas in other methodologies it is the researcher who represents the research subjects:

> This is theatre as methodology, theatre as a mode of devising a meta-world; to collaboratively and artistically frame a 'real' research problem or context in order to peer inside it. Engaging youth in research – theatrically – provides a robust environment for questioning, as the work deals in metaphor, or recreates 'real life' situations in which collaborators are able to more freely experiment with alternative strategies and perspectives in testing the validity of their own theories and insights about the world.[100]

In much of applied theatre, topics, themes or problems are explored through drama with a group of people. Participants can take on many roles: planning, acting in role, reflecting, critiquing out of role and presenting their work. Applied theatre might involve the participants working directly with an experience or issue from their own lives, or they might work analogously through a fictional frame. Either way, the theatre forms used are designed to create a safe and critical distance from a subject.[101] A variety of theatrical traditions might be used: researching, writing and performing a scripted play, verbatim theatre, and storytelling, participatory improvisation, contemporary performance-art, forum theatre, process drama or site-specific performance. Applied theatre can engage people in identifying problems, considering diverse issues, experience and perspectives and imagining/enacting possible solutions or futures.

Decolonizing research methodologies through applied theatre

'Aboriginal and non-Aboriginal researchers who tackle any facet of Indigenous study must have a critical analysis of colonialism and an understanding of Western scientific research as a mechanism of colonization.'[102] Earlier in this chapter we positioned research as a political practice and as part of the progressive battle for social justice. However, we also recognized that research for many Indigenous peoples 'remains inextricably linked to European imperialism and colonialism'.[103] Brown and Strega argue that 'historically, this has meant that those on the margins have been the objects but rarely the authors of research, and the discomfort that those on the margins feel about adopting traditional research processes and knowledge creation has been interpreted as their personal inability or failings'.[104]

Smith[105] argues that through research, both formal and informal, the West has taken ownership of Indigenous properties, knowledge and beliefs. At the same time, policies that are 'informed by research' impact on all aspects of Indigenous peoples' lives. She argues passionately that decolonizing methodologies mean Indigenous people might begin to reclaim the right to represent themselves in ways that envisage new futures, and to take control of the ways in which Indigenous issues are discussed and handled.

Indigenous researchers recognize how the arts provide different, and more appropriate, ways to represent knowledge than more traditional research forms. Brown and Strega argue how 'aboriginal realities are unique and diverse, and expressing these realities demands creativity and innovation. We encourage Indigenous writers to develop and utilize styles of writing such as narrative, self-location, subjective text, poetry, and storytelling that better reflect Aboriginal realities than do academic prose'.[106] Linda Tuhiwai Smith recognizes the importance of creativity and research as sites for resistance: 'The project of creating is about transcending the basic survival mode through using a resource or capability which every Indigenous community has retained throughout colonization – the ability to create and be creative'.[107] Denzin argues that: '. . . participatory performance work honours and respects local knowledge and customs and practices and incorporates those values and beliefs into participatory performance action inquiry'.[108]

We understand that central to the process of applied theatre is the manner in which dialogue is established through the aesthetic process. 'Dialogical performance is a way of having intimate conversations with other people and cultures. Instead of speaking about them, one speaks to and with them. The sensuous immediacy and empathetic leap demanded by performance is an occasion for orchestrating two voices, for bringing together two sensibilities'.[109]

The participatory, democratic processes inherent to applied theatre work can be understood as the bridge which allows for intimate conversations about things which matter to all participants. Applied theatre has, in this context, a particular strength for working within Indigenous communities. Kovach argues, the conversational method is a means of gathering knowledge found within Indigenous research. The conversational method is of significance to Indigenous methodologies because it is a method of gathering knowledge based on oral story telling tradition congruent with an Indigenous paradigm. It involves a dialogic participation that holds a deep purpose of sharing story as a means to assist others. It is relational at its core.[110]

Creating new research languages

All art, therefore, appeals primarily to the senses, and the artistic aim when expressing itself in written words must also make its appeal through the senses, if its high desire is to reach the secret spring of responsive emotions. It must strenuously aspire to the plasticity of sculpture, to the colour of painting, and to the magic suggestiveness of music – which is the art of arts. And it is only through complete, unswerving devotion to the perfect blending of form and substance; it is only through an unremitting never-discouraged care for the shape and ring of sentences that an approach can be made to plasticity, to colour, and that the light of magic suggestiveness may be brought to play for an evanescent instant over the commonplace surface of words: of the old, old words, worn thin, defaced by ages of careless usage.[111]

We have struggled at many junctures in the writing of this book with 'old, old words' that have conspired on occasions to rupture our ways of thinking and representation. We have struggled with reductionist scientific terms such as data, the ease in which we can slip into talking about *subjects of research, research populations, the researched, validity.*

We are very aware of Denzin's challenge to 'not use words like data, or abduction, or objectivity. These words carry the traces of science, objectivism, and knowledge produced for disciplines, not everyday people'.[112]

And yet, we have struggled to find other words to replace them that don't have the same taint. We recognize the manner in which scientific and neo-liberal language has colonized our own thinking and its expression. In struggling to elucidate new ways of thinking about research, we have privileged an academic discourse that has been largely prosaic and has attempted but mercifully failed to be dispassionate. We have been overt in our political motivations, we believe our aesthetic positioning is also clear, but we recognize we have largely failed to present our work in a way that creates the magic suggestiveness of the artist.

In many ways the history of the relationship between applied theatre and research has been characterized by the desire of many, to break away from old forms of writing and representation within academic journals and books towards new and exciting modalities of representation. Yet there has also been a clinging on to old paradigms, and even older and more defaced words, perhaps no more so in the relationship between applied theatre and evaluation.

Evaluation and applied theatre

The most common form of research in applied theatre has been evaluations of existing programmes. Evaluations are variously called measurement, assessment or research. In these instances, funders typically require an external or internal evaluation of the impact of the programme. These aims may or may not approximate the aims of the researcher. In this section, we do not intend to review the different methodologies that could be applied to the evaluation of applied theatre. Our intention here is to instead review the traditions and practices that have become habitus in the field, and to make some observations about how we might strengthen theory and applied theatre through evaluation practices.

As the experienced Australian researcher Lyn Yates says those who commission evaluations (or as she calls it contract research) '. . . are not interested in some abstract ideal of good research they want research that specifically meets their needs'.[113] This can compromise the research and the researcher in a drive to meet the needs of the funder, but any researcher that receives funds and works with people has a responsibility to be transparent. Evaluation is one strategy for making the impact of applied theatre transparent. Additionally, the evaluation accounts for the way researchers work with communities, how often scarce resources are expended. Baños Smith believes that it is a key part of their work with children to be transparent and accountable:

> We believe it is important to examine our impact so that we are accountable for what we do to those with and for whom we work, especially children themselves, and to our donors (both institutional and individual). In addition, assessing our impact can help us to learn from our experiences to improve our work, develop 'good practice', and to develop evidence based policy that can be used for advocacy. It is also critical that we share this learning with others both within and outside the organisation.[114]

This approach to evaluation balances the needs for programme enhancement, accountability and advocacy. A strong evaluation in applied theatre will meet several needs and courageous researchers who are able to admit their failings as well as triumphs are critical of the field. A more dangerous outcome in our view than misspending resources is wasting the time of our participants and raising false hope. The fear is that without effective methods of evaluation we will do more harm than good. As Etherton and Prentki argue, in the welter of effects and counter-effects in working with communities, understanding change is an imprecise science. They argue that equality and fairness can assist applied theatre practitioners as they aspire to ethical effectiveness:

> But how can these values be assessed and measured over a sustainable period, when the undermining global economic context in which they have to operate counteracts all the good intentions? How can we detect whether 'positive social change' involving greater equality has taken place? Or 'social justice' involving a fairer distribution of resources has been achieved? What are the indicators for a better world in these

terms? In order to contribute to a more equitable world, we, as applied theatre practitioners need to have ideas of how to reform our praxis in order to contribute to long-term solutions. We certainly don't want to continue to be ineffectual while we try to persuade ourselves we are doing some good.[115]

These are basic and irrefutable questions for transformative principles that are at the heart of applied theatre research projects. The chasm that emerges between elevated ideals and programme realities is not merely a fact of life in research with human participants. If the gap between theory and practice is not understood and allowed for, it is potentially injurious to the credibility of the field. We are not arguing here that we should dump our aspirations for critical hope, democratic change and empowerment but rather that our evaluations should be unflinching in their pursuit of 'what worked' and 'what didn't work'. On occasions, this evaluative honesty may come at the expense of credibility with those who fund the work. The alternative, however, is to pursue a style of evaluation that does little to support the enhancement of programmes and the maturation of applied theatre generally.

Advocacy and research

The struggle for applied theatre to gain traction in the community development sector has led to a predictable relationship between advocacy and evaluation. A young field like applied theatre relies on the communication of its methods and approaches through its successes. We are not arguing here that the link between advocacy and evaluation or research should be severed. On the contrary, one of the prime responsibilities of any applied theatre researcher is to search for the success stories in the programmes we design and deliver with communities. We are arguing here, however, that these kinds of success stories should not be at the expense of robust findings. The current cycle of research and advocacy in applied theatre means that there is often subtle pressure to tell the 'positive story' and ignore the difficulties and the failures. As Baños Smith argues there has been a tendency by some in the field to make unsubstantiated claims about their programmes suggesting change where the evidence does not exist for such change. She argues if we want to make claims for change or transformation these claims require solid, quality evidence. Baños Smith argues: 'Often reports discuss change, but these claims are not substantiated; in some cases comments are overly generic and unreferenced.'[116]

Baños Smith[117] suggests a mix of quantitative and qualitative methodologies is a persuasive approach in applied theatre keeping in mind the needs of the field and the funder. The quest to find data and findings that will satisfy funders, community members and participants will compel applied theatre researchers to employ a diversity of methodologies in evaluative research. As we mentioned earlier all research methodologies carry their own assumptions and cultural meanings, it is the role of the researcher to understand and locate these assumptions and to design research/evaluation that suits the needs of the communities and of course the requirements of the funder. Above all there is a need to understand the impact we are having on communities whether that supports our advocacy of applied theatre or not. As Baños Smith argues, '. . . we are not only interested in positive changes, but also in negative changes that may have resulted from our work, and in unintended changes that we had not anticipated.'[118] If applied theatre practitioners ignore the whole story of the research we are likely to perpetuate the myth that applied theatre is a 'silver bullet' miraculously healing all manner of social and economic problems. As we mentioned earlier we prefer, Michael Balfour's concept of 'little changes'[119] where modest but sustainable claims are made about the impact in the community.

Methodological complexity

Typically, impact in the kinds of projects that applied theatre practitioners engage with are complex and notoriously difficult to measure.

These projects working as they do on resilience, empowerment, democratic citizenship and critical hope all rely on sensitive yet robust methodological strategies. As Prentki and Etherton argue, the community development sector has appropriate measures for the delivery of basic human needs, but less so for the other needs of attitude and behaviour change over time:

> For instance, food is either provided or not with the consequence that there is or not starvation. However, where the interventions fall within the focus of rights and culture, as is the case with the processes of applied theatre, the assessment and measurement of impact is much less clear-cut.[120]

There is also at times a distrust of impact assessment that may be 'disciplinary inheritance' that is suspicious of evaluation of methodologies imported from other disciplines; at the same time it inherits a general reluctance to developing and systematizing its own.[121] Faced with this conundrum, applied theatre practitioners may be tempted to rely on what we've always done. However, researchers such as Osterland[122] are calling for more 'scientific' approaches (suggesting 'control groups' to understand change over time). These traditions carry with them assumptions, sometimes colonizing, that can prove problematic for applied theatre programmes and the communities they serve.

Dichotomizing research strategies will not assist our ongoing viability as a field. We believe there is intrinsic value in choosing from traditional and innovative methods, mindful of their embedded assumptions that most clearly fit the needs of the participants, communities and the evaluation/research. The challenge to innovate in relation to research is for us to understand and engage with traditional research methodologies where they are useful and appropriate and work more innovatively and creatively at developing our own responses and our own languages in research. The applied theatre as research section in this book is our contribution to the challenge of methodological innovation in the field.

Understanding change over time

Recently applied theatre researchers have called for evaluation strategies that embrace a diversity of methodologies and borrow from long-standing traditions of longitudinal research. Longitudinal, quantitative and qualitative designs respond to the challenge of demonstrating the ebbs and flows of community change. In this sense the research remains with the community perhaps long after the applied theatre programme has left. This approach has the advantage of understanding the immediate effect as well as the remnant impression when applied theatre programmes leave communities. Osterland argues that the time is now right to apply the longitudinal design to: 'prove what we might believe – that drama affects participants in a deep and lasting manner'.[123] Advances in the understanding of longitudinal qualitative design[124] now make this type of evaluation design a viable strategy for applied theatre researchers. As Etherton and Prentki argue, while immediate effects might be measurable, change over time requires sustained and therefore expensive evaluation strategies:

> But are there are also alterations in attitude and behaviour that are registered in the long term, sometimes over years and generations? Assessing this longer term impact of applied theatre differs from concepts of monitoring and evaluation, which are an immediate assessment of achievement . . . showing up the need for more sophisticated tools of measurement at different stages in a prolonged intervention into human development.[125]

While programmes and funders rarely have the resources to sustain long-term design, applied theatre as a field needs several of these kinds of projects to move us from the one-off ad hoc case (as valuable as those might be) to sustained and enduring research that 'allows evaluation sometime after the final euphoria'.[126]

Effective evaluation in applied theatre

In applied theatre evaluation, the initial buzz after the euphoria of performance can provide very positive outcomes for an evaluator. This however, does not constitute the whole picture in applied theatre research. What is required is deep analysis (often over time) of how the process has made 'small change' in the lives and the communities of the participants. This kind of research feeds the growth of applied theatre by asking and responding to intractable and wicked problems. Working in this way is not always simple and requires methodological flexibility and sensitivity.

The growth of our field in breadth and depth is only sustainable if we can look the difficult questions of community change and effectiveness in the eyes and attempt in our own small way to describe how we make a contribution. The fruits of this kind of research will also assist us to develop theoretical positions that can be applied across international programmatic and institutional boundaries. This kind of praxis, born of the connection between theory, research and practice provides the opportunity for growth and development in our sometimes under-theorized field. Our ongoing sustainability depends on our ability to, through innovative, appropriate and flexible research and evaluation, create theory-related practice that builds credibility with funders, bureaucrats, governments and critically with those engaged in applied theatre programmes.

Applied Theatre as Research

In the next section of this chapter we outline our claim in more detail that applied theatre has a place not only as a site to undertake research but also as a methodology *for* research. Up to this point we have been providing a historical, political, cultural and methodological context for applied theatre and its place in research. Our approach from here on in changes gear a little. While the discussions up to this point have been largely conceptual we would like to spend some time reflecting on the tangible processes of the approach we refer to as Applied Theatre as Research (ATAR).[127]

In presenting an argument that applied theatre can be a research method in itself we are not suggesting in any way a transferable model of research. ATAR calls first and foremost for a politically and socially committed approach that requires research to be responsive to and driven by each unique setting. However, we believe that there are commonalities to approach and method that can be usefully drawn together to exemplify the way in which ATAR can be considered a new and distinct research approach.

Our research journey into ATAR has separately stretched over 30 years of engagement with applied theatre and research and 5 years of working together on several research projects. We have known and written about on several occasions the power of drama and theatre for education and social change, and it seemed to both of us that there was potential for these approaches and methodologies to be applied to the research questions that presented themselves to us on a daily basis. Of course, we were not the only people thinking along these lines. Going back to first principles we wondered how we could conceive of a research method that responded to the multidimensionality of human experience and offered the potential for critical hope. We both were interested in how we might use our skills in making theatre to inform research that perceptively and cogently generated data but simultaneously had the power to reflect that data back to the diverse audiences and communities from which it sprang. The question for us was not whether ATAR was a viable method, but rather why applied theatre was still a fringe dweller in the methodological metropolis. For us, Dixon and Senior's call for arts-based researchers to imaginatively and rigorously engage with the growth of methodologies struck a chord:

> Art based research is in its adolescence. We need ongoing, critical reflection on goals, criteria, and limitations, and equally important,

compelling examples of ABR and DBR to understand possibilities and contributions to knowledge and understanding.[128]

To us, this seemed like a logical progression from the process of performance ethnography where the data is collected using qualitative means and then communicated using drama and theatre. We were keen to see how ATAR might unify process and communication by using drama, theatre and other arts forms as the method of data generation and research communication within marginalized and displaced communities of need. Barone and Eisner claim that the unification of arts in the process and dissemination of research is a public service:

> A better reason for doing arts based research may be this: to the extent that an arts based research project effectively employs aesthetic dimensions in both its inquiry and representational phases, to that extent the work may provide an important public service that may be otherwise unavailable.[129]

For both of us ATAR coheres arts-based research and performance ethnography into a potent, sensitive and responsive methodology for research with diverse communities. For instance, in a recent project, the data collected provided the raw materials for a video documentary but also was presented to the funder and the community to explain the outcomes of the research. This is a powerful by-product of the research that not merely supports the communication of the research that allows funders and the community to advocate for policy and practice change. Our first research partnership began with a conversation with one of Michael Anderson's PhD students and colleagues. Costa Loucopoulos had extensive experience working in schools with drama education and had recently begun a programme with young Indigenous people in a skills development and leadership programme called Young Mob. Costa introduced us to World Vision, Australia (WVA) to assist in understanding how well the programme was meeting the needs of the Young Mob group and to advise on the redesign of the programme from the young peoples' perspective. At the time we were excited by the funders' openness to using methodologies that engaged young people in a different kind of research relationship. WVA was interested in research that provided the young people involved with arts-based skills that also developed a vision of what worked in the Young Mob and the potential for a renewed programme based on the needs and desires of the young people who were at the centre of the programme. This seemed like an opportunity for us to use the skills we both had developed in the classroom and in communities through applied theatre programmes in the other sphere of our professional lives.

The underlying principles of ATAR

Performance is an act of intervention, a method of resistance, a form of criticism, a way of revealing agency. Performance becomes public pedagogy when it uses the aesthetic, the performative, to foreground the intersection of politics, institutional sites and embodied experience. In this way performance is a form of agency, a way of bringing culture and the person into play.[130]

We have used Denzin's words here as they nominate the power of the dramatic process as an active, morally engaged, aesthetic form that reveals power, status and agency. While Denzin is referring to performance ethnography we would nominate all of these qualities as sitting at the heart of ATAR.

ATAR is an act of political and cultural resistance that creates through the fictional frame a set of propositions that are co-constructed, analysed and then re-presented to communities as a method of creating new knowledge and forging social change. Like arts-based research, ATAR unifies the processes of data generation, data analysis and the dissemination/communication of findings using the rigour and discipline of multiple art forms. However, ATAR has two primary and complementary motivations, the creation of theatre and the performance of political and cultural resistance. As we claimed earlier, research, in whatever form it takes, is never politically or culturally neutral. As Conquergood argues, 'There is no null hypothesis in the moral universe. Refusal to take a moral stand is itself a powerful statement of one's moral position.'[131] Researchers using ATAR enter the research space with a desire to see power and power relationships made visible and to 'give voice to those who have been marginalized as a result of their race, ethnicity, gender, sexual orientation, nationality, religion, disability, or other factors (as well as the interconnections between these categories)'.[132] When we engage in ATAR or any other research for that matter we enter a moral and political sphere where our intentions should be transparent.

Finally, Denzin's nomination of the aesthetic is central to our interest in ATAR. The power of the dramatic form to engage, uncover, amuse and teach is well understood. Despite the efforts of many[133] we believe there remains potential to explore in greater depth the power of theatre aesthetic in the research sphere. Perhaps there remains a lingering distaste for mixing the arts with what has been considered the 'scientific' sphere of research, but this bifurcation has hobbled the potential of the arts and research to enrich each other. There is much potential in using the arts to engage in the post-normal problems and challenges that we face. We believe that ATAR should take its place among the other arts-based research approaches so that we might contribute to understanding and resisting the challenges our community faces now and into the future.

Earlier in this book we contextualized ATAR in terms of its relationship to PAR and arts-based research. ATAR in our view uses the resources of theatre to generate data that can then be analysed to interrogate human experience. It relies on the creation of a 'meta-world'[134] to support the understanding of actual worlds. While all art forms can be appropriated as research strategies, like how theatre can be done so, ATAR has at its core the fictional frame that engages participants in a 'dramatic conceit'. We use the term 'conceit' cautiously. We are not suggesting that in this kind of work participants should be distracted or unaware that they are partaking in research. The fictional frame is present as a way of accessing emotions and understandings at a deeper level that engages and provokes the imagination beyond what might be possible in other research methodologies.

The following discussion maps ATAR as a methodological approach. Intertwined throughout that mapping is an attempt to contextualize and reflect on this approach within the broader context of arts-based research approaches and is exemplified by the case where we both worked together for the first time on an ATAR project.

Co-constructing research: Mapping the questions

Classically, discussions of research begin with a definition of the question or the problem by the researcher. By contrast, arts-based research methods frequently are characterized by a co-constructed understanding of the research question. We are not suggesting here that the researcher is absent from the research but rather that the communities involved in the research are more likely to have a sophisticated understanding of the research questions having lived with and through the issues that prompt those questions, in some cases for lifetimes and generations. Our role as researchers is not to tell communities what the questions are but rather to support the construction and design of research methods that respond effectively to the challenges, as they are understood by the community from which they emerge. In this regard, researchers are designers: selecting the right materials, surveying the scope, understanding where and when to engage and knowing how to present the research at the conclusion of the project. This has been a persistent concern of arts-based researchers, Sean McNiff argues:

> a defining quality of art-based researchers is their willingness to start the work with questions and a willingness to design methods in response to the particular situation, as contrasted to the more general contemporary tendency within the human sciences to fit the question into a fixed research method. The art of the art-based researcher extends to the creation of a process of inquiry.[135]

McNiff's suggestion is that methodology and research questions should intertwine through the design of the research. This in some ways is anathema to the current methodological careerism that positions researchers not in terms of their ability to respond to a problem but rather in terms of their methodological expertise. While we are not arguing that methodological expertise is a problem in itself, there is an issue with research methodologies and researchers who cannot engage with problems because their methodological stance and expertise are too rigid to respond to the complexities of modern human experience. The arts and drama, in particular, have a shape-shifting form that allows for these complexities. The history of theatre and performance demonstrates the flexibility of the art form to wrap itself around different political, social and historical epochs to create meaning for diverse communities over time. This inherent formic flexibility makes drama and theatre suited to complex research questions.

This co-constructed mapping of the research question and the subsequent research project creates a shared ownership of the research in all of its phases. As McNiff argues:

> Since artistic expression is essentially heuristic, introspective and deeply personal, there needs to be a complementary focus in art-based research on how the work can be of use to others and how it connects to practices in the discipline.[136]

There are shared responsibilities here between the researcher and the communities to ensure that the research has integrity and is investigating relevant questions for that community. The researchers role is to attend to the scope, shape and design of the research project in response to the questions that have been mapped by themselves and by the community.

By way of example and explanation we have contextualized the discussion of the approaches and principles of ATAR. The following case study and the examples that follow through the remainder of this section relate to the Young Mob project undertaken with young Indigenous people in Sydney and funded and overseen by World Vision, Australia.

Exploring applied theatre as research:
Young Mob, Sydney, Australia

The ATAR process was undertaken on 21 and 22 November 2011, but the preparation for the process began long before then. This is a narrative account of the development of the relationships between the assessment team and the Young Mob programme participants (including teachers, Young Mob leaders, officers of World Vision) that made the 2 days possible. The evaluation programme began with a meeting at World Vision on Monday 27 June 2011 where WVA agreed to use ATAR approaches as part of the assessment process for the Young Mob project. Members of the project team then arranged and convened consultation meetings with Young Mob stakeholders including WVA, teachers from YM, (YM schools and participants) in Young Mob to create a *research network* for the project. In contrast to extractive research approaches, the research network approach identifies everyone involved in the research as a co-researcher. This included Indigenous community members who assisted in the assessment processes and gained experience in implementing ATAR approaches. A series of five meetings of various members of the research network were held to co-create the assessment project.

As the research/evaluation chief investigators, we negotiated with the key stakeholders the development of a 2-day applied theatre programme for Indigenous young people involved in the Young Mob leadership programme to understand what they thought the future could be for the YM. The ATAR approach was explained and members of the research network contributed ideas and approaches to be incorporated into the 2-day assessment process.

The Young Mob assessment took place in the Faculty of Education and Social Work at the University of Sydney. On day one, *Qualities of Young Mob* the YML were asked to participate in a process drama to help WVA understand what the future of Young Mob could be. The focus was to explore the deep qualities that make YM successful.

Figure 1 Still from the video pretext.

To introduce the drama a video pretext was created and delivered (see Figure 1). A pretext sets up the dramatic action and introduces the participants to the task to be completed. The pretext in this programme was a fictional video message from the minister of education from New Zealand, Trevor Tolley, who had heard how successful YM has been and wanted more information on how it could be deployed in a more effective way in Australia and in New Zealand in the future. Tolley introduced a teacher in role, his chief of staff, Peter O'Connor to investigate the programme and report back.

The teacher in role is a technique used to allow the facilitator to investigate an idea or issue within the fiction of the drama. In this instance it allowed Peter O'Connor to take on the role of the unknowing second in charge. This allowed O'Connor to ask questions about Young Mob from a naïve perspective and to elicit responses from the standpoint of someone who 'doesn't know' but is under pressure to find out. O'Connor is deliberately framed by the minister as being keen but not overly bright or quick on the uptake and would clearly need assistance to get his task completed. This role was designed to alter the traditional researcher/researched power dynamics common in research with young people.

The fiction attempted to establish that the participants were more knowledgeable experts on Young Mob and there was clearly no 'correct answer' the researcher had in mind. The dramatic frame literally asked them to be co-researchers on the programme for the fictional minister. The YML accepted the fiction quickly and enjoyed the idea of having to 'pretend'. In role the first task for the YML was to create a series of freeze frames that depicted the issues confronting Aboriginal youth, what they liked about YM and how YM helped them to overcome their issues. Using the dramatic construct that the images would be sent by video text to the minister, the freeze frames were filmed and questioned so that the ideas could be translated clearly to the minister. O'Connor was able to ask genuinely naïve questions in role that produced data which deepened and provided useful nuance to the images created. For example, when approaching a group of young people who were struggling to create images that stressed ideas about the importance of elders, O'Connor asked if his New Zealand ones would be OK for them to borrow in Australia. The gaucheness of the in-role question allowed for a detailed response from the participants which clearly revealed the nature and importance of elders within a local context. One of the participants responded by saying 'No they belong to the land here, you will have your own ones in New Zealand' (Zach, aged 16).

The images and the responses then became important parts of the assessment data set. After this session concluded another video pretext from Tolley was delivered that thanked them for their initial work and requested that the YML create posters about 'what makes Young Mob special' for three places:

1. an elders' meeting,
2. a deputy principal's office and
3. a community centre

The posters detail the qualities that YML value in the programme and they were additionally used by O'Connor to probe (in role) the nature and features of the YM programme.

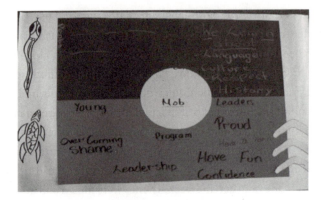

Figure 2 Poster produced by Young Mob leaders.

The posters generated (see Figure 2 for an example) became part of the data and were analysed thematically and spatially. The YML were asked to help O'Connor load the images for relaying to the minister by explaining and detailing the choices they made for the poster. Again, this in-role questioning provided a richer set of data about the issues under examination.

Young Mob had been using a variance of the enhanced forum theatre to examine issues of importance to them over the previous year. This was a theatre form that the participants were familiar with and so it was used to question and provide further information for the minister about Young Mob. Scenarios were developed by the planning team and the YM participants ran the forum session using the scripts given to them. The scenarios dealt with issues of shame and bullying.

On the second day participants said they had gone home to search the internet for the minister of education in New Zealand to double-check if the programme was indeed fiction. One participant said that even though he understood the research was framed as a fiction, he wondered if was a double bluff and that he thought O'Connor probably did work for the Ministry. Regardless, the group was introduced to a final video pretext from Trevor Tolley who congratulated the participants on their work. He informed them that they would be meeting the Creative Director of Light Bulb Advertising who would like to create a campaign for Young Mob that included songs and videos for the website. Michael Anderson took the role of the advertising executive and played a stereotypical somewhat shady role, offering 'rewards' for a job well done. The allure of 'rewards' proved a strong motivator for the participants for the day.

The remainder of the active research was spent in YML developing a piece of arts-based communication with local Indigenous artists for the YM website. The group split into two, with one group producing a video and the other a song about YM. This process was developed to deepen the research team's understanding of what the participants felt YML could be into the future. The arts-making processes were fun and engaging research activities that involved the students in a process of attempting to crystallize their understandings. One of the teacher participants commented on the approach:

> The research approach worked really well. I was really surprised they worked so hard over the 2 days and didn't want to split up. They mixed in really well with the other kids. It showed that they could be really capable and inquisitive and it showed that side of themselves to themselves.

The final pieces of film and the song became important parts of the data. However, so too did the conversations that occurred during the making.

The research document

The research presented to WVA consisted of a traditional text-based document with over 20 programme recommendations that had been developed through a thematic analysis of the data generated over the 2 days of the project. We were able to use the multiple sources of data generated to provide a multi-layered and rich presentation of the participants' ideas, thoughts and feelings that used a range of multi-modal forms of expression. The data sources included stances and gestures in the freeze-frame works, the drawings, colours and shapes in their posters, their in-role answers to naïve and bumbling researchers, the theatre making captured on film and the lilt of the music created. All of these forms were used to create a very nuanced and rich text to address the questions of WVA.

We also provided an 8-minute DVD which captured the ATAR process and the many ways the process addressed the research questions. This showed the participants making the freeze frames, drawing and talking about the posters, engaging in the x-change game and making the video and music. The DVD only used the voices of the participants and acted as a powerful addendum to the more traditional text. An interactive e-book was also created which allowed for the performativity and the embodied nature of the research to be presented. The e-book integrated some of the interview and performance materials (integrating video and audio files) in an attempt to make the research 'come alive'.

Designing the project

As we discussed earlier, the research question is a collaborative mapping process including researchers and participants. The design of the next phase of the research project, while still collaborative, often relies on the expertise and experience of the researcher. The task of selecting appropriate and relevant research strategies that can be crafted into a responsive and affective piece of research is the main aim of the initial stages in designing the research project. As Leavy[137] argues researchers are shaping and 'sculpting' new approaches to research that connect communities to their issues and enable ventilation of them.

The planning of an ATAR project is an active crafting of aesthetic tools to meet the needs of the research participants in answering or addressing the research question.

In this way ATAR projects can never be 'off the shelf' projects. Much of their strength as a method is in the manner in which they arise from within communities, are co-constructed and realized in different ways. One research project will not look like another, as the research strategies employed will be specifically designed for a specific research question and a unique group of research participants.

In the Young Mob project we spent considerable time discussing the questions and planning the research with the young people who would be generating data with us. These discussions were crucial to the project being viable for several reasons. Primarily they helped the research team to understand the approaches that these young people disliked in research. Many communities suffer from research fatigue. Our initial discussions with these young people confirmed what we had suspected – that they had not been consulted in previous data collection and had inappropriate methodologies foisted upon them. For instance, researchers had used survey-based instruments to collect data from these young people, many of whom had very low levels of literacy. These initial discussions also helped us to identify the arts practices that these young people were familiar with and enjoyed. These discussions began to give shape to the research design. It acknowledged and took account of their preferences and needs rather than the restrictive methodological predispositions of the researchers involved. An additional benefit is that the research team has the opportunity to 'break the ice' with research participants. Communities who have research fatigue often have preconceptions about the ways researchers will engage with them. In this instance, discussion with participants broke down these barriers and preconceptions and signalled that we were committed to the co-construction of research with them. Another related issue with these kinds of communities is the need to 'do no harm' through careful preparation and sensitive engagement:

Preparation is particularly important when the research involves sensitive inquiries as child abuse or family violence studies. Individuals may become emotionally triggered. If it is indeed a sensitive topic, the researcher needs to be aware of the supports in the community and how to support research participants if the need arise.[138]

Part of the work of planning and preparation is to consider the impact of the research on the research participants. In the preparation stage care should be taken to engage with stakeholders to ameliorate the risks that the research could have on the mental health of participants. Arts-based research has consistently engaged with vulnerable participants, and it is the responsibility of the researcher to understand the power of the methods being employed and ensure that precautions are taken to avoid harm.

This co-created approach requires care and time and resources in the initial stages of the project. As a result the research is richer because of the investment the community has in the development of a collaborative endeavour with mutual benefits. The next phase of the research, the design phase, allows the ATAR researcher to select and wrap the arts forms around the research question.

Creating a symbiotic experience

Before the research team can be recruited and before the project can be designed, the research investigators must consider how the research experience will be a symbiotic rather than a parasitic experience that benefits everybody involved. What we mean here is that the research must have mutual benefits for the researcher and the research participants. Of course the primary beneficiary must be the research participants. In our view, this is one of the moral obligations that researchers have to those who are involved in the research. There are two main ways in which this symbiosis can occur.

In the design of the research, capacity building can be integrated into the research methods. Considering the kinds of skills that might engage and enrich a group of participants is likely to ensure stronger and more sustained commitment to the research project. This approach also inverts the common research practice of entering a community and mining data from 'subjects' and then leaving the community without offering anything in return.

In the Young Mob project the young participants had a 2-day intensive arts programme that involved them in theatre making, talking with an Indigenous stand-up comic, working with an Indigenous musician and then working with an Indigenous videographer. These skills were to be later picked up and further developed in ongoing arts activities with the participants as they expressed their interest in the different art forms.

The research took place at the University of Sydney. We spent considerable time discussing the venue with the participants. They were keen to see where we worked, it was a foreign landscape for them. We were keen for these young people to experience a few days on the campus. We deliberately held our workshops adjacent to the Koori Centre, where images of Aboriginality and Indigenous rights decorate the walls. The participants toured the campus with their facilitators. One young woman commented that it was the kind of place she could come to.

For the participants we wonder now if they considered these days as research or whether they saw them as theatre making. Their engagement with the process was evident however, not because they were being polite to the white fullas who were there to collect information about them for their own arcane use, but because we spent 2 days together making theatre, music and video.

The second strategy increasingly employed by arts-based researchers is to support symbiotic practice in the dissemination and communication of the research back to the community. Arts-based researchers have a proud tradition of communicating by using appropriate aesthetic forms reflective of their communities. Patricia Leavy claims that this approach to communication breaks down the barriers between researchers, communities and participants.

The use of arts-based representational strategies [such as performance ethnography, verbatim theatre] brings academic scholarship to a wider audience. Free from discipline-specific jargon and other prohibitive (even elitist) barriers, arts-based representations can be shared with diverse audiences, expanding the effect of scholarly research that traditionally circulates within the academy and arguably does little to serve the public good.[139]

Performance ethnographers and verbatim theatre practitioners have used research processes to collect data and then presented the findings of their research back to the communities that they entered to collect that data.

In the Young Mob project we failed to do this. We simply didn't feed back to the wider community nor did we find a time to bring the group back together to review what we had said on their behalf. It is easy to excuse this failing by saying that we weren't funded to do this and it proved logistically difficult to do. These are however, merely excuses. If we had prioritized this process we would have made it happen. We could be harshly accused of continuing the age-old process of raiding Indigenous knowledge without sustaining any kind of relationship with the community beyond our funded project. We have sought funding to go back and continue working, but perhaps we should have made any work with Young Mob conditional on this approach before we began our work. Despite our genuine desire to create work that was truly in partnership with the community, we doubt whether we truly achieved this.

Building a research team

Once the research question has been mapped and the plan for the research has been negotiated a team to deliver the research can be assembled. In ATAR projects it is common to work with multidisciplinary teams that include researchers, artists, teachers and cultural experts to assist in the generation, analysis and representation of data. Artists often provide specialist knowledge that is useful in the development and delivery of research projects. For instance, community musicians can assist in the design of a songwriting activity that generates data for a specific question. While artists are often highly skilled in the area of expertise they sometimes require detailed briefings relating to the research process. They, like the participants, may have preconceptions about research that are not consistent with the ATAR approach. While many artists are favourably disposed to this kind of work there is often a difference between the traditional role of the artist and the role of the artist in arts-based research. Where possible recruiting artists who have worked within the community context previously, or on other research projects, will reduce the degree of briefing required to have them prepared for these specific investigations.

In the Young Mob project, we worked closely with Costa, who had a long-standing relationship with the young people, largely established through applied theatre projects he had engaged them in. We worked with the Indigenous facilitators who ran the programme and spent considerable time in the planning phases discussing the best approaches and attempting to come to terms with the subculture of the group.

We worked with several Indigenous artists who we met and discussed the project with on a number of occasions before the research workshops. They included a musician/songwriter, a stand-up comedian and a videographer. We also had two videographers from the University of Auckland and Molly Mullen a doctoral student who acted as a research assistant to the project.

The Aboriginal artists were recruited to support the data-generation process. While the research team had drama-based skills they did not have skills in developing and delivering arts-based sessions on songwriting, documentary making, radio plays, hip hop or design. Working with the young Aboriginal artists on the project had multiple benefits that included creating positive role models, cultural experience and understanding, capacity building for participants and expert understanding of skills relating to Aboriginal art-making processes. They also developed relationships quickly with the young people through their arts making that was clearly based on their shared Aboriginality.

There was a connection made with the Young Mob participants based on an unstated shared experience of the cultural devastation and racism experienced by the Indigenous people of Australia. We believe it would have been impossible for any of the white people in the project to create this trusting connection that resulted in strong commitment to the work. The natural ease of both Indigenous groups working together meant at various points throughout the project we deliberately retreated into the background.

In our experience, the careful preparation of artists to this kind of work is essential. While artists may have community arts development experience, the specific requirements of research (data generation and findings dissemination) is often a new experience. We found that some of the artists had a better understanding of the process than others. Given our time again we would devote more resources to supporting the development of these artists as part of the research team and integrating them more thoroughly in the project.

Yet as Leavy argues there is more that unifies artists and researchers than divides them.

> Theatre practitioners and qualitative researchers share many critical characteristics, including keen observational skills, analytic skills, storytelling proficiency, and the ability to think conceptually, symbolically, and metaphorically. Moreover, as indicated, both practices require creativity, flexibility, and intuition, and result in the communication of information that generates meaning.[140]

It is for these reasons that in ATAR projects it is not uncommon for artists to act as co-researchers and valuable contributors to the applied theatre research journey.

There are several other groups of people that may be involved from time to time with the research project. Teachers, social workers and psychologists often provide advice and support in the design and delivery of ATAR. That is useful with sensitive issues or if they have specialized knowledge of the 'research population'. Their insights can help researchers avoid common pitfalls and design and deliver research that attends to the needs of the participants as co-researchers in the project, not only benefiting the needs of the researcher.

This kind of external censoring, while well meaning, had the effect of limiting some of the responses and potentially lessening the authenticity of the data in the YM project. This experience serves as a valuable reminder that roles in the research need to be clearly defined and understood before the research begins.

Any research has the potential for tensions and difficulties. ATAR is no exception and has potentially more opportunity for misunderstanding. A tight definition and discussions of how those roles will be played out in the research may alleviate tension before projects begin and remove the opportunity for misunderstanding. Crucially, however, the selection and definition of roles will mean that the research can reach its potential unhindered by intervention from others.

Attending to rigour: Anticipating the challenge

The accusation often levelled at arts-based researchers is that their approaches lack systematic rigour. ATAR, using as it does, fictional dramatic structures is likely to be critiqued on the same basis. The use of the fictional frame in research allows, as in the arts generally, participants to create meaning through distance. This meaning is not less valid because it is obtained through fiction, rather, this fictional frame reflects a different approach to data generation. We would argue that the arts are themselves highly rigorous and disciplined processes. The arts have within them their own forms and systems that can be readily applied to research. Our aspiration as researchers is to be rigorous in the pursuit of knowledge that is hard to discover. Often those who dismiss arts-based methodologies have limited methodological strategies in their own traditions to understand the multidimensionality and complexity of human experience. As Chilton argues, 'Artistic, expressive forms bring inner experience into consciousness and encapsulates and transforms complex experience and ideas' (This is how beauty answers terror, transforming the wounds of our history).[141]

While this approach may not appear rigorous to some, expressive forms such as drama and theatre foreground and transform the complexity of modern human experience into knowledge that can be applied for the good of diverse communities. What we require in ATAR and other arts-based research methodologies is a departure from traditional definitions of rigour. We should work to make our own standards and our own definitions of rigour that suit the needs of our communities rather than the research industry. As Eisner argues the arts do not relate easily to mainstreams conception of validity. The arts seeks patterns of meaning that contribute to a fuller deeper understanding of the human condition.

Rather than being chained to outmoded constructs ATAR must arrive at relevant and appropriate definitions rather than being defined by others. The strength and discipline of our aesthetic is a good starting point in setting our own boundaries for the research journey ahead.

One of the challenges that ATAR researchers face is the authentic reflection of the multiple perspectives embedded in both the arts-making and data-generating processes. We find Laurel Richardson's[142] construct of crystallization a particularly fitting metaphor for this multivocal process. Crystallization is a process that allows multiple perspectives to contribute to the presentation of the research. In ATAR there are often multiple voices, participants and therefore perspectives on the research. Crystallization allows the researcher to make the democratic principles that are foundational in ATAR a reality in the research analysis phase. Triangulation is the use of a variety of data sources in a study.[143] It is a useful term but does suggest limitation. We prefer the crystallization method as it has greater scope to validate the data. Laurel Richardson (1994) says the '. . . central image for "validity" for postmodernist texts is not the triangle – a rigid, fixed, two dimensional object. Rather, the central image is the crystal, which combines symmetry and substance with an infinite variety of shapes, substances, transmutations, multi-dimensionalities, and angles of approach. Crystals grow change, alter but are not amorphous'.[144] Crystallization allows the authentic voices of participants to emerge and acts as a bulwark against the researchers overwhelming other voices.

Selecting a fictional frame . . . entering the story

Fictional frames are at the heart of an effective ATAR project. They are perhaps its most defining feature. The success of a fictional frame often lies in the time and effort expended in ensuring that it has scope and depth to respond to the research question. By fictional frame we mean the dramatic conceit that participants take roles within to provide distance from the real world. Fictional frames use theatre conventions to move participants away from actual engagement in the event (in research this might be the central question or issue under study) to what O'Toole[145] calls the first order drama through a range of roles from guide (I show you how it was) to critic (I interpret the event) to the final and most distanced frame of artist (I transform the event). Bowell and Heap[146] pick these ideas up in *Planning Process Drama* creating a grid with eight frames that shows how framing creates emotional distancing, labelling the frames as hot to cool, again moving from the first order, the recreation of the focus event, through to symbolic or artistic representation of the event.

John Carroll described framing and distancing as providing participants with the possibility to 'test out ideas, try them over again and generally examine them, without necessarily having to fulfill, in actual life situations, the promises they have tried out in the depicted one'.[147] This means that fictional framing provides the freedom to experiment, to try out new ideas in what Carroll called a 'no-penalty zone'.[148] The no-penalty zone describes how inside the fictional frame there is no risk in the real world for the decisions that are taken, although there are always consequences in the fictional world.

We suggest fictional framing provides participants in research the safety for them to engage emotionally, aesthetically and through the body to talk honestly about matters of significance. In designing the fictional frame it is necessary to design spaces for research participants to be sufficiently distanced from their real lives to be free to work within the fiction, but close enough to the fictional world so that their engagement with the fiction resonates with their real lives.

The features of an effective fictional framework

In our view the fictional frame must have the following features:

1. A fictional frame must suit the participants and the researchers
In ATAR the creation of a fictional framework is actively negotiated between the researcher and the participants. In other words, the frame must be engaging for all those involved and should also be within the capabilities of the research team. In the Young Mob example, the fictional frame was the use of the outsider or other in the form of the second in charge character (Peter O'Connor) seeking help from the Young Mob participants. The young people were able to use their real expertise to inform their work within this fiction. This is a deliberate inversion of the traditional researcher/researched paradigm that privileges the researcher above the research 'subjects'. This inversion was designed to change the usual relationship in the research transaction by altering the agency of the research participants. In other words, the fictional frame allowed them to act as if they were experts in the fiction, using the expertise they had in the real world. As we've mentioned in a collision of realities, on the second day of the research project with Young Mob, one of the young men approached O'Connor and said, 'I've done some research on you just to check that you don't really work for the Minister of Education in New Zealand.' His total engagement in the programme the rest of the day was in response to knowing that the work was fictional.

2. A fictional frame must provide the potential for metaxis.

Drama and theatre allow all participants to distance themselves from the action and content of the performance by inhabiting a character or role. This allows all those involved to distance themselves from the research by inhabiting a meta-world. This meta-world provides the potential for metaxis. Augusto Boal[149] uses the term 'metaxis' to describe the process whereby a person in role is able to both perform and view that performance. In this sense the person is always the actor and the audience simultaneously. Vygotsky[150] describes this process as a dual affect, where the person is both engaged directly with what is happening in the drama, and at the same time is distanced from it as he or she watches his or her own engagement in the drama. Using improvisational forms derived from theatre rehearsal and practice, Boal was intent on breaking down the gap between actor and spectator, creating instead a theatre form where the separation diminished so that Boal's 'spect-actors'[151] became, in Bolton's terms, both the participant and percipient of their own actions.[152]

Like Bolton, Boal recognized that the dialectic between the fiction and the real was the central and most powerful agency for changed understanding through drama. Boal describes this as metaxis 'the state of belonging completely and simultaneously to two different autonomous worlds: the image of reality and the reality of the image'. In metaxis

> the oppressed artist is able to create an autonomous world of images of his own reality, and to enact his liberation in the reality of these images, he will then extrapolate into his own life all that he has accomplished in the fiction. The scene, the stage, becomes the rehearsal space for real life.[153]

Boal's analogical induction hypothesis had resonance and linked with Heathcote and Bolton's insistence on a distanced, framed or analogous approach to drama.

> The function of analogical induction is to allow a distanced analysis, to offer several perspectives, to multiply the possible points of view from which one can consider each situation. The oppressed must be helped

to reflect on his own actions. A disjunction of action and reflection on that action must be brought about.[154]

Metaxis describes the process where participants are encouraged to engage in a role while simultaneously retaining a sense of themselves, in essence, maintaining their own identity while playing another. They also simultaneously reflect on the way the other roles are interacting with their role. This process provides space for reflection on interactions, and their implications that are beneficial for the research process. Metaxis allows for an exploration, consideration and reflection of the 'other', at a distance from the real, lived experiences of the person taking on the role.

Metaxis matters in ATAR because the content of research often touches on areas of high sensitivity such as family violence, sexual behaviour, criminality and bullying. The fictional frame and the subsequent character/role distance provide a safer place for participants to engage with the research questions. This distance does not mean that participants do not reflect on their own experience, but rather allows them to do so from the safety of the role which is 'other' then their actual identity.

3. A fictional frame must provide the potential for imagining a different future

Fundamentally, fictional frames must be able to provide ways of not only describing current realities, but also providing spaces for imaging different futures. When working with the dispossessed and marginalized, this framing provides an opportunity within the safety of the fiction for them to rename their worlds. If, as we have argued previously, research must be based on, and also engender, critical hope and provide for an imagining of the future, the fictional frame can provide the aesthetic space for such work to occur. We argue that making a different world visible and creating our roles in that world differently is a form of active resistance, a matter of reclaiming stolen voices.

In the case of Young Mob the general outline of the story was fictitious, which allowed the young people present to expertly design and integrate their experience of the existing programme, and their lives, into the design of the new programme. The fictional frame delivered, in this case, rich data, because the task was well defined and simultaneously open enough to allow new ideas to emerge and be integrated with other ideas. In some ways the ATAR process is similar to open dramatic forms, such as improvisation. There is freedom to invent and create within a context that allows the 'actor' to use their experiences. These stand in contrast to a more closed form, such as scripted drama, where the background and experience of the actor is limited to the constraints of the character the actor is playing.

4. A fictional frame must generate meaningful data

If a fictional frame is not planned carefully enough, it is possible that the data will be too narrow or will not be sufficiently rich to generate findings. When planning the fictional frame researchers should carefully consider generating diverse data on several different aspects of the research question. To enable this process to occur efficiently on the Young Mob project, we mapped the research question to the fictional frame, and then to the data-collection strategies we were employing in the project. This element of planning helped us to collect diverse types of data. This meant that if one stream of data was not productive, there were several other streams for the research team to rely on for the research findings.

In the Young Mob project, multiple sources of data were generated through the different arts processes. The frozen images provided an opportunity for us to then consider and reflect with the participants on what they showed us in their posters. However, we perhaps attempted too many art forms over a short period of time. It meant that the level of satisfaction for the participants in the quality of their art making was sometimes low. We are unsure what the relationship is between the quality of arts making and the quality of the data generated. We have a sense that the level of technique in arts making does not have a correlation to the quality of the data generated. For example, although we could have spent much longer working on the freeze-frame images and worked harder to improve their aesthetic quality with the fictional conceit of filming them to send to the New Zealand Ministry of Education, they lacked any emotional punch for either the students or us. However, when questioned in role by O'Connor as the Ministry official, it was clear by the detailed responses from the participants that the freeze frames had provided a process for them to reflect deeply on the issues. To facilitate a fuller understanding of how the Young Mob Workshop proceeded we have attached the table below.

Table 1.1 demonstrates the flow of the research-generation sequence and the embedding of the fictional frame throughout the 2-day research generation of the project. The third column provides some explanation of the process.

Table 1.1 Sequence for YML research

Day one		Notes
9:00–9:30 a.m.	**Breakfast** **Welcome to country**	A welcome to country acknowledges the land as Aboriginal land and pays respects to the Aboriginal people present on that land. The research participants delivered the welcome to country.
9:30–11:00 a.m.	**Deadly Participators** Minister of Education NZ addresses Young Mob and sets up research 'frame'. What is it that is deadly about this programme and what is it that makes the participants victorious. Students work on tableaux that represent a problem, overcoming that problem and being victorious at Young Mob. Discussion and presentation.	The fictional frame allowed the participants to celebrate their success through the programme. This set a tone for the research that we were interested in hearing their stories about their success through the programme. Minister of Education NZ addresses were delivered through a short digital pretext. 'Deadly' is a term used by Aboriginal people in NSW to describe something that is excellent.
11:00–11:20 a.m.	**Morning tea**	All of the breaks were used by the research team to check in with each other about the effectiveness of the research.

Table 1.1 (Continued)

Day one		Notes
11:20 a.m.–1:10 p.m.	**Young Mob Qualities** Minister of Education NZ thanks the students for their work in the morning. It is so impressive that she would like them to work as Educational Advisors. She requests that the students develop posters that can be downloaded from the Young Mob website for deputy principals' offices. These posters will remind Deputies why Young Mob is deadly and how participants need to be treated. Students present their work advisory subgroups.	In the next session the digital pretext is developed further to deepen the responses from the young people present and assist in the data generation. One of the key issues identified in the planning meetings for this research was that Deputy principals were resistant to the Young Mob programme. This pretext was planned with this understanding and to engage the young people participating in this research. The aim of this pretext was to understand the qualities of the current programme that they felt helped them to succeed.
1:10–1:35 p.m.	**Lunch**	The lunch breaks were used to review the research data that had been generated to ensure that it was responding to the research question.
1:35–2:40 p.m.	**X-Change Game** Minister requests that educational advisors show how the game works and then discuss implications beyond the classroom.	The x-change game is a modified forum theatre approach that was used to generate success stories from the participants.
2:40–2:50 p.m.	**Wrap Up** Minister is impressed and will ask Light Bulb Advertising to contact students to do further work tomorrow.	The third digital pretext summarizes the day and sets up the fictional frame for day two of the research.

(Continued)

Table 1.1 (Continued)

Day two		Notes
9:00–9:30 a.m.	**Breakfast** **Welcome to country**	We used this time to recap and remind participants of the progress and success of the first day. Almost all of the participants who attended day 1 returned on day 2. This was a major concern of the research team and their continued attendance suggests that they were motivated to return and engaged in the research project.
9:30–10:30 a.m.	**Light Bulb Advertising** The President of Light Bulb Advertising congratulates Young Mob for their work because the minister of education has contacted him requesting that they be employed to develop a website that takes what is already in use and develops it into an effective, modern and future website. It must work 5 years into the future so students are to think about how Young Mob will look. The participants must now enrol into two of five options for developing the website: 1. Develop answers for FAQs 2. Develop tableaux of the future participants victories.	The second pretext assisted the research team to generate data with participants that imagined the future for the Young Mob programme. The various data-generation methods, including rap, documentary, dramatic tableaux, mixed various data-generation methods to ensure that the team had enough data to create a strong and cogent set of findings for use in the dissemination phase of the research.

Table 1.1 (Continued)

Day two		Notes
	3. Video promotional infomercial work. 4. Rap and music that advertises the work. 5. Radio interviews of a facilitator, student, deputy and a World Vision staff member from the future.	
10:30–10:50 a.m.	**Morning tea**	The breaks were used as a time for the researchers to give feedback on the data that had been generated at each session.
10:50 a.m.–12:15 p.m.	Session one	Participants rotated through the data-generation sessions. In the first part of these sessions the skills of each area were taught. For instance in songwriting, participants learnt from an Indigenous songwriter the skills of songwriting and then wrote a song as a group that reflected their feelings and aspirations for Young Mob.
12:15–12:55 p.m.	**Lunch**	This break was also used to check in with all of the researchers and review the depth and scope of the data being generated.
12:55–2:25 p.m.	Session two	Participants rotated in small groups into another data-generation session.

(*Continued*)

Table 1.1 (Continued)

Day two		Notes
2:25–2:45 p.m.	**Wrap Up** President thanks the participants on behalf of Light Bulb and the Minster.	This session was used as a plenary to evaluate the processes used in the data generation and to get responses from the participants on how they thought the data generation could be enhanced.

Generating diverse data: Making theatre in multiple ways

In the planning phase of an applied theatre as research project, diversifying the data is one of the core requirements of the research. First, it allows participants to engage with the data-generation strategy that best suits their needs. Secondly, experience has taught us that not all data-generation strategies provide the depth of data required. Often an idea for data generation that seems compelling in the planning falls flat at the research-generation stage. Employing a diverse range of data-generation strategies makes room for this kind of risk. In the Young Mob project we designed several different approaches to generating data/arts making. These data-generation strategies were built around the discussions with the young people and the stakeholders we had engaged within the planning phases.

As we mentioned earlier the data generated in ATAR can encompass any arts-based products and processes. In the same way that drama and theatre can include any and all of the arts in performance (narrative, film, design, music and songwriting, dance, etc.), applied theatre and research can employ any and all of the arts as a strategy to generate data. Deploying the arts in research provides access to communication and understanding that is embodied, affective and imaginative. As Leavy explains, the arts promote communication:

> Arts-based practices can also promote dialogue, which is critical to cultivating understanding. The particular way in which art forms facilitate conversations are important as well. The arts evoke emotional responses, and so the dialogue sparked by arts-based practices is highly engaged. By connecting people on emotional and visceral levels, artistic forms of representation facilitate empathy, which is a necessary precondition for challenging harmful stereotypes and building coalitions/community across differences.[155]

In the following section we will discuss some of the arts-based strategies that we have used together for data generation. The selection of different aesthetic approaches will reflect the kind of research data that are required and the specific preferences and needs of the participants and the particular arts skills of the research team. This list is neither exhaustive nor definitive but the discussion is intended to inspire new strategies for data generation that employs the arts in appropriate and engaging ways that suit the needs of the communities and the needs of the research. In the design of any ATAR project there is a significant amount of choosing and carving to be done.

Drama

The use of improvisation and playbuilding techniques in research has been used extensively for many years. It can provide data that are embodied, narrative driven and reveal motivations. Participants need to be provided with a well-planned structure that is accessible but also provides scope for rich data to be collected. For instance, in an ATAR project addressing bullying, a drama that considers possible reactions to critical incidents where tension arise could generate valuable data to understand how adolescents embody and respond to situations of conflict relating to bullying. Augusto Boal's[156] approaches also provide opportunities for data collection. Forum Theatre, where the researcher takes the role of Joker and guides the drama, has been used in several projects to collect data successfully. These approaches ask participants to intervene in community problems to uncover oppressive practices and generate consensus in solving community crisis.

In the Young Mob context we used a variant of the forum theatre process that the participants had already been working with. It provided an insight into how the Young Mob saw Indigenous students being treated at school. The tension of the work was heightened when O'Connor took the role of the racist and officious deputy principal. There were heated exchanges when the participants took the opportunity to engage O'Connor in role and talked passionately about their experiences of school and the importance of Young Mob in shifting their expectations. We did not plan on this researcher-in-role intervention, but it arose from our desire to lift the aesthetic quality of the forum piece by deepening the belief in the role of the antagonist. The flow-on effect of this was to generate richer data.

Songwriting

There are some groups who do not feel comfortable engaging in drama. In these cases it is wise to understand the kinds of art forms that these participants most connect with. Songwriting is a structured way of creating meaning with the added challenge of setting that meaning to music. Again, structure that provides a dramatic pretext such as 'can you write a song that explains why this program helps you at school?' allows participants to understand the brief and then work with the songwriter to craft a song that often has within it the narrative qualities that can be analysed. The role of the songwriter, facilitating this process, is crucial. They must support and provide skills for the creative process without interrupting or interfering with the data emerging in the room. There is also a balance to be struck between teaching skills, working within the aesthetic and developing data that can be analysed at effectively.

One group in the Young Mob project engaged in a songwriting session that ultimately proved disappointing for all involved. We did not give enough time to support the process, build in training and support with our Indigenous songwriter who clearly needed that to sort through the complex process of devising music with this group. The end result was aesthetically poor and we retrieved minimal data from the process.

Documentary

Allowing research participants to present their own voice through documentary making connects those generating the data with their audiences in a direct way. The structure required here is for young people to create a reflection of the experience and presented in a short-form documentary on film or radio. Obviously, sensitivity is required if this option is selected. Many young people do not have the power to give consent to the release of this material, and in some cases this material cannot be released because of ethics requirements. Even with these qualifications, this approach can be very effective in providing participants with agency and control in the presentation of their views on a given research question. A fictional frame will support the relevance of these documentaries to the research question. For example, if the research project was considering respectful relationships, a documentary maker could investigate what they consider to be 'respectful' in different cultural and social contexts. This approach mirrors Dorothy Heathcote's commission model[157] that 'commissions' students to take on a fictional role but to deliver a real-world outcome. In the research context, the role of documentary maker and the real-world outcome is a documentary (the commission) on what respectful relationships look like. These documentaries provide a uniquely authentic perspective with little intervention from the researchers.

The participants in Young Mob found this the most satisfying art form to play with. They enjoyed the power of holding and working the camera, of creating small scenes that they could then quickly replay and then reshoot. These were scenes of the future. There was much animated discussion as they worked and we recorded these rich conversations as part of the data.

The project would have been strengthened even further if we had provided an opportunity for the participants to edit and produce the final video. This would have signalled a genuine devolution of control over these pieces of art to the participants. This would have also mirrored a genuine power-sharing over the final results of the project.

Design

One of the approaches that we have used to good effect in the past has been visual design. While some participants feel self-conscious about their artistic ability, many involved in research projects do not feel comfortable taking on the role or engaging in any depth with physical forms of representation. Design process, if framed effectively, can heighten the importance of communicating a view or an idea above the aesthetic quality of the work. In the Young Mob project participants were asked to take the role of a designer and create a poster for a principal's office that reflected the values and qualities these young people valued in the Young Mob programme. The designs that the participants created not only reflected these values but also integrated (without being asked) the elements of their culture they took pride in. The process of design and its aesthetic discipline had the effect of condensing the ideas that these young people had about their culture and presented them in a visual form. In essence, this provided a visual summary of the collaborative focus group's discussions around the valued features of the Young Mob programme. There was much pride in these visual representations and they were used in the reporting phase back to the funder a valuable reflection of the research-generation and findings process.

The role of technology

We have not, to this point, discussed in any length the opportunities that technology provides for the generation of data. As we mentioned before, ATAR is a relatively new field and emerging technologies will provide new possibilities for producing rich and diverse data. While we have not personally seen any use of game design, gameplay, graphic novels or film-making, there are obvious applications for this kind of work, given an appropriate fictional frame, artists skilled in these areas and participants who have these interests. In the same way that technologies are revolutionizing what's possible in the professional arts sector, art-based research in general (including ATAR) also has the opportunity to extend what might be possible through the use of these innovations.

Technological advances have assisted with the development of arts-based innovations. Quite simply, new technologies have allowed for the construction, preservation and dissemination of many new kinds of 'texts'.

What we have witnessed in our own research is the use of video and still cameras (often integrated within phones) to collect data. These materials are often collected directly by participants and they provide researchers with an opportunity to collect authentic data that is controlled directly by those participating in the research. This is a kind of agentic shift in the research which places those who have often been the 'subject' of the research as the generators of the research.

These data-generation strategies are just a sample of what's possible. Artistic practice in all its hybrid and evolving forms is the wellspring of continuous inspiration and opportunity for arts-based researchers. If researchers have an appropriate framing and an understanding of the preferences and backgrounds of participants, any range and combination of these and other practices can yield rich data. In the next section of this chapter we would like to turn to analysis processors for ATAR approaches.

Data analysis

Analysing data in ATAR requires the researcher to understand the qualities (dance, drama, documentary) of data generated and apply appropriate analytical methods that capture the meaning from that data.

In this section we would like to suggest some approaches that we have employed for the analysis and crystallization of data. This section is not intended to be a comprehensive discussion of analytical methods but rather reflect some of the approaches that we have found useful in the use of ATAR analysis methods.

Interim data analysis

ATAR projects are often complex and sometimes feel unwieldy. The integration of drama, dance, songwriting and film would be difficult in any project, but when they are used for research purposes, another layer of complexity is added. To manage this complexity we have used the process of interim data validation midway through the research process. In the Young Mob project we had several data-generation/arts-making sessions taking place at the one time that meant that no one researcher could understand the totality of the data being generated. To overcome this we used the lunch breaks as a way of 'checking in' with members of the research team and presenting the data from the sessions that we had been coordinating. This process allowed us to understand the quality of the data we had generated (depth and scope), but critically indicated gaps that were emerging in the coverage of the research questions. We allowed time in the programme (see Table 1.1) for extra data generation to cover the emergent gaps. In practice, this was a meeting where the research team

- looked at the video,
- looked at the posters created in the design session,
- talked to the artists,
- listened to the songs created in the songwriting session

and generally discussed the coverage and depth of the data that we had collected to that point. This process also allowed us to check in with each other to ensure that participants were engaged and able to respond effectively. This process has several advantages from our perspective.

Primarily it allows the researchers in a complex process to monitor the shape of the emerging data and respond. Any large-scale research project must monitor the relevance of the data collected to the initial research questions. In these kinds of projects this is made possible through these kinds of validation processes.

Analysing the data

The multiple streams of data that emerge from an ATAR project provide some analytical challenges. Analysis of dance and film are obviously different to the analysis of drama or songwriting. In our projects we have used simple thematic analysis to deal with the diversity of data streams in the project. By analysing all of the data streams we were able to generate findings that connected directly with the research questions. An additional advantage of collecting data that is recorded (as posters, films, scripts or song lyrics) is that the data can be reanalysed at a later time. We also used ethnographic observation strategies to attempt to capture the 'atmospherics' in the room and to capture the silences. In a busy research project, ethnographic observation can assist researchers to understand the meaning of the action, the dialogue and the silences. In the research projects that we have been involved in, these silences have often been as telling as the other data that have been generated.

Qualitative software such as NVIVO is ideally suited to managing these diverse data streams. These packages now allow for the integration of field notes (from ethnographic observations), video files, sound files and other media in one unified database. Data can then be coded and analysed in a systematic and cohesive manner to generate findings that respond directly to research questions. Recent innovations in qualitative software have made the management of multiple data streams reasonably simple. This particular tool has been extremely beneficial for researchers as it allows researchers to summarize data and draw findings from diverse and large data sets.

There are of course many other approaches that can be employed to analyse ATAR data. Researchers use ethnomethodology, quantitative analysis, discourse analysis, linguistic analysis, image analysis, semiotic analysis to name a few. Paramount in this process is the fit of the analytical strategy to the project. One of the most prominent research contributors who intersects the arts, qualitative research and analysis strategies is Johnny Saldana.[158] His work demonstrates the potential for reconciling traditional research paradigms with innovative and performative approaches to data generation, analysis and representation.

Disseminating, communicating and presenting the data

The arts in general teach us to see, to feel, and indeed to know. What we are proposing is that the means through which the arts function as illuminating vehicles may find expression and utility in research activities as well as in the arts themselves.[159] The power of the arts to be a 'vehicle for illumination' and communication is unparalleled in human history. Performance ethnography has served the research field by reminding researchers of their responsibility to connect communities with research and has shown them, in a sense, how to build and operate the 'vehicle'. This is not only a contractual necessity, but also a feature of symbiotic research approaches. As researchers, we have a moral obligation to connect the research we have undertaken with our research participants. In ATAR projects the form of the data generation will often lay the groundwork for the communication and dissemination of the research. For instance, if the process involves the creation of documentaries by participants these could naturally be developed into a compilation that is presented back to the participants. In the Young Mob project this was done in several ways. At the end of the 2-day data-collection process the data generated were presented back to the participants. Additionally, each of the participants received the final video demonstrating their work on the project. However, as noted earlier, we failed to maximize the potential of presenting the report that included DVDs, written report, visual material, etc. back to the community as a whole.

Again, the approach taken to the communication of findings should be responsive to the needs of the community that generated the data. For some communities a performance is neither appropriate nor desirable and a short written report is more appropriate. For other communities that are geographically dispersed a short documentary film distributed over the internet may suit their needs.

Multiple ways ahead

We would be the first to acknowledge that this methodology is in its infancy. The explosion of opportunity that has arisen with the arts-based research movement has connected the power of the arts with the requirements of research. In many ways, we are just beginning to understand the potential of this marriage. As Elliott Eisner suggests (talking here about schools), there is still significant potential in these approaches:

> Arts-based education research will have a future depending upon our ability to reach for the heavens by crafting research that reveals to us what we have learnt not to see and on the public's willingness to accept what we have made visible as one useful way to understand and renew schools. In opening our eyes, arts-based education research may become something of a revolution in awareness, epistemology, and in method. But it will not be without its battles.[160]

The salience of this methodology will continue to evolve as ATAR researchers continue to innovate within the form. What we are suggesting here is not a rigid set of protocols, rather a set of principles to guide the ongoing development of this exciting methodology.

These principles are situated within an understanding that new paradigms of research are necessary because of the extraordinary times we live in. Although not exclusive, these principles can be briefly summarized as the following:

Personal and political motivation

We understand that the personal and the political are inextricably linked. Now is not the time to demand objectivity and truth, now is the time for researchers to stand alongside the silenced and the marginalized. Now is the time to understand the manner in which research is manipulated and distorted for financial, political gain by the powerful. These times demand critical researchers who are committed to agendas of social justice. Post-normal times demand a fresh and invigorated research agenda that still believes in the possibility of change.

Critical hope and imagining

As an interventionist ideology, the critical imagination is hopeful of change. It seeks and promotes an ideology of hope that challenges and confronts hopelessness. It understands that hope, like freedom, is an ontological need. Hope is the desire to dream, the desire to change, the desire to improve human existence. As Freire says, hopelessness is 'but hope that has lost its bearings'.[161]

ATAR demands of its researchers a personal commitment to the creation of critical hope. Research cannot satisfy itself with simply describing or analysing the disasters we presently live in. Communities who live in despair don't need any more research to tell them what their predicaments are. These are already painfully obvious. What *is* required is research committed to an agenda of social change and social justice, research that provides not only the visions of what different futures might be arrived at, but also positive, meaningful and constructive steps to achieve change.

Democracy

The greed of global capitalism is a direct threat to the possibilities of democracy. ATAR positions itself alongside those other forms of resistance, determined to hear the voices of the deliberately silenced. It positions itself alongside others involved in community-based struggles, which understands that at the heart of democracy is the power of talk. Talk, which disrupts, which challenges, which rejects the current hierarchies of power that destroy the lives of millions.

The aesthetic

In ATAR, while we are researchers, we are also theatre makers. We are committed to making theatre that is in itself powerful statements of resistance. We recognize and understand the power of beauty in a world made ugly through greed. We understand that the theatre provides a means to unmake the everyday, the ability to both think about and represent the world in startlingly different ways. We understand that the participatory nature of applied theatre provides opportunities to engage in theatre making for those restrained from arts making because of their class. We understand that theatre can speak powerfully by the dispossessed, *to* the powerful.

ATAR is not about using elements of applied theatre in research, it is about the centrality of the participatory theatre form within all phases of the research process. It is about making applied theatre in all forms *as* research. It is research *as* theatre. We understand that the metaxial relationship found in applied theatre within fictional framing provides safety in distancing for communities to speak honestly and truthfully to themselves.

The research gatekeepers will continue, as they have with arts-based research, to look with suspicion on ATAR. This is to be expected of any innovation, but especially an innovation that seeks to uncover power, privilege and status. This resistance cannot become a reason to stop innovating within this approach.

While there will be counter resistance, there will also be organizations within communities and funders that continue to understand the profound opportunities of ATAR. These opportunities do not lie in the stories that can be generated, and in the findings that can be delivered. Nor in the startlingly powerful moments of theatre that will be created. For us, the opportunity is to change the way we 'do' research. It is the opportunity to change the place of the 'subject', of the research putting them at the centre of the research process. It is the opportunity to negotiate the process and the product of the research with communities, not to just have research imposed upon them. It is the opportunity to be in partnership with communities, seeking to respond to questions that matter to them, not merely the questions that matter to us. In essence it is the opportunity, through critically departing from traditional research, to remake research that urgently addresses the post-normal world.

ATAR in practice: Complexity, hope and engagement in applied theatre as research

As anyone who has been involved in research knows, it can be a messy, complicated and sometimes frustrating business. We wanted in this book to give some of that flavour to working with ATAR. We wanted to go beyond our own experience and provide perspectives different from our own that provide spaces for contrast, consideration and reflection on the qualities of ATAR. The research that is described here is not the kind readily available in research textbooks or handbooks, but it does attempt to deal honestly with the challenges and joys of this kind of research. The next section of this book brings together a collection of six researchers who, in different ways, exemplify the underlying principles of ATAR. Although they exemplify the principles they are not models of exemplary research. They weren't selected with any pretension of modelling a standardized approach to ATAR, rather they demonstrate the eclectic manner of arts making that constitute the tools of this approach. We are delighted that the writers took our instructions to write honestly and reveal their work 'warts and all'. This approach recognizes that we have as much to learn about research when we admit our mistakes as we can by focusing on successful work. Monica Prendergast reminds us that 'false starts, wrong turns and dead-end disasters that are a natural part of the process of both performance creation and research'.[162] They also demonstrate the way in which the flexibility of the form means that ATAR processes shift throughout the course of any research endeavour. It is what they share in common that drew us to select these case studies and these writers to be included in this book.

The cases are all written by authors with a deep commitment to the use of applied theatre as a liberating, humanizing, research agenda. This commitment is deeply personal and political. There is no one in this collection standing in the splendid lost land of objectivity, validity and truth. Each writer speaks of his or her personal commitment to providing the space for marginalized, disenfranchised individuals and communities to resist. There are no hero narratives that pretend that the research has transformed lives, but there remains in each chapter a hope for a better world. This hope is placed within a realization that 'hope is necessary, but it is not enough. Alone it does not win. But without it my struggle will be weak and wobbly. We need critical hope the way a fish needs unpolluted water.'[163]

Each writer creates research projects where theatre and other art forms are used to generate, analyse and present or represent data. All the researchers are deeply concerned about the quality of the aesthetics of their arts making with their research participants. In each case there are moments of beauty where potent theatre distils new understandings and knowledge. Each writer is a careful researcher who ensures that there is almost a seamless interface between applied theatre and research. The political, ethical and aesthetic dimensions and their interrelatedness in ATAR are revealed in the honesty of each writer's account of his or her work.

Fictional framing is used in different ways in each of the chapters, sometimes the frames inform all the work and at other times they are a smaller part of the overall research design. In all cases, the fictional frames provide a form of distancing for participants to engage with the realities of their lives. Sometimes the framing occurs in and through performative processes and at other times through the establishment of fictional roles and tasks established in an ongoing improvisational form. Regardless, the fictional framing in each case is revealed as a central strand of ATAR.

In our selection of case studies, we made a number of other conscious choices. Other than Brad Haseman, who is a highly experienced researcher, our other studies provide the space for emerging scholars to present their work. We have also attempted to provide a diversity of cultural and political contexts, with ATAR showcased with children in care in England, in the highlands of Papua New Guinea, the site of ethnic massacres and reconciliation in Australia, retirement villages and alternative education sites in New Zealand.

We begin the case study section with a chapter written by Claire MacNeill. MacNeill examines the use of ATAR within the context of British Child Welfare systems working with 'looked after' children (LAC). In many ways MacNeill's work exemplifies applied theatre research at its best. Through a detailed analysis of her distinct use and application of ATAR she examines the ways in which this work creates a framework for a critical departure from research done *to* groups.

Claire has been developing research with what she describes as 'misrepresented' young people for many years. As an applied theatre researcher-practitioner her work has been committed to examining where and how applied theatre can integrate into the worlds of these young people and be of best use. MacNeill's chapter is based on her long-held interest in the social and political uses of drama, theatre and film as tools for research and development. Her analysis of the lives of these children's lives is chilling.

MacNeill's personal political commitment to this work is obvious as she struggles to make a difference in the lives of some of the most vulnerable children in England. After her initial work with LAC, she came to understand that the state system in the United Kingdom brutalizes these children. LAC are regularly confined in care homes, affection is deemed inappropriate and creativity and/or therapeutic intervention is non-existent. She realized that she could not walk away from these young people and has continued working for the last 12 years to find ways through ATAR to provide a space for their voices to be heard. MacNeill considers that the core of this research has been the evolution of child-centred, reflexive emancipatory research methodologies. She has been committed to discovering new languages, processes and research frames *for, with* and *by* young people as the collaborators of the research. She uses a wide and eclectic range of media and aesthetic frames to achieve this.

Her work reveals the manner in which the war on young people is the context for her research as a site for resistance in a post-normal world. MacNeill reflects on how her research aligns itself with decolonial thinking when she describes in disturbing detail how children are colonized through cold corporate approaches to their care. She usefully links the relationship between theatre and play and asserts that the various research projects may have provided children with the possibility and beauty of reclaimed childhoods.

Adrian Schoone's work is also set among marginalized children, but his work focuses on the nature or essences of those who work as tutors in alternative education settings. He contends because of their lack of formal training as educators they are marginalized within the education system and yet offer a highly relational and intuitive pedagogy. Adrian's research is informed by a phenomenological approach and he uses poetic enquiry as an arts-based methodology. However, his research takes a performative turn when he decides to use drama techniques with his tutor participants to generate both research data and poetry. His research starts out as simply attempting to blend theatre elements with his poetic endeavours but he ends up with research that embodies many of the elements of ATAR.

The delicate fictional framing whereby they get the chance to re-programme a robot that has been set up to replace them by the Ministry of Education provides a space for participants not merely to reflect on their own lives, but to consider them within the neo-liberal takeover of education in New Zealand. The fictional frame invites the participants to be subversive, to resist the dominant discourse that dehumanizes the teacher and the student in schools. In doing so, it provides a no-penalty zone for the tutors to be playful with their contributions. The form of found poetry that Adrian uses adds to the group's intense playfulness. Although playful in form, Schoone recognizes that the work is deeply meaningful for the participants and through the work they are able to challenge a range of disempowering processes within the education sector. Finally, in the workshop, the participants themselves take the opportunity to perform their work. This is not a planned, rehearsed performance but one that is generated spontaneously from the playfulness of the previous theatre processes.

The performance embodies the poetry found through the participant's playbuilding with the robot and awakens the robot within the fictional frame, but as Maxine Greene suggests for all the arts, it also 'awakens them to new possibilities' for their work with some of the most marginalized and dispossessed young people in New Zealand. Schoone creates a space of resistance where the tutors are able to reclaim their 'intimate uniqueness' which is stolen from people in post-normal times. In their romanticizing of their roles they reject cynicism, they reject hopelessness and instead find, through the theatre process, themselves in a community of resistance.

Jane Luton's description of the applied theatre work that she researched appears at one level a standard piece of reminiscence theatre with an attached research project.

However, there are many features that draw us to viewing this as ATAR. The multiplicity of research frames are used to capture rather than generate stories, retrieved through embodied reflection processes and then held in the temporary space of performance. The residents of the retirement village are encouraged into embodying their stories with the applied theatre facilitator using a range of pretexts as ways into the work. Video recorded, these then become the springboards for the young actors who will play these stories in the performance to interview the older people or to engage in further improvised work with them to devise the performance. The young actors take the role of researchers and they use applied theatre processes to then embody the stories that belonged to the older people. The final performance which brings both the young and old onto the stage together becomes a celebration of community. A community where young and old come together through the process of applied theatre as research, finding in each other's lives a connection neither group had expected. For many of these older people, their stories, their lives were recognized, told and heard and acknowledged for the first time. As an antidote to the dehumanized world of the twenty-first century, this is highly politicized work. The tears which flowed both on and off the stage are potent reminders of the impact of applied theatre on all involved. The ongoing relationship that was created through the project reminds us that applied theatre research displaces the traditional research relationship with one of mutual respect and trust. Honouring the stories became a mutual honouring of each other.

Linden Wilkinson's chapter which tells the story of the horror of colonization in Australia in the 1800s and beyond is also a story of critical hope and courage. The details of the Myall Creek massacre and the breath-taking humanity of the Aboriginal people who act as guardians on her research journey are powerful testaments to the divide between settler and Indigenous populations in Australia. Wilkinson reminds us that greed sits at the heart of colonization as it does in its current mutation as global capitalism.

Importantly however, Wilkinson chooses to place her research not in the site of colonial trauma, but at the site of the memorial to mark the massacre because as she says 'something positive had happened there' nearly a hundred years later. The memorial was a place of reconciliation in a 'silenced' landscape where that has seldom happened. Wilkinson avoids telling a story of false hope. She focuses instead on how her research sought not only to define a shared, equitable and sustainable future but also to find ways of confronting and addressing the wrongs of the past. Ultimately though Wilkinson reminds us that the arts reveal our common humanity, not homogenized and commodified, but a way of knowing each other across cultural and historical divides.

Esther Fitzpatrick also addresses postcolonial relationships, but works with the way in which descendants of settlers come to terms with their colonial histories. Fitzpatrick uses Derrida's call for researchers to speak to the ghosts. Defined as 'hauntology', this methodology involves interrogating relationships with the dead to examine the elusive identities of the living. Embarking on an auto-ethnographic project Fitzpatrick proposes that hauntology was particularly relevant to make sense of emerging and in-between identities in postcolonial situations. Throughout her study Fitzpatrick employs a/r/tography and ekphrasis as particular methods to summon up the ghost and disrupt the traditional narrative of Pākehā (white New Zealand) identity. Pākehā, representative of other white identities in postcolonial situations, often struggle with a sense of belonging and being able to articulate a positive ethnic identity. Using the ghost as a form of fictional framing, Fitzpatrick uses multiple art forms to trouble and disrupt the narratives of her own past, to challenge the racist attitudes and hegemonic behaviours of Pākehā. Fitzpatrick uses a range of arts-based approaches that culminates in an embodied performance of her poetry and paintings.

Brad Haseman has been instrumental in rethinking the relationship between arts practice and research over many years. He argues that we are at a pivotal moment in the history of research and that a third performative research paradigm is a critical departure that moves beyond either qualitative or quantitative methodologies. Using the folk opera forms developed by the *Raun Raun* Theatre company in Papua New Guinea, Haseman shows how the distancing fiction of this form acts both as a data-generating tool and a process for addressing significant cultural and sensitive issues.

Part Two

Case Studies in
Applied Theatre as Research

Applied Theatre as Research Working with Looked-After Children

Claire MacNeill

The chapter will explore the uses of Applied Theatre as Research (ATAR) within the context of British Child Welfare systems working with looked-after children. I will examine the ways in which this work creates a framework for a radical appraisal of research done *to* groups.

I have been developing research with misrepresented young people for 14 years. As an applied theatre researcher-practitioner my work has been committed to examining where and how applied theatre can integrate into the worlds of these young people and be of best use. I trained at the University of Winchester through an undergraduate degree that examined the social and political uses of drama, theatre and film as tools for research and development. I went on to teach in this area and to undertake a PhD into the specific uses of this work with looked-after children. This research took 12 years to develop and underpinned my journey in a range of institutions and settings.

Forming the foundations: The mainplace pilot project

In 1999, I embarked on a final-year student project within a residential children's home called Mainplace.[1] The project spanned 4 months and was facilitated by myself and four other student facilitators. We initially visited the home on a weekly basis with this increasing to three times a week towards the end of the project. As a final-year degree project we were required to work towards a conclusive event that showcased the work in some way and demonstrated the specific use of applied theatre in our chosen context. We worked with five young people who were residents at the time: Lila, Aaron, Emily, Leon and Helena aged between 10 and 12 years. This project established the foundations of my research over the subsequent 14 years.

We began by facilitating basic drama games in the games room within the home. Using improvisation and energy exercises we became familiar with the group, the setting, the young people's relationships with one another and the daily rituals within the children's home context. Improvisation-based role-play games provided useful frames for the young people to demonstrate their worldviews. We were able to explore the 'real context' through the 'fictional contexts' created through the drama.[2] The young people's choice of characters and scenarios were insightful representations of their real experiences. Aaron played a policeman arresting another young person in one scene. His use of terminology and his portrayal of power and authority suggested a familiarity with this process.

What became immediately apparent were the levels of tension, resentment and competition between the young people. These were exasperated when we introduced the idea of creating a group piece. Although they were enthusiastic to perform, the group struggled to agree on a shared idea or format. In an attempt to resolve escalating disagreements we suggested working on individual camera interviews to capture their different ideas. We themed these interviews around a Big Brother diary room with reference to a popular television programme at the time. Working on a one-to-one basis revealed how positively the young people responded to having their own space and opportunity to speak.

Away from the rest of the group the young people were philosophical about how they felt about living in Mainplace and the real causes for the problems within the home. They shared their hopes and dreams for the future and talked about their lives outside of the home, at school or with their families. This process illuminated the young people's need to speak independently from each other about how they felt and *who* they were. We realized that the group had been resisting working together because they needed to be heard as individuals. This was a pivotal phase of the project's process in becoming reflexive and responsive to the group's needs.

We built on this new knowledge by setting individual challenges such as giving each young person a disposable camera with which to take pictures of the things they liked and disliked. These photos revealed scenes that happened within the home in our absence and beyond the workshop context.[3] One photo showing a young person being arrested by two policemen within the home was a startling realization into the criminalization of looked-after young people.

Individual pieces

The groups' need to tell their own stories in their own ways informed a specific approach to adapting the work to create individual pieces with each participant that was unique in style and content.[4] The project became focused on the ways in which creative media could be used as tools for reflection, self-determination and expression. There was a fundamental shift in the leadership of the project from the facilitator group introducing different media, games and techniques *to* the group, to the young people leading the work with us working as their assistants. Each devising process was unique to each young person. They made decisions about the content and style of their piece and the type of assistance they wanted in producing it.

The refocus on these individual pieces had a dramatic impact on the group's dynamics. They demonstrated a sense of pride and commitment to their individual projects and praised each other's work. By owning something independently of one another, they began to respect each other as artists and co-creators and not feel the need to compete with or criticize one another, as they had done before. Some of the young people required additional cast members in their pieces. This helped to build bridges between the group members as they approached each other for help.

> The changes I saw in the young people were that they interacted for the better with each other and they OWNED the work it was theirs not staff/carers. The atmosphere was 100% improved whilst workshops were being done.[5]

The themes within their pieces explored issues of belonging, peer acceptance and the stigma related to being in care. They represented their relationships with staff members and the other young people in the home, the ways in which rules and regulations impacted on their lives and how they felt about the physical, aesthetic environment of the home. Helena's piece told the story of a holiday she had been promised and how it felt to be told a day before she was due to go that it had been cancelled 'by the people above'. Lila created a fictional piece about a girl struggling to hide the fact that she was in care from her friends at a new school. Aaron's piece spoke of how people look at him on the bus as a mixed-race kid and what it means to be in care. Lee created a mockumentary within which he played a number of different characters advocating for aesthetic changes to the home and surrounding garden.

The young people were unanimous in wanting 'the top people' of the local authority to be their audience. We sent invitations to the director of Hampshire County Council's Children Services and managerial teams from varying departments. The young people's individual pieces were performed to a large audience of senior management staff, residential social workers and wider members of the public. The response from the audience in the form of public apologies and the recognition of inefficient practice cultures was an alarming insight into how removed managerial teams were from the young people's immediate worlds.

Audience member: What do you think you got out of it yourselves?

Adam: The freedom to express ourselves.[6]

Everyone in social care should see something like this![7]

I think the directness of the approach meant we saw it as it is and just how immediate it is for young people. We recognise it in our own children but may not be as aware for children who are looked after.[8]

I was deeply affected by this work and all it had illuminated in relation to an *institutionalized upbringing*. The realization that looked-after children are regularly arrested in care homes, that affection is deemed inappropriate and that creativity and/or therapeutic intervention was non-existent, was compelling. The outcomes from this project inspired an expanding research project over 14 years. In this time I explored the relationship between research and practice in child welfare arenas, the ways in which systems and institutions are designed and structured and their impacts on those they 'care' for. I used applied theatre as a multifaceted tool to research these contexts, to develop work with participants and to examine the 'parodies, ironies and contradictions' within these settings.[9]

Expanding the research in related settings

The Mainplace group remained as my focus group by formulating the foundations of pedagogy and praxis and continuing to advise me. These techniques were expanded and adapted throughout my work with other young people in related settings.[10] This research interrogated *who* looked-after children are, the types of backgrounds they come from and their journeys into and beyond care. At the core of this research was the evolution of child-centred, reflexive and emancipatory research methodologies using a range of media and frames. This work was committed to discovering new languages, processes and research frames *for*, *with* and *by* young people as the collaborators of the research. I used grounded theory and hermeneutic cycles to inform my decisions about what to look at/do next and reflexive practice to recognize emerging patterns and trends.[11] Each individual project represented different

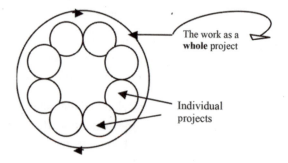

Figure 3 This research as an expanding action research model.

stages of a wider action research model (Figure 3) and enhanced the work in different ways as explained here:

> Action research starts with small groups of collaborators at the start (Mainplace group), but widens the community of participating action researchers (other children in residential homes and front-line staff) so that it gradually includes more and more of those affected by the practices in question (young people on the estates and within prisons).[12]

I continued to visit Mainplace and develop different projects within the home until 2007. I became a part of their community. Visiting the home over a number of years gave me an insight into the lifecycles of the home. The practice became an adaptive methodology that was able to respond to these lifecycles. We used it to mark different occasions, work with new residents, document celebrations, create pieces for staff members and young people who were moving on. The staff and the young people became comfortable and confident with how it could enhance life within the home.

I facilitated another 4-month project in a children's home called Crosstones after receiving external funding to do so. Using the practice as an adaptive methodology in this setting revealed the diversity of applied theatres' uses. I was alerted to the pitfalls in assuming one model fits all after initially assuming that this group of young people would also want to create a performance for managerial staff. As a younger group it was more important to the young people to play, experiment with props and costume, create sets and imaginary worlds and use film-making to tell their stories.

In both Mainplace and Crosstones the practice created different research frames through which the young people were able to reflect on and critique their worlds. The young people produced performance pieces for different internal and external audiences as well as creating pieces for their own personal processes of self-discovery. The themes from the pilot project in Mainplace resonated throughout this work. Through ongoing projects and discussions I achieved a deeper understanding of the sources of their oppressions.

Working within the institution

The resistance I experienced as I navigated my way beyond the homes into organizational frameworks revealed the paradigmatic contrasts between applied theatre practice conventions and social care cultures. The act and art of negotiating the use of this type of work within these frameworks became another fundamental strand of the research. As Thompson helps to explain:

> Theatre is a method of identifying possible and assessing existing interventions. Theatre is the research method itself. . . . Theatre is an action that is research. . . . Theatre becomes the enquiry, not the object of the enquiry.[13]

I was employed as a participation development officer for two different agencies. In both of these settings my efforts to create spaces for young people to own and influence pieces of work that helped them to *tell their own stories* were strongly revoked. As a research tool the act of trying to develop applied theatre work provided useful insights into the belief systems and cultures of these contexts.

Blinded by these agencies written commitments to empower and enable young people, I saw these employed roles as opportunities to expand this work and create a multitude of *individual pieces* for relevant audiences. As I attempted to develop collaborative creative workshops whereby young people owned the agenda and could define different routes for the work I experienced resistance, sabotage and reprimand from my employers. In the first setting I was advised to resign and criticized for not providing young people with a script. In the second setting I was told that I was interested in 'pure participation' and that is not what they were looking for. As Etherton helps to highlight:

> Agencies often say that they want children's participation in 'their' projects when they actually mean, the 'agencies' projects.[14]

These experiences were crucial in realizing the significance of applied theatre as a discipline in settings that view participation as a fragmented activity to affirm and stabilize the necessity of the organization rather than to empower participants beyond the reach of its institutional arm. As I was shoved about and manipulated I realized the ways in which these cultures can obscure and distort your ability to envision an alternative by being overwhelmed by agendas, timelines and bureaucracy. The 'organization of the organization' closes in and fills up the space to think critically or creatively.[15] It became apparent that it is these power techniques that keep frontline workers and social workers trapped by the myth of procedurally correct practice, through the colonization of their minds, time and imaginations.

These experiences highlighted the dissonance between rhetoric and reality and the value of applied theatre as a research process in action. If only ever reading the policies framing these agencies their real parameters and boundaries would have never been truly understood.

Housing associations

Working on different estates in London for a housing association revealed concurrent trends in how young people are viewed and treated by organizational structures. Young people were largely seen as 'the problem' by the housing association with teams dedicated to issuing 'anti-social behaviour orders' (ASBOs) and dealing with vandalism.

These cultures reflected the same provider–user relationships and segregations and distortions between young people and the decision-makers. In this context I was able to find spaces to develop and demonstrate emancipatory models. Many of the techniques that emerged from the children's home settings were expanded and adapted in this context.

Closed penal institutions

My work in children's prisons as an advocate illuminated the structural matrix of the care system and the traps children in care find themselves in. My work within this setting revealed the cycle of deprivation. I would continually meet young people from the children's homes and from the estate settings I had previously worked in. This setting exposed the manifestations of institutional abuse within a closed setting. The journeys of the children of the poor as cogs to the institutional wheel were laid bare.

Through projects, workshops, observations and negotiations in a range of interconnecting settings I began to construct an understanding of the care system and its complexities. The sources of repression and distinct trends of dehumanization were pieced together through the insights and representations the young people offered and the ways in which different organizations responded to the practice. My initial hypothesis that performances to managerial staff could radicalize the care system, in light of the pilot project, was informed through the research. Using applied theatre as *research in action* I realized the interwoven agendas inherent to child welfare arenas and the multiple needs and uses for the practice.

Power paradigms

The care system is a complex web of services defined by governmental agendas and deep-seated socio-political ideologies. O'Toole and Carroll's notions of framing is a useful tool in visualizing the different contextual and concentric frames that circumscribe looked-after children's lives.[16] At the centre of this matrix, fixed firmly at the bottom of an inward-facing hierarchy, are the care settings within which young people live. Each interlinking frame represents the different sources of oppression that engulf looked-after children's worlds. Set against a backdrop of Western, imperialistic research traditions these frames delineate the specific power paradigms that define their childhoods.

The outer frames represent the sociopolitical history that has established the British care system. The next consecutive frame represents contemporary assumptions within wider society fed and provoked by media, moral panics and political agendas. The next frame represents the power relations and power techniques as strategies used to deliver the 'care agenda' and the dissonance between policy and practice. The inner frame represents the immediate settings looked-after children are subjected to, the iron-homes, detention centres and prisons and the distinct cultures that govern each of them.

The origins of the care system dates back to the nineteenth century where the fear of Britain's slum and street children and the threat they presented to social order prompted the founding of new laws and institutions to contain, control and make use of this 'vagabond mass'.[17] It is within this period that 'delinquency was created' and a series of

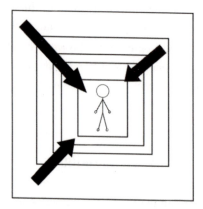

Figure 4 The power paradigms that circumscribe looked-after children.

new laws were established that explicitly focused on the punishment and correction of the children of the poor.[18]

Children's deficiencies became a growing national trend with government subsides feeding a multitude of mushrooming agencies and experts. Science and law provided a protective umbrella under which this web could proliferate.[19] Those who were not sent to work in England were exported in their thousands to overseas colonies to fight at the front line.[20]

> the time is approaching when this seething mass of human misery will shake the social fabric unless we grapple more earnestly with it than we have done.[21]

My research explored the ways in which relationships of dependency are fostered through the institutionalization of children and the uses of propaganda, othering, research and policy to mask and justify the brutal realities of care settings. Foucault, Freire and Smith help to narrow the focus on the *power relations* and *power techniques* manifested within institutions. Foucault examines the use of history-making to silence the voices of the institutionalized. He is interested in the catalogued myths that construct and stabilize institutions' power and control over others (figure 4).[22] Freire echoes these ideas with particular emphasis on the techniques used to exclude the learner in participating in their own development.[23] Smith's research into the colonization of Māori peoples examines the impact of alien institutions of thought and theory on the lives of those 'othered' by these systems. She examined how the foundations of their entire being were eradicated through the eyes of the Western researcher and the dominant voice of knowledge and power.[24] She states:

> they had theories to prove, data to gather and specific languages by which they could classify and describe the Indigenous world.[25]

My research revealed the ways in which looked-after children are colonized by corporate approaches to their care. Their opportunities to be children and explore the world are supressed by rigid, mechanical systems designed to feed them through administrative machinery.[26]

Looked-after children are trapped within ideological and physical frameworks dominated by science and expert cultures. They are disconnected from their childhoods and development and prevented from being able to *be* children. Complicated legal proceedings and meetings dominate their worlds, the language and cultures of which prevent these children from being able to communicate or participate in any meaningful way.

Science, surveillance, policing and the rationalizing of abuse and neglect through procedurally correct practice is integral to contemporary social care practice. The ever-increasing pressure on social workers to maintain professionalism in their management of 'caseloads' and their treatment of young people as 'clients' systematically removes and makes strange the basic premise of communication and care. By creating a system that is defunct and devoid of human emotion and opportunities for natural connection – order is maintained. By objectifying young people and making front-line workers 'the administrators' of these processes the care system is programmed to self-regulate rather than *enable* those embroiled within it. The dangerous act of communications, empathy and natural relationships are supervised and disrupted.[27]

Looked-after children are robbed of their identities, childhood spaces and imaginations. They are treated as empty vessels to be filled with dominant ideas. They live with the labels they have been issued by these systems, believing they are bad, worthless and unlovable. Their lives become a revolving cycle of abuse and neglect. Goffman, Wolfensburg and Tullman theorize this as 'the principle of normalization':

> How a person is perceived and treated by others will, in turn, strongly determine how that person subsequently behaves. The more consistently a person is perceived as deviant, therefore, the more likely it will be that he or she will conform to that expectation and emit the kinds of behaviour that are socially expected, often behaviours that are not valued by society.[28]

Their alienation from decision-making processes means looked-after children struggle when they are effectively spat-out of the care system most commonly aged 16. They have been 'un-trained' throughout their institutionalized upbringing.[29] There are approximately 60,000 young people in local authority care at any one time in Britain.[30] Children in care make up 49 per cent of the young offender population and 23 per cent of the adult prison population.[31] Forty per cent of young people taken into care have a criminal record within 6 months of entering into the care system.[32] The young people at the centre of these perverse and profit-obsessed systems are those most *in need* of protection and support.[33]

> Katherine: Sometimes I feel like I'm trapped and squashed into a little box and I can't get out.[34]

The reality is looked-after children are indeed trapped within a boxed network of political apparatus resonant of the power relations and use of policy and science on a global scale.

The review meeting, drama as a research tool

My research examined the impacts of these systems and cultures both by creating frames within which these experiences could be demonstrated and critiqued by the young people as well as creating opportunities for this work to create a counter to these processes of subjugation.

The Review Meeting is a pivotal example of the ways in which apparently depoliticized processes used to monitor the progress of looked-after children are embroiled with dehumanizing power techniques. How these meetings *feel* was powerfully conveyed during a drama workshop with looked-after children. After hearing a great deal of anecdotal evidence about review meetings the young people elected to recreate the experience so that I could understand, first hand, what it felt to be them in this situation. In role as 'the professionals' they set about creating the meeting context. I was cast as 'the young person'.

The mechanics of the meeting were made immediately clear as each 'professional' delivered a long report detailing their observations and recommendations about 'the child'/'me'. In role as a social worker, teacher, foster carer and doctor the young people adopted a distinct persona and spoke in a clipped, curt manner. I was not permitted to comment until every professional had spoken. 'My' hygiene, recent aliments, school performance and behaviour were listed as though I was not only *not* in the room, but that I was *sub*-human. Throughout the meeting I felt embarrassed and silenced. The use of my real name, rather than a character name, made the experience more immediate. The 'doctor's' recommendation that I should wash more regularly and for this to be more carefully monitored was particularly mortifying. There was a long discussion about which budget would support this new target.

Review meetings, in theory, exist as an opportunity to review the young person's progress and make decisions contributing to their 'care plan'. In reality, these meetings disconnect young people from their own lives and stories and treat young people as an object of enquiry.[35] The young person's privacy and personal preserves are violated as the professionals openly discuss intimate details about their lives. Each of these reports is added to a case file that follows a young person through their life in care. This power technique reflects the use of the dominant voice to create a 'culture of silence'.[36] A young person's story is *re*written from the perspective of the professional and in doing so the young person's own knowledge and experience is erased and deemed irrelevant. Goffman expands on these ideas by discussing trends of 'looping' punishments whereby past behaviour is replayed to inmates distorting the natural separations of time and experience and making it impossible to move on.

Applied theatre as emancipatory research

If we return to the established paradigms of power, as I have outlined above, my research examined how ATAR can impact on these frameworks and re-centre agendas around the ideas and identities of participants.

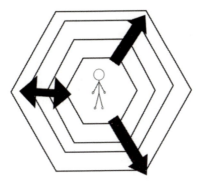

Figure 5 Subverting relations of force, re-centring young people within power paradigms.

My work used applied theatre to create radical spaces within these institutions to allow young people to reclaim their childhood spaces and provide an escape from the daily routine and administration (Figure 5). Within these spaces we explored new languages and devising processes that were unique to those involved. I used applied theatre to create sites of resistance and help young people to rediscover who they are and what they want to be. This work has therefore represented both method and goal.

> Self determination in a research agenda becomes something more than a political goal. It becomes a goal of social justice which is expressed through and across a wide range of psychological, social, cultural and economic terrains.[37]

What the work became and how it was adapted within each example reflects a site-specific relationship with where it was placed. As Balfour explains this is 'because the work is constantly changing in response to the practical experience'.[38] Prentki helps to further define the relationship between the context, the participants and the evolution of applied theatre praxis in this extract:

> [T]here is no 'correct' model; no workshop manual on how to do process. Again context is all. Specific circumstances give rise to specific

strategies for realising the purpose of using theatre as a means for marginalised groups to represent and/or change their social reality.[39]

Much of this work involved creating fissures within which to try to introduce a different way of thinking and realize an alternative to dominant organizations of power.[40] Sometimes these fissures were created through workshops within the children homes with different groups, other times through performances to different audiences. O'Toole describes the 'moments of awe' when the audience understands the significance of a performance in relation to its connections to the wider contextual frameworks and complexities engulfing that moment.[41] Through this research journey I realized the importance of the work was in creating these 'fissures' rather than trying to find *the* ideal context from which to launch the practice.

As with the review meeting workshop we used the practice to create fictional frames to explore and/or subvert the real context. As O'Toole helps to explain:

> In drama there must always be some congruence between real context and the fictional context . . . whether subversive or reinforcing of contextual values and attitudes.[42]

This use of the work represented the potential for this work to *merge the gap* between rehearsal and performance/fiction and reality and the ways in which a fictional framework can create a safe place to explore real experiences. These uses reflect Boal's ideas about 'rehearsing the revolution' while bearing witness to Bundy's concerns that those growing up in care do not have the opportunity to make sense of their experiences.[43]

Radical creative spaces

The younger children responded particularly well to games that transformed the space aesthetically. Through basic props and costumes we created space ships, weather rooms, 'fictional' children's homes, basketball arenas, supermarkets, talent shows and exhibition spaces. These different processes of transformation suspended the conventional confines of these contexts to create radical spaces for play and exploration. Through fictional frameworks we were able to celebrate the skills of young people, alter power imbalances and collaboratively participate in shared experiences. By entering to new imaginary worlds the young people and staff were liberated from the pressures and expectations that curtail their ability to interact and play. As Nicholson helps to explain:

> It is creative moments of transition that enable participants to move out of restricted spaces – literally or symbolically – and beyond identities that are fixed and codified by particular spatial practices into new forms of social identification.[44]

These activities were symbolic in relation to subverting the rigid frameworks that envelop these settings and in demonstrating the efficacy for this practice to create physical and ideological spaces of resistance. An example of this use of the work to engage both staff and young people while responding to the specific needs of one young person was achieved through the making of 'Keith the World Famous Basketball Player' film.

Keith was new to the home and experiencing difficulties settling in to this new environment. When asking him about his interests he told me that he liked playing basketball. By drawing in the other young people and staff members we created a mock basketball championship where the title of 'world champion basketball player' was being defended. Simon, a member of staff, acted as the opposition while the other staff members and young people swapped between the roles of the crowd, managers, reporters, score-keepers, basketball officials and deranged fans. I filmed and facilitated the development of the story by acting as the commentator behind the camera. This allowed me to alter the focus between each group member and facilitate the development of the story by acting as the narrator and stating what was happening and seeing it being played out and/or capturing the story as it unfolded. This mock film helped to raise Keith's status among the group and demonstrate his skills and interests as well as making him the champion. Simon acted brilliantly as the opposition who lost his title as world champion. This prompted a whole other storyline through which Joel, another young person, acted as Simon's manager and had to *look-after* him as the press demanded a statement about his downfall. This theme of reversing and exchanging the role of the cared-for and the carers/those *in-charge* recurred through the work as a context-specific technique of power-sharing.

These full group workshops brought the whole home together in a fantasy world where everyone was someone different and the home became a stage through which they could all interact with one another and play out different characters. Through basic props and costumes we transformed different spaces within the home into dressing rooms, press-release conference spaces and the garden as the basketball pitch. These types of techniques revealed ways of entering into the worlds of young people and creating new worlds within them. Through fictional frameworks we were able to celebrate the skills of young people, alter power imbalances and collaboratively participate in *shared experiences*.

Mini-me's

The lack of opportunity for looked-after young people to be seen as individuals and own processes of self-determination informed different strategies for representation through varying art forms. Mini-mes (see Figures 6–9) emerged as a technique within the children's homes and was later adapted in work with other groups on the estates. Using plasticine we created abstract representations of *who* we are and *why*. Different colours and shapes were used to represent different aspects of our identities helping participants to consider all the unique attributes that make them who they are. The use of plasticine to *mould* an identity was aesthetically significant and instigated important discussions about the ways in which we are shaped and influenced by our experiences. These processes helped to facilitate a deeper sense of 'self actualization' with looked-after children and produce miniature declarations of their identities.[45] As a counter to the homogeneous treatment of looked-after

Figures 6–7 Mini-me's created in a range of settings with young people.

Figures 8–9 Mini-me's created in a range of settings with young people.

children these processes celebrated diversity and individualism and facilitated important processes of reflexivity.

Leaving videos

Looked-after children experience a sense of no control over what happens to them, where they are placed and for how long as well as being disconnected from their pasts. Their timelines are dictated to them with no opportunity to make sense of what has and is going to happen. In one of the children's homes I visited, the manager banned previous residents from returning to the home to visit even if they had lived there for most of their lives. There is a culture of fragmentation that distorts and disrupts normal development processes in care systems.

In both Mainplace and Crosstones we began to make films to document the lifecycles of the home and to mark specific occasions. As members of staff moved on and young people were placed with foster families or left care we created good-bye videos. The process of making these films created a frame through which the immediate community within the home were able to document and research their shared cultures and experiences. Power imbalances were equalled as staff and young people became film-makers engrossed in processes of individual and collective reflexivity.

To create Louisa's leaving video the young people interviewed each other and staff members about how they viewed life within Crosstones and what they will miss most about Louisa. Even Louisa became part of the project when she was interviewed, in role as her own social worker, about how 'Louisa' felt about the move. Louisa, as Louisa, was also able to leave messages for the staff and young people via the film. This use of film subverted cultures of disconnection and the treatment of young people as 'passive recipients' of things that happen *to* them.

Critical drama and video processes can provide opportunities for people to explore existing representations of themselves and the culture they/we live in. . . . In considering practices that counter such marginalisations, opportunities exist for forms of representations to be placed in the hands of those who are normally spoken about[46]

Individual pieces

The use of ATAR to transcend multiple power paradigms and encompass the core considerations of emancipatory research as both method and goal was most succinctly encapsulated through the creation of individual pieces. Originated within the Mainplace pilot project I continued to use this approach and structure with different young people.

The devising of these pieces encouraged participants to consider *what* they wanted to say (their message), *how* they want to say (the specific form and frame) and *who* they wanted to say it to (the audience). Young people were encouraged to think critically and creatively and *own* processes of self-determination, self-actualization and communication. The strength of the use of the applied theatre practice as a research tool in this example is grounded in its adaptability and ability to place young person at the centre in the search for a suitable language, frame and format. These processes helped young people to regain control over the authorship and ownership of their stories and have a genuine influence over producing something unique to them. As opposed to case files written about them and reports only ever telling the professionals' version of events individual pieces created a context to capture the counter-narrative.

The individual pieces we collaborated in the children's homes took on many forms including: films, animated poems, photography exhibitions, clay animations using animal characters to depict different ideas, speeches, mini sets of worlds, posters and plays. We used these pieces to educate specific audiences on things that were important to the young people through a language and frame that reflected the young person's chosen mode of communication. This extract for Aaron's individual piece demonstrates how he elected to adapt Martin Luther King's 'I Have a Dream' speech. As the only black child living in the children's home in a predominantly white area his piece was significant in celebrating positive black role models and in identifying parallels in his own struggle to be seen and treated differently:

> I have a dream that people won't hold their bags closer to them as I walk by,
>
> Just because I am of mixed race doesn't make me a criminal,
>
> Just because I am from a care home, it doesn't make me a bad person.[47]

Foucault, Freire and Smith deconstruct the use of *autobiographical* and *culturally specific* processes to liberate participants from processes of colonization. Their combined theories for a liberatory praxis helps to construct a framework for the specific efficiencies of applied theatre as a research tool within social care settings.[48]

By magnifying the individual stories and theories of those trapped and objectified within these institutions the 'myth' of the unified state can be contradicted and destabilized. It is this annihilation of stories, cultures, rights and identities that applied theatre practice as a sociopolitical tool of intervention has been committed to rediscovering, and, in the process of rediscovering, has developed culturally appropriate, context-specific and person-centred strategies. Applied theatre as a research methodology has focused on ways to explore and respond to the specific needs and cultural diversities of those within the contexts in which it is operating. The uses of these strategies in social care settings realized the ways in which, as a collaborative research tool, the practice could *re*-humanize young people by subverting practices designed to objectify and demonize them.

> I understand Julie more from watching that [her individual film piece] than I have done in the last 18 months of working with her.[49]

Conclusion

Since the beginning, children of the poor in Britain have been treated with contempt. The manifestations of these attitudes in contemporary cultures are evident throughout the routine processes of dehumanization and institutional that shape and define child welfare settings. The specific techniques and relations of force used to objectify young people and create divisions between young people and their carers are magnified within children's homes, exasperated in children's prisons and detectable throughout wider social contexts. My research illuminated the lack of opportunity for these young people to engage in processes of self-discovery, critical thought and/or play. Looked-after children are disproportionately criminalized for acts that in a different context would surmount to growing up and making mistakes as part of their learning and development.

These young people are neglected by parents, systems and society and left to struggle in dangerous and hostile environments. They are stigmatized and demonized; they therefore often look for acceptance and protection in gangs.

> I was raised all my life to think I was worthless. . . . A lot of middle-class people think that gangs are untouchable and youths are unreachable, but that's not the case-these 13 and 14-year-old boys are scared, they are looking for guidance and they're going to anyone who can provide it, whether that's a 30-year-old gang leader or a 20-year-old church member.[50]

We need to develop a critically conscious practice that creates radical spaces for young people to be reflexive of their specific and shared sources of oppression and can inspire systematic and attitudinal change. The youth riots of August 2011 in London signified the union of young people across normal territorial divides through the shared objective to reclaim all they are excluded from. Unfortunately this protest collapsed back into notions of zero-sum power and an obsession with materialistic entities.

My use of applied theatre as research in child welfare settings created frames through which participants could demonstrate their ideas and experiences. In contrast to closed decision-making processes this work was able to treat young people as active participants in research processes and as experts in their own lives. The evolution of new methods and techniques in response to emerging ideas enabled applied theatre to act as a context-specific counter practice. In settings where systematic and scientific processes are symptomatic of how young people are excluded, collaborative research processes and co-designed research methods were particularly poignant.

My experiences in attempting to develop and transcend this type of work within organizational frameworks as an employee was crucial in illuminating dominant theory and the complex web of power structures. The act and art of negotiations was a fundamental component to better the understanding of how these webs function and the ways in which they interrelate.

Applied theatre as a research project has the ability to focus on processes of self-discovery, the development of 'innate skills', 'inner resourcefulness' and opportunities for critical reflection within and through the aesthetic space.[51] This work can offer new modes of comm-unication and the reflexive distance to articulate and make thought visible by equipping young people with the ability to see and make sense of their worlds. Workshop spaces, creative processes and access to new languages can provide young people with control over processes of self-determination *beyond* the stigmas and voices of authority that label them day to day. As a form of resistance beyond an attempt to simply counter-impose oppressions, applied theatre as research has the potential to reconnect young people with their 'identity kits' and their 'home-worlds'. This work can re-humanize. Radical freedom can take place through escapism and the opportunity to imagine and develop imagination as an internalized tool for survival.[52]

> there are some forms of resistance that decisively are not articulated
> to the dominant structures of authority and power in ways that make

them automatically recoupable by those structures, and those forms may produce a radical freedom that is not just negatively against a regime but positively for some value or ideal that lies well beyond its ideological territory.[53]

Mead's research into the use of theatre and art making in Balinese culture that treats young people as 'small human beings' and active participants in rituals and parallel participations is useful in imagining an alternative for our own young people. The cycle of neglect and abuse evident across my sites of practice highlighted a Westernized attitude towards contemporary poor law children.

> the ritual world of art and theater . . . is rather a real world of skill and application. . . . Children not only have precocious postural participation in prayer and offering . . . but also a whole series of parallel participations.[54]

Applied theatre has the ability to radicalize research cultures that treat young people as objects of research and passive receivers of inter- vention. ATAR can enable participants to become active participants in processes designed to meet their real rather than assumed needs and reassert their voices within society.

Finding Maximus in Fragments of Playful Intensity

Adrian Schoone

transform your whole life
lift hopes
shaping tomorrow together[1]

Every year in New Zealand up to 3,500 students are educated in alternative education centres. These students have been alienated from regular high schools due to exclusions, multiple suspensions or truancy. In many alternative education centres tutors are given primary responsibility for teaching these students the New Zealand curriculum, while also attending to students' pastoral needs. My phenomenological study seeks to understand essences of tutors, exploring their unique pedagogies that have emerged in the absence of tutors receiving any formal teacher education. I have used poetic inquiry as a method of both collecting and representing tutor experiences. In giving voice to tutors through poetic inquiry I wonder if their voices are a new sound of 'teaching', or perhaps their voices have a familiar ring to them, reminiscent of pedagogies we once knew.

In this chapter, I describe the closing act of my research inquiry when I brought together my research participants to explore the inter-subjective understandings of tutor essences. In the workshop I aimed to generate discourse among tutors through a series of drama exercises. I invited the tutors to infuse their essences into a 'tutor robot', made from cardboard boxes, which they named Maximus. The tutors worked playfully within the dramatic framing. Poems were enacted in both word and physical gesture to represent their collective self as 'other' through Maximus. The workshop progressed beyond a purely data-generating activity and opened opportunities where tutor identity was affirmed as the tutors saw themselves reflected on and in one another. Inadvertently the tutors romanticized their role, which became a critique of neo-liberal teaching practices. In this article I describe the workshop process and present four fragments of playful intensity that brim with tutor essences. I begin by describing the context of my research project.

Alternatives in education

All forms of education are alternative to each other. For instance, the onset of compulsory public schooling in the late nineteenth century for many 'Western' nations was alternative to pre-existing and localized ways of organizing learning, conceived as a 'private or semi-private charity' rather than 'social necessity'.[2] However, the idea of 'alternative education' emerged in the early 1920s as a response to the hegemony created by public schooling. For example, Summerhill School in England was founded in 1921 as a place where 'kids have the freedom to be themselves'.[3] Today alternative education generally refers to either those alternatives informed by progressive philosophies, or providers of education for youth 'at-risk'. The former emphasizes a humanistic, child-centred curriculum tailored to students' needs and interests and informed by democratic values.[4] My study focuses on the latter, where I seek to understand tutor pedagogy that aims to engage alienated secondary school-aged students in learning again.

From the late 1980s, community initiatives for education arose in response to increasing numbers of students not attending secondary schools due to exclusions, multiple suspensions or truancy. Creative Learning Scheme is one example of an early provider, established in

1997 by the youth pastor of an inner-city Auckland church who found that some students in her youth group who were not attending school.[5] Her effort to help students re-enter schools was unsuccessful and so she began a 'creative learning scheme' by offering these students a range of learning experiences focused on developing literacy, numeracy, cultural and life skills. The scheme also made use of the Mercury Theatre, where the centre was based, by working with students on creating a dramatic production retelling their life stories.

These initiatives took shape in the wake of a neo-liberal agenda to transform education through the policy of 'Tomorrow's Schools'.[6] As a result of this policy Vaughan observed that schools were 'becoming more conservative and competitive, and therefore less amenable places for students "at-risk."'[7] By 1996 there were 500 students in alternative education in up to 60 settings.[8] In 1999, these grass-roots initiatives were made legal through the Ministry of Education's Alternative Education policy. Milbank, Ministry of Education project manager at the time, described the policy as 'a combination of the community approach utilising people who can work alongside these young people, and the school's expertise and formal support'.[9] Currently there are 1888 alternative education student placements across the country, with an annual turnover of 3,500 students, in approximately 150 off-site providers and a handful of school-based programmes.

The alternative education student, aged between 13 and 16 years, is likely to be Māori (61 per cent), and male (70 per cent), and urban (93 per cent), and socio-economically deprived.[10] A health survey of 335 Auckland and Northland alternative education students found 'considerable health, education and social disparities are evident among young people in alternative education, demonstrating a broader failure of services to meet the needs of this group'.[11] A study on the background of 41 alternative education students, reported that most experienced significant problems in their family life, for example: violence, drugs and alcohol, poverty and sexual abuse.[12] Students explained they disengaged from secondary school because of 'teachers . . . not knowing them or developing effective relationships with them' and a 'mismatch between their levels of achievement and teaching levels'.[13] Alternative education tutors work with these students to help restore their confidence in relationships and learning again.

Finding the alternative education tutor

> you're their educator
> you're their driver
> you're their shoulder to cry on
> you're their   emotional punching bag
> the list goes on . . .[14]

The key protagonist in many alternative education providers for teaching these students is the tutor. The tutor is not usually a trained teacher but instead the one who draws from life experiences and other qualifications, such as youth work or trade skills, to provide holistic learning opportunities. The tutor role is therefore vulnerable to take over from competing conceptualizations of youth work and youth mentoring because of the broad range of outcomes that the tutors seek for their students, both academic and social. Although qualified teachers support tutors with curriculum planning, the role sits tentatively in the context of increasing professionalization and standardization of pedagogical practice; the 'positivist discourse that is concerned with the mastery of pedagogy techniques'.[15] However, because tutors tend to lack teaching qualifications they have become as marginalized as their students. In one report, tutors were described as: 'the least trained to work with difficult students', regardless of 'how well meaning they might be'.[16] These types of comments motivated me to understand how tutors were re-engaging students in education. I suspected that due to tutors' lack of formal teacher training, alternative education may be one of the few spaces left where a more intuitive and relational pedagogy manifests.

Informed by phenomenology I seek to find tutor essences, to understand their shared experiences and discern the distinctive contribution that tutors bring to the teaching and learning relationship. Phenomenology researchers seek to 'slow the research down and hold his or her gaze on the phenomenon itself . . . to illumine its special quality as an experience'.[17] My research quest is not to find the definitive but as Heidegger maintains essences reveal the manner in which something pursues its course or how it endures its presencing.[18] In the Māori worldview essences can be thought of as *iho*[19]: 'heart, essence, inside, inner core, kernel, pith of a tree, essential quality, nature'.

One research method enabling a view of essences is poetic inquiry, an arts-based methodology that privileges poetry as a way of knowing.[20] Within this research method, I chose to take the particular approach of 'found poetry', pioneered by sociologist Laurel Richardson.[21] In her study of unmarried mothers Richardson told the story of Louisa May, transcribing the tape into 36 pages of text. She then fashioned the text into a three-page poem using only the words of Lousia May, her tone and diction, but relied on 'poetic devices such as repetition, off-rhyme, meter, and pause to convey her narrative'.[22] Finding poetry is a phenomenological pursuit. Heidegger's view that 'men dwell poetically', a phrase he found from the poet Friedrich Holderlin, implies that poetry does not merely reflect experiences of dwelling, but also creates dwelling.[23] My examination of alternative education tutors focuses on understanding the language that tutors use that sustains them as 'being tutors'.

My research involves eight alternative education tutors, comprising six males and two females, six Pasifika (three Cook Island, two Samoan, one Tongan), one English, and one New Zealand European, who range in tutoring experience from less than 1 year to 12 years. These tutors work in alternative education centres across Auckland. I interviewed the tutors and worked with the transcript to craft poems from words and phrases I highlighted. I restricted myself to only using the language of the tutors. I also sought to find poetic utterances of tutors in their everyday language at the alternative education centre. Over the course of three months I visited the centres where the tutors' worked and observed them in classrooms, corridors, vans and meetings, taking note of the words and phrases tutors spoke. In my final research activity with tutors I aimed to bring them together to explore shared understandings of tutor essences, and this was when Maximus was created.

Blurring boundaries between poetry and drama

Originally, in my research, I used poetic inquiry conventionally, that is, content in collecting the spoken word and creating verse. I wondered, 'isn't this alternative enough?' Through conversations with colleagues who use drama as a way of generating data, I was encouraged to consider the performative and embodied nature of the arts, at large. Methodological boundaries began to blur as I explored the use of drama as a way of framing workshops to bring my research participants together to explore shared understandings of tutor essences.

At first I struggled with incorporating drama in this way because I did not see myself as a 'drama person', thinking it was something for expert drama practitioners. I soon appreciated the same argument, perennial in the arts, could be levelled at my use of poetry in research. Just as I recognized the poetic nature of what it means to be human, I acknowledged the dramatic and playful impetus in us all. This reflects the democracy of the arts, without dismissing 'artists' as master craftpersons. Furthermore, I began to realize this alternative approach to research sat well with a study on 'alternative' education, for in order to know about different things we need to explore in different ways. From these ruminations I developed a framework for a drama workshop that elicits poetic discourse.

In this chapter I present the workshop and outline its key features. I weave excerpts from my research journal, the workshop script and poems with reflections and theoretical links. There was a sense in which the activity was both playful: experimenting, risk taking, playing with language; and mindful: thinking about what we do, taking the human content and context of our work seriously, considering how what we learn might change us.[24] The workshop began more playfully, but as it progressed the participants were confronted with revelations of their essences. I now 'step inside' the workshop to describe how the workshop transpired to be a transformational moment for tutors.

Elements of the workshop

This is how the workshop begins:

> 'So what are we doing here?' – says one tutor, a few others agreeing with his statement. This made me apprehensive, conscious of not wanting to waste the tutors' time. All but one of the participants had driven across the city in heavy traffic, after a long day with their students.

After some refreshments and warm-up activities I gather the tutors to stand around a hidden object, covered by a sheet. I frame our time together with:

> Today let's imagine that the Minister of Education has decided to do away with human teachers, replacing them with robots. We have managed to get one of these robots through the 'Institute for the Preservation of Real People in Education' (IPRiE). We are charged with infiltrating the robot with the essences of the AE tutor. We have one of them; it will become one of us.

The script framing echoes Mantle of the Expert[25] in that the teacher, in this case the researcher, presents an enterprise and enables participants to take on the role of experts to solve a problem. However, in this case the participants are not fictional experts and neither is the context. The Minister of Education 'doing away with human teachers' in favour of robots is symbolic of neo-liberal education reforms, where positivist pedagogical discourse based on best evidence syntheses coupled with the introduction of initiatives such as standardized student benchmarking in reading, writing and mathematics, is liable to reduce teaching to a series of scripts and rules for the narrow curriculum.[26] Illich sees this growing 'algorithmization or mathematization' within society as people renouncing their 'intimate uniqueness'.[27] Perhaps the workshop will go some way to recover the 'intimate uniqueness' of the tutor.

Lifting off a sheet, I introduce the tutors to the crudely constructed robot with its body made from cardboard boxes, arms of polystyrene and cardboard-cups for eyes. The tutors are:

Amused	at the box-like robot
Astonished	that this is research
Apprehensive	what shall we do?

We stand around looking at the box robot. I ask the tutors to think about what they could do with it, and they give answers such as 'short circuit the robot', or suggest turning him into a Dalek from the *Doctor Who* television series. As a starting point, I encourage the tutors to think of a name for the robot.

The tutors throw around a few names. One tutor, seeing the company logo 'OfficeMax' on the box, suggests that the robot is named Maximus, Latin for 'greatest'. With the group agreeing with a name a tutor scribes 'Maximus' across the forehead of the robot with a black marker. I notice that once Maximus is named his status rises beyond an inanimate object, to become a type of personality among us who we could get to know. Life proceeds from the name, according to the storyteller Phod-lohk, 'in the way a river proceeds from its source'.[28] From the onset, his name gives two pieces of information: he is male, and he is 'great'. This slim revelation resonates with Rousseau's declaration about tutors from his eighteenth-century treatise on Education: 'A tutor! What a noble soul!'[29]

Moreover this dramatic workshop creates an environment where an implicit naming occurs, a phenomenological naming. Maximus is the explicit name, but the sum of his character, skills and experiences ascribed to him is a process of implicitly naming the tutor. It is a chance for the tutor to 'come into the Open *as*', which is a 'renunciation of all the dim confusion' that surrounds the tutor role.[30] As Freire says 'to exist, humanely, is to *name* the world to change it'.[31] Naming, which occurs from encounters of dialogue with mutual love and trust, brings significance and dignity. It is to turn 'anybodies, faceless men without qualities' into 'somebodies', who are 'positively characterized and appropriately labelled'.[32]

Next, I ask the tutors to search for words and phrases from the weekend newspaper that they feel describe themselves as tutors. I toy with the idea that the experiences of tutors are somehow encoded through this large selection of language, as Merleau-Ponty suggests 'language has all our future experiences written in to it, just as the destiny of men is written in the stars'.[33] I ask the tutors to cut these words and phrases out and paste them on the robot, making Maximus a type of three-dimensional concrete poem. This activity bears similarities to a drama strategy 'Roll on the Wall' where words and phrases that describe a certain character are written on the outline of a person drawn on a large sheet of paper. In the workshop tutors are not completely free to brainstorm, as they are restricted to use only the words and phrases they find in the one newspaper.

The act of selecting particular words and phrases is an initial distilling for essences. The room is large and open, some tutors sit at tables; others sit on the floor or remain standing, continually moving. One tutor decides to find music on his iPhone to play while performing the activity. Most tutors cut and paste words and phrases, one after another. Many joke about. One tutor makes a pile of words in front of her, carefully considering each one, distilling further essences. Another tutor decides to paste images on the robot from a catalogue: a coffee machine, walkie-talkie, GPS and charger. He explains that the robot is getting an 'upgrade'. This moving, standing, cutting, pasting, music listening, sorting and joking are ways of thinking, considering, sorting and engaging.

I caution the tutors to pay particular attention where they paste these words, mindful that their position will enhance meaning. One tutor intimates she seeks my approval as she gingerly straddles the word 'opportunity' across the two eyes, and pastes the phrases 'new look' and 'in the heart' as eyelids.

Maximus

Eyes of:	opportunities
Speaking:	tender respect
Hands:	help, create, fun
From a heart of:	substance, inspiration

After about 40 minutes Maximus is clothed with over 80 separate words and phrases. I give the tutors time to walk around Maximus and read the various phrases. It is as if he is speaking to us; as we speak the words on him we enliven him: 'the spoken word is genuine gesture, and it contains its meaning in the same way a gesture contains it'.[34]

In order to further explore shared meanings I proceed by giving each tutor seven stars to place on statements that resonate most with them. I explain that when the robot is mass-produced the words

Figure 10 Maximus.

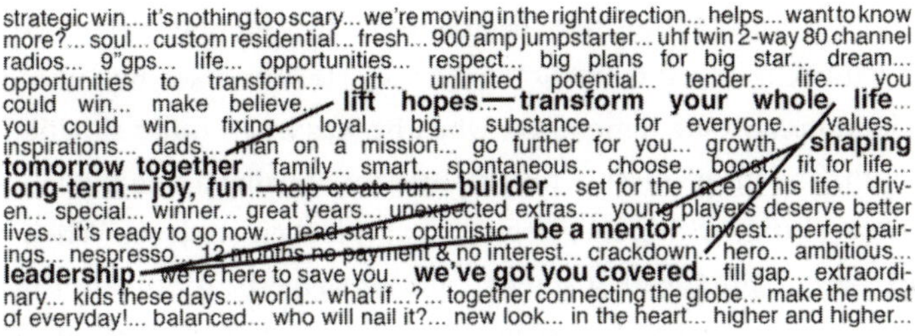

strategic win... it's nothing too scary... we're moving in the right direction... helps... want to know more?... soul... custom residential... fresh... 900 amp jumpstarter... uhf twin 2-way 80 channel radios... 9"gps... life... opportunities... respect... big plans for big star... dream... opportunities to transform... gift... unlimited potential... tender... life... you could win... make believe. **lift hopes.—transform your whole, life**... you could win... fixing... loyal... big... substance... for everyone... values... inspirations... dads... man on a mission... go further for you... growth... **shaping tomorrow together**... family... smart... spontaneous... choose... boost.. fit for life... **long-term.—joy, fun**. help create fun... **builder**... set for the race of his life... driven... special... winner... great years... unexpected extras.... young players deserve better lives... it's ready to go now... head start... optimistic... **be a mentor**... invest... perfect pairings... nespresso... 12 months no payment & no interest... crackdown.. hero... ambitious... **leadership**... we're here to save you... **we've got you covered**... fill gap... extraordinary... kids these days... world... what if...?... together connecting the globe... make the most of everyday!... balanced... who will nail it?... new look... in the heart... higher and higher...

Figure 11 Words and phrases pasted on Maximus by tutors.

that have stars will be illuminated. They are able to distribute the stars as they wish, for example they can put more than one star on statements they think represent depth of tutor essences. In the chart above I have listed all the words pasted on Maximus. I have made bold the words that are given two or more stars. I suggest that these illuminated words present an intensity of tutor essences. I play with lines connecting words. It is as if I am making constellations with language to find meaning.

These connections create the following found poem:

long-term – joy,
fun – builder leadership
be a mentor
shaping tomorrow together
lift hopes
transform your whole life
we've got you covered

We sit down together to discuss some of the words and phrases that appear on Maximus. I pick out certain phrases, which we discuss as a group, tracing the nuances of meaning in the alternative education context. For example, one tutor explains he commits to his students for the long term in the same way he remains loyal to the Warriors; a rugby league team that has had successive losses all season. When the group discusses 'lifting hopes', another tutor states that 'a lot of students come to us broken, they have been rejected by a lot of different people, and I think we need to show them hope'. He says 'I see myself as the student', because he remembers when he was in a similar situation as a youth. The tutors discuss the importance of being a role model; one who transforms within themselves, alongside their students. When you work on one thing with a student, a tutor suggests, it can affect many areas for the student. He explains that when a student learns to show respect to him or herself, he observes that the student then usually respects others.

The workshop continues with tutors interacting with Maximus in four ways. First, the tutors depart from using only the newspaper to adding their own words to Maximus. Secondly, the tutors make their own found poem together, reciting this into the heart of Maximus. Thirdly, as Maximus leaves impressions, the tutors make a one-word print for him to imprint on his students. Finally, the tutors give Maximus some advice before he departs to infiltrate the other robots.

In the following section, I will explore elements from these four activities and present fragments of meaning arising from playful intensity. I observe this intensity occurs when playfulness gives way to mindfulness. These moments disrupt linearity, enabling research participants to take greater ownership of the experience.

Fragment one: 'It's the love that's missing'

The first fragment of playful intensity occurs during the discussion with my research participants regarding the phrases on Maximus and the sense that there are things that the tutors want to say but feel inhibited by the limit of words and phrases available in the newspaper. Curious to explore what is silenced I decide to break my rule of only finding words and phrases from the newspaper, allowing the tutors to write their own words on Maximus too. I feel if I give voice to tutors in one

open... **listener**... loyal... available... someone to talk to... advisor... buy them a feed... **encourage**... persistent... **love**... **role model**... be an example... believe in yourself... respect 4 yourself... care... integrity... genuine... real... honest... tenacious... "seeing is deceiving, dreaming is believing"... positive... opposite... speaking truth... equipping for life...

Figure 12 Additional words and phrases on Maximus generated by tutors.

hand, I cannot take it from them with the other hand. I am surprised at the response to loosening the rules, as the tutors readily write out words on paper and then paste them onto Maximus.

I give the tutors a few extra stars that they can place on their words. In the chart above I have made bold the words that were mentioned either more than once or had two or more stars on them. The tutors' new words focus on relational concepts – 'love', 'care', 'encourage' and 'listen'; personal qualities – 'loyalty', 'honesty', 'integrity', 'persistence'; and resilience-building factors such as 'believing in yourself'.

Tutors caring for their students, and loving them as a parent would, recurs as a theme in the research project. Indeed the word tutor derives from Latin '*tueri*': 'to watch, guard'.[35] Noddings contends that caring is central to pedagogical practice.[36] The tutors' parental-type love for their students appears in my interviews, and they are keen to have these traits represented on Maximus also. The following poems are made from interviews with tutors:

i felt these kids need a mother
i want to protect them, you know, from what's going on
i am not a teacher, as such
i learn that these kids need more than *this* teaching
just care for them
full-time, going on six years now[37]

i could have easily chucked it away, but
i do love them and if i didn't
i couldn't be here
i would never call myself a teacher
i am more of a father[38]

With the ongoing professionalization of teaching, there is increasingly less consideration of teachers as *loco parentis*. Max van Manen suggests there is a deep connection between parenting and teaching as they 'derive from the same fundamental experience of pedagogy', which is to 'empower children to give active shape to their life contingencies'.[39]

Fragment two: Seeing the self in other

The next fragment of meaning occurs when we sit around Maximus. The tutors discuss his various attributes, and at times they contemplate him silently. Just before we move on to the next activity one tutor says: 'Maximus could be a manager.' I ask the tutor to explain further, to which he directs me to 'look at all the skills Maximus has', and I reply 'that *you* have.'

> *Found poem from Maximus*
> extraordinary leadership
> unexpected extras
> 5-inch GPS, 2 way channel radios, 900 amp jumpstarter
> shaping tomorrow together

This is a self-actualizing moment for the tutor who, by looking upon his array of skills and dispositions pasted on to Maximus, realizes his own value and essences. The tutor declaring Maximus 'could be manager' is a metaphor that expresses worth, where being 'management' is what the tutor sees as valuable. Our exchange resembles Boal's analysis of *metaxis* where simultaneously the participant belongs to two different worlds: 'the image of reality and the reality of the image'.[40] It is in within this nexus of interplaying forms that Boal describes the potential liberating effect of 'enacting his liberation in the reality of these images . . . then extrapolate into his own life'.[41] Although there is no time in the workshop to explore this tutor's comments further, at a fundamental level I find that the experience of creating Maximus affirms tutors in their identity and value.

Fragment three: The heart of Maximus

I ask the tutors to create a found poem using the words and phrases pasted on Maximus and to speak this poem into his heart. This will be recorded and then played back as if Maximus himself is speaking to us. I am surprised at the ease with which tutors organize themselves, working together by brainstorming various phrases from Maximus and then arranging the phrases. They add a new phrase: 'finding that diamond in the rough.' The tutors are given time to rehearse and then, rather than deciding to take separate parts, speak the following poem in unison into the recording device:

> believe in yourself to see beyond your current reality
> to lift hopes, love, integrity and fresh ideas
> move in the right direction – transformed lives: *finding*
>   *that diamond in the rough*
> be a role model and a mentor
> be someone who builds with the long term in mind
> we've got you covered

The chorus of tutors reciting the poem into the recording device is performative and ritualistic. Austin points out a performative sentence 'indicates that the issuing of the utterance is the performance of an action – it is not normally thought of as just saying something'.[42] Therefore, as the tutors recite the poem it is as if Maximus is receiving his soul. The found poem reads as a two-fold imperative. First the tutors direct Maximus to act in certain ways, and secondly when Maximus speaks this found poem back it is an imperative towards his students. This reflects the observation a tutor made earlier that transformation occurs with both the tutor and the student simultaneously.

The tutors speaking in unison into the robot's heart also demonstrates the agreement of tutor essences, where their individually chosen phrases appear to 'pluralise of its own accord'.[43] When the recording is played back it is as if Maximus speaks, his voice and words are familiar yet strange.

Fragment four: Leaving imprints

Because Maximus leaves impressions, I ask the tutors to make a small printing block with the one-word impression that they want Maximus to make. I explain that as teachers imprint grades on their students, what sorts of impressions do tutors make on their students? The words

Figure 13 The one-word prints tutors make.

the tutors choose are: 'confidence', 'hope', 'restore', 'caring', 'ready', and 'ripple'. Using adhesive cut-out cardboard letters the tutors create a printing block. To test the imprint, tutors are able to make crayon rubbings from their prints.

The tutors discuss among themselves that this is an activity they would like to do with their own students. On a separate occasion I discussed with the principal of the alternative education provider that a similar process could be used to explore the graduate profile of an alternative education student. In these ways the workshop could become a pedagogic gift to tutors and others.

To end the 90-minute workshop I ask the tutors to give Maximus some advice before he leaves to infiltrate schools and alternative education settings. In giving their advice, I ask the tutors to make sure they include the word from their print in their advice. As the tutors give their advice, in turn it soon becomes a dramatic and ritualistic performance. The tutors perform this poem:

whatever he imprints, he *restores* – digest it!

> *The tutor approaches Maximus,*
> *and as he says, 'digest it' he*
> *thrusts the word into the*
> *mouth, a cut out hole.*

caring . . . Maximus, you are more than a robot, you have a heart now, we anoint you, and appoint you

> *The tutor takes the print and*
> *places it in his mouth as another*
> *tutor acts to sprinkle anointing*
> *oil over Maximus.*

Maximus, this is your mission: instil and impart *hope!*

> *Like the first tutor, he places the*
> *print inside Maximus' mouth.*

a person who is going to make *ready*, i knight you

> *The tutor enacts knighting the*
> *tutor, by tapping Maximus on*
> *each shoulder.*

ripple . . . generational impact . . . go!

> *The tutor waves his hands*
> *upwards to 'shoo' Maximus off.*

At this point I put a sheet over Maximus and the workshop ends. The physical actions and interactions with Maximus are an unexpected innovation from the tutors, lending insight into their pedagogy which values embodied learning experiences, humour and encouraging language. The rich discourse of the tutors is far from robotic auto- mations. I will now briefly consider the essences of tutoring that appear from the lines in the tutors' poem.

whatever he imprints, he restores, digest it!

A tutor essence is to restore confidence in self, and in learning again.[44] This imprinting occurs through poetic utterance, *poïesis*, bringing forth. This is not a summative academic judgement, but often appears as words of encouragement, such as 'believe in yourself to see beyond your current reality.' Buber observes that 'teachers who want to help the pupil to realize his best potentialities must intend him as this particular person, both in his potentiality and in his actuality'.[45] The poetic utterance is made possible by the tutors having positive relationships with students. This occurs when the student's 'resistance against being educated gives way to a singular happening: he accepts the educator as a person'.[46] The tutor directs Maximus to digest his advice, symbolic of Maximus 'taking it in'.

caring . . . Maximus, you are more than a robot, you have a heart now, we anoint you, and appoint you

A tutor essence is to care like a parent, which is elaborated on earlier in this chapter. The tutor demonstrates the importance of caring as an attribute of character that makes Maximus 'more than'. Caring becomes the prerequisite for his anointing and appointing for mission. The act of anointing Maximus with oil is a religious symbol to 'confer divine or holy office'.[47] There is a sense in which tutoring is vocational, a response to a call to make a difference. The Latin root of the word vocation, 'vocare', means 'to call'.[48] This hallmark of tutoring became an indicator of good practice in the Education Review Office report on alternative education: 'staff show enthusiasm about making a difference for students'.[49] The moral impetus of wanting to make a difference seems to integrate into tutor pedagogy ensuring their activity focuses on the achievement and well-being of each student.

Maximus, this is your mission: Instil and impart *hope!*

A tutor essence is to be an agent of hope. This is to think in terms of possibility rather than probability.[50] The manner in which this is accomplished is through instilling and imparting. Instil means to either 'gradually but firmly establish an idea or attitude in a person's mind' or 'put (a substance) into something in the form of liquid drops'.[51] Instilling drops of hope. Instilling is reflected in the following poem found from a tutor interview transcript:

> a little spark went on in his eyes
> the shoulders go back
> 'oh, this is easy'
> it is little steps of epiphany all the time[52]

Imparting hope occurs when tutors make students party to their own journeys of hope. This is reflected in the following found poem from a research interview transcript:

> i started sharing about my grandparents and how
> i was given up at three months old, but hey 'i'm still here, i'm still
> moving forward'

'don't lie about your life being the same as mine.'
i buried that, i didn't tell anyone
he knew someone else was on the same page as him
it kinda did justice to both of us[53]

a person who is going to make *ready*, i knight you

An essence of tutoring is preparing young people for their next educational destination. The knighting of Maximus, provocative and unexpected, ennobles the tutor.

ripple . . . generational impact . . . go!

An essence of tutoring is to view their work from a wide angle. The tutors commit to their students for the long term. This is no 'short fix for [academic] credits' according to one tutor. Also, tutors embrace the student in the context of *whanau* (family) where a generational impact can occur. Therein lies a hope that the positive change that occurs for the student will 'ripple' out messages of possibility to family members that may be in similar predicaments. Signalling that the tutors feel Maximus is imbued with enough essences, the last word of the workshop is 'go!'

Maximus: A romantic critic

make - believe
what if . . .?
dream great years
together

In this dramatic workshop the tutors inadvertently romanticized their role, mirroring Rousseau's declaration: 'A tutor! What a noble soul!'[54] From the beginning of the workshop with naming the tutor

'Maximus', greatest; then to labelling the tutor with words such as 'tender', 'loyal', 'inspiration', 'man on a mission', 'honest', 'genuine', and 'positive', with the final act of knighting him (tutors knighting themselves), it is as if Sir Maximus was about to mount his steed and proceed to save students thrust from a Dickensian/Coketown-type school. Maximus only briefly alludes to his challenges, with 'kids these days – 12 months no payments & no interest'. Novalis, a protagonist of the early German romantic period declares 'the world must be romanticised'.[55] In part, this charge arose as a reaction to Enlightenment where everything appeared subdued by reason. The early romantics became disconnected from their community bereft of customs and laws condemned as antiquated, disconnected from nature bereft of mystery, magic and beauty, and disconnected from religious faith, relegated as mythology.[56] Therefore, to romanticize the world, Novalis explains, is to 'give the commonplace a higher meaning, the customary a mysterious appearance, the known the dignity of the unknown, the finite illusion of the infinite'.[57] The romantic tutor emerges in response to the neo-liberal context of education and wider society reform that has resulted in students experiencing rootlessness themselves.

The workshop method was also romantic, promoting the tutors to work aesthetically, as they considered where best to place words on Maximus and creating and performing found poetry. This confluence of poetic inquiry and drama-as-inquiry provided an embodied research experience that tutors found unexpected, playful and pivotal for understanding their essences. Observing the tutors working together and listening to their conversations was a rich source of poetic utterance for my research project. Creating Maximus provided a safe distance for tutors to explore their identity and Maximus, being the accumulation of multiple voices, provided another level of distance again. Now and then tutors ask after Maximus, who sits in my office, and whenever I look over to him he continues to tell me something new about himself as a tutor. Perhaps there is a word that I had not yet seen, or a new combination of words that might provide another insight. Only the other day he told me to,

make the best of every day!
it's nothing too scary
we're moving in the right direction

Pretending to Research:
Young People at the Centre of Discovery

Jane Luton

Introduction

Just because you find that life's not fair
It doesn't mean that you just have to grin and bear it
If you always take it on the chin and wear it
Nothing will change

(When I grow up)
Just because I find myself in this story
It doesn't mean that everything is written for me

If I think the ending is fixed already
I might as well be saying I think that it's ok
And that's not right

The young actors stand on stage, beginning to perform the show's final song. A few members of the cast walk downstage to meet the seniors who are waiting in their front row seats, ready to be led into the spotlight to lend their voices to Minchin's 'When I grow up'.[1] As the song draws to a close, loud applause rings out as the cast and seniors take their bow. The seniors return to their seats with huge smiles. A large screen drops down, video and photographic images begin to play, displaying moments of the senior citizens engaged in the drama process that culminated in the performance. The audience get a brief taste from the video of the laughter and smiles, discussions, performances and the sharing of artefacts that were all part of the research journey which culminated in the performance of *Capturing the Tales*.

This intergenerational project began its life in a research hub on social justice during the International Drama in Education Research Institute in Limerick, Ireland, 2012 (IDIERI 7). Stephen Dallow of Applied Theatre Consultants and Sarah Woodland of Griffiths University, Brisbane, discussed developing an intergenerational drama project in Auckland, New Zealand. Sarah had previously devised and developed a similar project in Australia. In 2013, The Trusts Community Foundation provided funding for the project. After approval by the Residents Committee and Management within the Waitakere Gardens Retirement Village in West Auckland, several of the residents volunteered to become a part of the project. The plan was for the seniors to begin sharing personal stories through drama. Young people would collect these stories by working alongside them and translating their stories into a series of public performances. The young people volunteered to join the project from Kids 4 Drama (a community school of performing arts also based in West Auckland). Kids 4 Drama has been running for over 20 years at the Blockhouse Bay Community Centre in Auckland, carrying out weekly after-school drama sessions and presenting a wide range of devised productions. Many members of the group had spent several years working together, and were therefore familiar with the languages and strategies of educational drama and theatre. However, this was their first foray into using drama as a research tool and creating the subsequent ethnographic performance. Part of the introductory process required the students to become familiar with research approaches, and to develop an awareness of the seniors as real people – with real stories to tell.

The seniors were all residents at the Waitakere Gardens Retirement Village, an independent lifestyle retirement village in Henderson. The retirement village is a vibrant place, with many activities for the residents. Most of the residents who chose to take part had very limited previous involvement in drama. One of the residents in the project is an active singer, often giving public performances. Not all of the residents in the project were physically active; some used a Zimmer frame or a stick. During the process, two residents unfortunately suffered bouts of severe ill-health, pulling out of the project although remaining supportive of their friends who remained involved. Residents were given the opportunity to attend sessions without the need to be committed for the entire process. By the time of the performance there was a core group of 15 residents who took part in the weekly sessions. It was from this core group that most of the performance's stories were born.

Stephen Dallow led the devising workshops with the group of seniors and the young people and then directed the performance process with the young people. Briar O'Connor worked in a number of roles, including providing formative evaluation by attending all of the workshops. Briar also ran a series of focus groups with the seniors asking for feedback on their experience. As stories were shared, Briar also became the fact checker, ensuring historical accuracy.

My role was to help enrol the children as researchers. I ran two drama workshops which explored ways to generate stories and ask questions of the elderly. I then collected the story of the making of the performance with a particular focus on the seniors.

The aim of the project was to use Applied Theatre techniques to create a safe forum for generating stories from a group of senior citizens through developing a research relationship with a group of young people. After the final performance, Co-Director of Applied Theatre Consultants Peter O'Connor[2] thanked the members of the company, senior citizens and young people by telling the audience that 'applied theatre is theatre which has the capacity to create a sense of community in which participants can view the world as they would like it to be, rather than how it is'. O'Connor highlighted the last phrases of the song 'When I grow up', as indicative of the aims of applied theatre. He noted that 'If you always take it on the chin and wear it, nothing will change!' Dropping his academic guard and responding from within the highly emotionally charged end of the project, O'Connor perhaps understandably veered towards the hero narrative. Change of course is never linear and the ready assumption that we all agree on what change should mean and what it should bring is a problem that has bedevilled applied theatre.

The performance was created to be presented to an audience consisting of friends, family and the general public, on 1 October 2013, the United Nations International Day of Older Persons. Further performances were scheduled to be presented the following week, with a final performance planned for the third International Critical Research in Applied Theatre Symposium held at The University of Auckland. The seniors were to be the guests of honour at the first and final performances, and again at the Symposium, participating in the final moments of the performance.

Stephen Dallow had a very personal relationship to the project. Both his parents reside at the Waitakere Gardens Retirement Village, and throughout the process he continued to make discoveries about his own family narratives. Dallow[3] envisioned the drama project would help to create a new sense of family and community for those without close relatives, as well as generating lost stories, 'snippets to carry forward into a new generation'. The stated objectives of the project were to

- create a safe space and process,
- generate stories to be shared,
- create a sense of community to bring young and old together

Generating stories

Research processes sat at the heart of the project. The younger people, enrolled as researchers, used a range of research strategies to generate life stories from the seniors. The stories are described as being generated,[4] rather than being collected, as the dramatic methods used, enabled the stories to be recalled and mediated through other similar or contrasting stories shared by the others. Individual stories were actively developed and changed as one story led to another. Memories are not always precise and accurate as they are shaped by the intervening years and experiences. The dramatic strategies acted as the key to unlock some of the forgotten stories. One resident, Cindy, speaking to me after the performance said it was only as the process progressed that her memories began to return to her. On returning to her apartment after a session she would begin to remember her own stories.

My own research data about the process were gathered from observations and dramaturgical analysis of the workshops in action, particularly those of the seniors. The Facebook page dedicated to the project also provided a lens into viewing what was happening and a source for distanced data to be viewed and analysed. The entire process was photographed and video recorded by one of the young people who was given time out of school as part of his media studies course. The photographs were to be used as part of the performance but they also became a valuable data source for the research. Surrounding the whole process was the evaluative research which was used to inform the project as it happened.

Out West

Much of the theatre research sessions took place at the Blockhouse Bay community centre, where the young people concurrently undertook their drama classes, and the Blockhouse Bay Primary Performing Arts Centre in West Auckland. West Auckland is a solid, working-class suburb, with its own iconic sense of identity, informed by its settlement by Dalmatian farmers. West Auckland is represented in local television and literature as the home of white bogans, heavy metallers and boy racers, epitomized by the ubiquitous kiwi black T-shirt or singlet for men and leopard skin accessories for women. Young people in the area are routinely stereotyped as dangerous, untrustworthy and selfish. Left leaning in its politics, it also has a vibrant beach culture set among some of the country's wildest and most dangerous beaches. The Waitakere Gardens Retirement Village situated in the heart of West Auckland is a gated community with residents who are still intellectually able and mainly physically capable, although some are frailer than others and require mobility assistance. If West Auckland celebrates its bogan culture, conversely the retirement village is home to a largely immigrant middle-class community, with many of the seniors spending most of their lives bringing up their families in the more middle-class areas of the suburb. Politically however, most residents shared a healthy disregard for the neo-liberal revolution that had cannibalized New Zealand since the 1980s. Two married couples attended the workshops, however, the others came independently. Many had strong personal memories of their lives during the Second World War, with several having grown up in England – London in particular. Only one male resident had attended university, yet some had worked as teachers and principals. Some of the women had what they classed as large families. They had experienced life in New Zealand during a time when women did not usually attend university, and when family planning choices were not available. Through the workshops they often sought to place their own lives within wider historical and cultural contexts.

Preparing to research

At the start of the project I introduced the young actors to the concepts of research, and to working with the elderly. Two initial workshops were planned around addressing the concerns that Nicholson[5] has about the use of young people acting as researchers. She asks 'the dramatisation of oral narratives, particularly when students are involved in interviews and research, presents particular challenges. How are interviews conducted and interpreted? Whose stories are chosen for development in drama? Who controls the texts? Do the actors have the authority to fictionalise the stories? How are the narratives shaped into dramatic form? How is the work presented and received?'

The first research workshop was designed to introduce students to the idea that old people should not to be seen solely as a resource, and instead are seen as people like themselves; people who have stories to tell. During the introduction to research drama workshops, many of the young people said they had some form of contact with an elderly figure. Several spoke of living with grandparents, or spending periods of time with them, and they expressed a sense of love, admiration and pride. Schweitzer[6] has described how young people find imagining that seniors were once as young as themselves to be 'intriguing'.

After working with Dallow for several years, the young actor/researchers were both knowledgeable and proficient in the use of non-naturalistic drama conventions, and confident in the shaping and exploration of ideas. During the workshops, I asked them to imagine and dramatically represent themselves growing older. As they worked, they became aware of how and when stories are told, how and when some elements are forgotten while some grow and how and when, depending on the audience or how many times a story is told, reflection and perception are introduced. Through the drama, by considering their own aging, the young people were asked to visualize seniors as 'real people' who had lived 'real lives'. I sensed them begin to challenge stereotypical ideas about old age. At the end of the 7-month process, Raoul wrote in an article for the MetLife newsletter how 'stereotypes on both sides dissolved and both the young and the old opened their hearts to one another'. It would be easy to be sceptical about this claim, but the long term and enduring relationships formed between individual seniors and the young researchers suggest that genuine friendships were formed as a result of meeting beyond the stereotypes of age.

I asked the young people to ask for, and listen to, a story told by one of their own older family members so they could then explore it dramatically within the second workshop. In the workshop they played with a wide variety of conventions exploring their ideas so that they could 'break the pattern of linearity in their drama'[7] when shaping the work. This enabled them to play with the narrative, to include moments of reflection, or highlight moments of significance through freeze frame or repetition. They began to realize stories are altered as they are retold.

The majority of the storytelling and generation of data for the performance by the residents was done through the use of dramatic conventions. However, the young people were also going to do face-to-face interviews with the seniors. To prepare for this, the young actor/researchers took the opportunity to interview Dallow as he revealed a personal story. They were able to rehearse their skills in preparation for their visit to the Gardens, where they were to carry out their own research. They discovered the importance of making eye contact, and of engaging in conversation rather than relying on a series of pre-planned questions. Dallow asked the young people to listen and to think about the responses they were receiving. Using the improvisation mantra 'keep building – don't go backwards' the young people could see that their theatre training was useful in generating detail and colour to the stories.

Ethical approaches to research

The seniors agreed to take part knowing their stories would be mediated and used for a public performance – unless they requested otherwise. Dallow explained to the residents that the process provided the opportunity to discuss anything they wanted to stimulate ideas, but they all had the right of veto when it came to those ideas being performed. Briar O'Connor ran a workshop for the young actor/researchers on ethics, and how they should approach the research process. They were reminded to treat the participants with respect and dignity – the watchwords being to do no harm. This was supported throughout the devising and rehearsal stages where no careless or stereotypical work was permitted within the rehearsal room. Students were expected to take ownership of their characters from the first workshop, again in order to honour the stories. The young actor/researchers explored their own emotions about the upcoming project by drawing simple annotated stick figure pictures. Several showed mixed emotions,

concerning uncertainty 'how can I bond with this old group of people?'
However, there was also a deep feeling of excitement and interest
within the journey that lay ahead; 'I'm intrigued', 'this will be fun' and,
'I want to hear stories'. After their first conjoined drama workshop, the
young people expressed positive views about the seniors, commenting
how they had a lot to share, were physically bouncy, they said what was
on their minds, and how they were open with their stories. The young
people expressed great surprise at the seniors ability to remember so
much detail. Schweitzer suggests the experience for the young in this
sort of process is about far more than preparing for a performance

> As well as being creative participants in the production, they need to
> relate to older people, to empathise with their lived experience, and
> find their own dramatic idiom through which to express the material
> they have gathered[8]

In the same workshop, the seniors were given an opportunity to collect
their thoughts on a large sheet of paper about the project and the
young people prior to meeting with them. The comments reflected
a diverse range of feelings including: 'youth can be very complicated
these days' and a personal reflection describing youth as, 'something
I missed out on due to war years'. Other comments included 'we
only hear about the bad ones' and, 'my youth brings to mind social
awkwardness and the only time in my life when I knew everything'.
One resident expressed how she felt vulnerable about sharing her past,
and some mentioned the vulnerability of thinking about memories
long forgotten, those certainly never discussed with their families. One
resident asked the question, 'who wants to know about my story, it's
not very interesting?'.

Later in the project, as relationships between the young and seniors
developed, these views started to change. Some of differences were
captured in letters written between both groups. During the final
workshop two of the young people wrote to the residents telling them
how they should 'never underestimate the power your stories hold, and

the importance of the life you have lived'. As the letters were read out
to the circle of residents, applause broke out. Laughter soon followed as
one letter addressed them read: 'you lovely old bunch.'

Research with the seniors

Schweitzer,[9] who has worked within the field of reminiscence theatre
for decades, developing many projects with seniors, has suggested 'it
is highly desirable to bring them together as a group to share stories
before they meet the children'. Prior to the coming together of seniors
and young drama students, Stephen introduced some of the drama
strategies to the residents of the Waitakere Gardens.

During this first workshop, the residents were asked to share a
happy memory from childhood with a partner, simply by retelling the
story. The seniors immediately engaged in the activity, making eye
contact with their partners, using gestures and re-enacting aspects of
their story – the natural desire to embody was already apparent. The
residents took on the responsibility to present each other's stories to the
group, already beginning to use dramatic techniques. One pair chose to
speak in role. Many of the stories concerned war memories and their
own relationships with grandparents. There were stories from growing
up in London, a trip to Whipsnade zoo and an elephant ride. As the
stories were told, the seniors would touch and pat each other, looking
to each other for confirmation that the facts of the story were correct.
Throughout the process, there was a great deal of laughter. Raoul later
identified this laughter as important, 'increasing levels of enjoyment
and hilarity set the atmosphere for bridging the generational divide'.[10]

Over the next 6 months, Dallow led weekly sessions employing
applied theatre techniques, providing opportunities for the seniors to
embody their stories. I was surprised to see how quickly they became
confident in preparing and rehearsing their scenes. Each session began
with a game, often inspired by an artefact requiring participants to think,

speak and move within their degree of comfort. Then two or three themes would be used to inspire the session's drama work. The themes were often culturally or historically informed. They covered topics including work, employment, schooldays, family life, war memories, childhood and NZ historical moments – among many others. The themes offered dramatic potential, dealing with both the serious and humorous sides of life. At the end of the session Dallow would introduce the theme for the following week, which he hoped would be, 'useful, not a burden.' He invited them to bring along any artefacts or stories that they might think of in the upcoming days. This ensured the seniors could contemplate the theme at leisure, recalling memories in their own time.

Dallow employed not only thematic issues to elicit stories, but also the senses which included remembering the smells of bygone years. As Myerhoff[11] describes,

> Memory is a continuum ranging from vague, dim shadows to the most bright vivid totality. At its most extreme form, memory may offer the opportunity not merely to recall the past but to relive it, in all its original freshness, unaltered by intervening change and reflection. All the accompanying sensations, emotions, and associations of the first occurrence are recovered and the past recaptured.

By accessing the other senses Dallow sought to unlock further memories. The smells generated a discussion as the residents recounted the carbolic smell of hospitals, the smell of the salty sea, the smell of the bush, Johnson's baby powder, the smell of a dog, of fresh-cut grass, camphor, the smell of newly baked Hokey Pokey, sulphur phosphate from the factory in Penrose, a fruitcake with brandy, and one particularly pungent smell came from memories of a children's home.

As Dallow led the seniors through drama activities, he was not only stimulating memories but also stimulating the brain. The brain responds to the 'process of becoming different'[12] which a new process like drama can offer. Thus the drama sessions could be viewed as a kind of mental gymnasium, through which memory was accessed and the brain challenged. Throughout this process, Dallow moved around the groups, gently encouraging the participants by reminding them there are no right or wrong answers in drama. At the end of the session, one of the seniors concerned previously that she would be unable to participate or remember said, 'but we do – this is good for our grey power'.

Together, the seniors began remembering the stories of their lives. Myerhoff[13] writes that

> the term 're-membering' may be used, calling attention to the reaggre-
> gation of members, the figures who belong to one's life story, one's own
> prior selves, as well as significant others who are part of the story.

Through embodiment, the memories are further recalled and replayed. The seniors bring to mind those important events that make up who they are, and which are archived in their bodies.

A meeting of minds and bodies

On 2 April 2013, 30 young people and a group of about 12 seniors met for the very the first time. The students arrived early and began to talk about their own grandparents as their minds turned to the task in hand. The workshop took place in a large rectangular room with a glass front looking down over the resident's vegetable gardens. It was a shared space, meaning other residents came and went making coffee, sometimes taking the time to stop and observe the activities. Both the young and old had been asked to bring along an artefact to help stimulate discussion, and potentially a dramatic scene. From the introductions conducted around the circle of participants, it became apparent the ages ranged from 6 to 89 years. As the seniors introduced themselves the young people spontaneously applauded. Dallow began with a drama game, he had played with the seniors previously and they approached it with a high degree of confidence. Dallow used a torch, a floppy hat, a cloth flower and large paper bag to inspire imaginations and to encourage physical activity. There was a large round of spontaneous applause for one of the oldest residents who took the role of James Bond 007 clearly and enthusiastically. There was a great deal of laughter within the group, as the seniors and young people responded imaginatively to the variety of props. All were required to think outside the square. The game ran fluently passing from participant to participant, young to old without pause. Contrary to my expectations, the seniors were actively involved throughout, even at one point lying on the floor to mime an underwater hockey match. The game required both cognitive and kinaesthetic skills. It broke down the barriers between the age groups through laughter and applause. Both young and old listened, responded and supported each other's contributions.

The first theme explored memories of going to the movies. As the young and old began to talk together in small groups, much information was shared. Students gained an insight into a communal context, separated only by time. It was apparent through the head nodding, eye contact and smiles that there was respect on both sides as the stories were told. Some of the seniors chose to sit on the floor with the young people. Together they began to create a scene, moving from discussion to action. They set up their chosen spaces with chairs and began to rehearse – the dramatic process embodied by young and old. In rehearsal and performance, the seniors engaged in a range of physical activities: moving, stooping and bending. This was to be an important part of the whole process as the seniors participated with growing confidence over the following 6 months. Their stories, trapped in their bodies, were released through their bodies in movement and play. Many of the videos and photographs taken during these workshops at Waitakere were then used in the final performance. The images tell a story of the seniors actively engaged in the creation of dramatic moments. One photo captures Raoul hiding under a chair, while video images capture Dena dancing and singing 'tiptoe through the tulips'. Lorna can be seen and heard recounting trips to the outdoor lavatory in the night. Bill insisted on participating physically within the drama, entering the space either with his Zimmer frame or with his stick. A number of the videos and photographs capture the pleasure this movement gave him. A video of one participant, who became more frail as the months drew on, shows how her 'youthfulness was mysteriously but undeniably apparent'[14] as she joined in the activities. Myerhoff [15] reminds us that 'the body retains the experiences that may be yielded, eventually and indirectly, to the mind' while Nicholson[16] reminds us that our bodies hold the archive of our lives. The video footage of a senior galloping across the floor, head held high with his face beaming while he uses a large purple flower as his horse, encapsulates the vibrancy, energy and imagination prevalent within the group during these research sessions.

Artefacts

The first session in which both young and old came together was full of laughter, and poignancy. Everyone had been asked to bring along a significant artefact to be shared within the group. The artefacts were explored through hot-seating, a convention which places an actor in a seat to be questioned by the audience. This requires the ability to ask deep, meaningful questions, a skill the seniors became more confident using throughout the process. The artefacts provided a focus for sharing stories and included a King James Bible, a wedding photo and an old suitcase of papers. One young man shared his beads of hope, colourful beads given to young cancer patients to mark each procedure they experience, and recounted his story of childhood cancer. The seniors used artefacts to recount memories of war and depression which they wanted to be remembered. Mackey[17] feels that artefacts are often given less importance, as people use online multimedia to archive their lives. It became clear however, that these physical objects hold a residual power as 'solid, material traces of the past provoke a distinct emotional response'. The artefacts were to become an important component of both the process in terms of data generation and then used again as part of the performance ethnography.

In many senses the seniors, the young actor/researchers, myself and the ATCo team were engaged in a whole-group research process.

Stories were generated, questioned, analysed, appreciated and cele-brated as we worked as co-researchers into each other's lives. These stories frequently offered significant insights into the social, historical and political history of New Zealand as well as personal stories. The collapsing of power relationships through the listening and sharing of stories provided an opportunity to talk about issues of deep concern to both groups. For example, the seniors' fear of unemployment occasioned through the Great Depression and a series of recessions since, resonated with the young people who in the working-class suburbs of West Auckland understood their own vulnerability.

Understanding the aesthetic

The seniors had limited experience of the drama process, having only been introduced to some of its conventions in the initial sessions. However, with Dallow's guidance confidence grew rapidly, and the first work created by the seniors and young people demonstrated understandings about aesthetic images and drama. This included the use of freeze to end a performance, flashback, dialogue and an agreed ending. One group physicalized an old bath tub by using students to create the imagined tub within the space. The seniors took active and equal roles with the young people, and at times they led the scenes. There was an understanding that the final line needs to confirm the end of the scene as well as leaving an audience wanting to know more.

The relationship in the creation of the stories meant each group could bring their difference expertise to the theatre making. The actor/researchers had more knowledge of theatre making, and the seniors had the knowledge of the past, their life stories to flesh out the dramatic forms. This symbiotic relationship empowered both groups to develop rich dramatic moments which captured and honoured the stories even as they were generated.

The seniors and the young people met on several occasions throughout the process. On one occasion the students were invited into the homes of the residents so they could gain further insights into life at the Waitakere Gardens. The seniors visited The Blockhouse Bay Primary Performing Arts Centre where they engaged in dramatic activities and rehearsed their song with the young drama students.

The performance approach

I never thought of years to come
In later life when youth has gone
I was young and I was gay
I only lived from day to day[18]

The above poem was written in 1954, offering a moment when a young woman looks to the future and celebrates her life. The poem remained hidden and unshared for nearly 60 years until Dena mentioned it in one of the sessions. Nathan, a musically talented young actor put the poem to music. In the final performance a group of the actor/researchers find the poem in a box hidden in the basement and this then leads into the entire ensemble on stage singing the newly composed song. The words bring with them poignancy, finally recognized and given value, 60 years after their initial creation. The shift in meanings of the word gay, provoked an opportunity for the two groups to discuss issues of sexuality in a manner I had not suspected. In the performance ethnography there was a temporal collision for the audience as they grappled with 30 young people on stage celebrating being gay. There was something immensely powerful in the double meaning in the phrase and the pride with which the song was performed.

Making choices/mediation

The seniors were asked to recreate stories from their teenage years. They were each given a character sheet where they wrote the name of their created character, listing three key things that had happened during those years. The residents were required to state a problem which needed to be resolved, list something the character had loved to do and describe a situation when they found themselves in trouble before giving a title to their performance – as if it was film. Rather than focusing on one story, they were asked to find a way to blend and juxtapose stories to create one new story. The groups discussed the values and ethics which appeared to have changed since their teenage years. By creating imagined characters, the seniors could blend aspects of their stories to find shared moments. These moments, drawn from several sources, contribute to the validity and authenticity of the stories. The titles chosen, *the circle of life, Knight Rider, Mary Mary quite contrary* and *from respect to rebellion* act as Brechtian placards, highlighting the main theme of each drama. Each story was then passed to another group to work on which enabled further distancing to occur. Rather than the simple retelling of one person's story, the stories became a mediated, dramatized view of society often containing reflections from the present on the past.

Ethnographic performance

The ethnographic performance used verbatim, scripted or devised processes to present as Saldaña[19] suggests 'a live or mediated performance event of research participants' experiences and/or the researcher's interpretations of data'. Some researchers use verbatim presentation, which is where the exact words of the participants are spoken. The introductory statement in the programme for the production explained that 'where possible, actual phrases have been used'.[20] It can be argued that verbatim gives a sense of authenticity by capturing and replaying the voices and language of the research participants. Other practitioners, including Saldaña,[21] believe the shaping of the data, or collected stories, should pay more attention to the aesthetic qualities inherent in a theatre piece as theatre should not only educate but also entertain. *Capturing the Tales* had been devised from a juxtaposition of stories, as they intersect, connect and diverge. This was a result of the students working 'with recordings and notes to devise vignettes from their interpretations of stories they have heard'.[22] The word interpretation is important in this context and Nicholson[23] highlights that young people in this kind of work can look 'for the "myth of origin", for the single, unmediated presence of truth'. Schweitzer[24] suggests the need for an 'artistic licence,' as the seniors need to 'accept the idea that exactitude is not required and that the young people's response has its own validity'.

The stories are in effect, retellings of events many years later. They were already mediated by the tellers, who remember what they choose to tell and who also comment on the action through a reflective lens. As Myerhoff[25] comments, 'life experiences are not swept away as if they had never been. They are rewoven into the present'. Drama is never an exact representation as it is always, to some degree, shaped for poetic or dramatic effect. The old adage that drama is life with the boring parts removed is usually true.

This was particularly apparent in a story told by Jim. He recounted the air raid drills at school as a child in London, when he was made to lie on the ground in the middle of the school field with an eraser between his teeth. He commented that the intervening years since the war made him aware of the ridiculous nature of the situation. When the young actors worked with this scene they chose to play Jim as his young self, but also using the words of his older and reflective self. As the young actor lay on the stage, he looked up and spoke directly to the audience, voicing his opinion that having an eraser between his teeth in an open field may not be the best way to cope with an air raid. The scene ends as the 'teacher' places a foot on his back and asks, 'What was that young James?' In the performance it is as if the young James was speaking the words of his older wiser self. Rather than a realistic representation of a past event this becomes a stylized moment where past and present collide. The development of this scene with its playful reflection on Jim's stories reveals how they have not merely retold the story but also begun to make their own sense of its importance in Jim's personal narrative.

The performance ethnography was not a mere re-collection of stories. Van Dijk[26] argues theatre should 'make us feel alive, to stimulate our imagination and to appreciate the totality of our humanity'. The laughter, tears and responses of the audiences during the performances suggest they felt both alive and engaged with the stories being re-told. The stories were not just happy stories but ranged in emotional depth. Perhaps the saddest moment in the performance was the story of a father's death during the war, retold through reading the original telegram. This particular narrative was shared during the final session at the Gardens. The senior reflected on the story through the lens of her adult self. As a measure of the success of the programme it can be argued that this represented a significant moment of trust as a difficult story could finally be recounted and shared with the group, and then be entrusted to be performed within the public arena.

Bill's book

One of the key moments in the process occurred early on, when Bill gifted a copy of a green folder containing a brief yet personal life history put together by his wife for his 70th birthday, 10 years earlier. The book contained pictures and personal stories of the life they had shared together following their wedding day. Bill was extremely keen for Dallow to find a way it could be used. The book contained insights and details about his life, intriguing the young people who eventually mediated the stories into a series of scenes. Using dramatic conventions which allowed several actors to portray the roles of Bill and Sylvia, scenes were developed which highlighted key moments in his life. In the final scene, a stylized enactment of passing years was shown as each of the actors playing Bill and Sylvia crossed to centre stage, held hands briefly before exiting. As they moved, the actors spoke Sylvia's written words in chorus:

> You have gone through 6 houses
> 3 swimming pools
> Numerous jobs quite a few I haven't counted yet
> Same with your cars
> But you have not traded me in yet

It was a touching moment where the non-naturalistic transitions emphasized the passing of the years, capturing the commitment and loyalty of the couple that were ended only by her death a few years previously. The scenes weaved verbatim speech with imagined scenes developed by the young actors to communicate the moments they had read about. The students added depth through further research about Bill's job, which contributed more information about the social history of New Zealand. After the performance one of the young actors noted how 'watching Bill react to his scene was great, he was so animated'. Bill had become a committed member of the project and when speaking with him after the performance it was obvious he was both moved and touched by the experience. He described to me in a conversation how seeing his picture on the front of the programme was something he never imagined would happen to him.

The framing device

Drama uses framing devices to tell stories while acting as a protective device for participants. The participants recalled stories knowing they were to be shaped for a public performance. By using framing and distancing in the way Dallow does throughout the workshops, the seniors were given the opportunity to bring memories forward through a process of shaping and reflection – rather than as 'open wounds'.[27]

For the final presentation, Dallow and the actor/researchers contextualized the stories as an imagined day when the seniors moved into their residences within a retirement home, placing their artefacts into the basement. This basement serves a similar purpose to a loft, which Mackey[28] describes as a 'form of archive and a place which, on the whole, remains highly personal and private'. In the loft lie 'iconic artefacts that reference a life'.[29] For the performances, the floor of the hall represented a basement in a retirement village. A table positioned at downstage centre held the iconic artefacts previously shared by the participants in workshops, separate to items used as props. A range of items took pride of place – including Malcolm's flight log and wings from an air force career, Lorna's toasting iron, photographs of parents and weddings and personal telegrams. At this moment, reality and fiction were woven together as the items were given pride of place and set apart as something special, each artefact representing the life of a resident.

In front of the audience at last

To act without an audience is like singing in a room without any resonance.[30]

Figure 14 Seniors and youth rehearse for the final performance at Blockhouse Bay Primary Performing Arts Centre, Auckland.

It could be asked why the seniors did not participate in the performance, aside from the singing, when they had obviously enjoyed the experience of improvisation with the young actors? Schweitzer[31] has suggested that seniors can begin to lose their enjoyment of the project when faced with remembering lines and the order of scenes – and some of the seniors *were* more than a little nervous about learning the lyrics to the song. Dallow made the decision not to pressure the seniors, but to include them in the performance where the affect of their appearance would be the most powerful (see figure 14).

Projects such as *Capturing the Tales* highlight the contrasts between the lives young people lead today with those the seniors lived. Schweitzer[32] argues,

> people did not have an inside toilet when they were growing up, or that the majority of them left school at 14. They may need to know that most women stopped working when they married and that housework and cooking took a lot longer without vacuum cleaners, washing machines and microwave ovens.

The stories were generated through Dallow's skilful choosing of themes and leading the seniors through dramatic activities. Perhaps the most political juxtaposition was created from the theme of opportunities available to young people after leaving school. During the final performances, the stories of the seniors and the young actors were contrasted in split stage form with a scene set in an employment office. The young actors demonstrated the wider range of possibilities available to them while pointing out the higher level of educational requirements placed on them. The scene highlighted and challenged the simplistic notion that change is always for the better.

Conclusion

What are we going to do now it's over? I enjoyed being down there for 9.30 every Monday morning.[33]

I can't sing dance or act, but I've had so much fun. I enjoyed being a kid again.[34]

We were looking from two sides at each other and then bridging the divide.[35]

These three comments sum up some of the most important aspects of this project. The regular drama sessions provided both a focus within the lives of the residents and a time to come together to share embodied stories. It was also an opportunity for the young and old to have fun and play. O'Connor[36] believes that 'play is important for us as individuals but it is vital to the success of communities. Play is the beginning of hope. Hope is a leap of the imagination, a playful joy in realising you do not have to live and die in the world you were born into'. People need opportunities in their lives to play and imagine and this forum provided just such an opportunity of returning to the playful state we know as children but often lose in adulthood. Drama sanctions the playful state and becomes the playground in which all can play regardless of age.

Myerhoff reminds us childhood memories often provide strong images and that 'one may experience the self as it was originally and know beyond doubt that one is the same person as that child, still dwelling within a much altered body'.[37] Through the process of dramatic play, the seniors were revelling in being themselves – the person they have always been, but who are now housed in an older body.

These two words, play and fun, were frequently used throughout the project by the participants and they sit alongside learning, love, respect and participation. As Raoul expressed, the divide had been bridged, from the tentative first feelings on both sides, and shifted to the outpouring of emotions expressed on the last night of performance. Raoul described this moment vividly in the village newsletter:

The excited students... formed a loving arch of farewell for the departing residents as they headed for the bus. As the bus departed the students gave a lusty rendition of 'When I Grow Up'. It was a powerful and wonderful moment![38]

The emotions were apparent within many of the positive comments posted on Facebook, as one of the actor/researchers, Ella described:

> Seeing all those bright, happy faces of the residents, especially Bill's, seriously brought home to me how much this meant to them, I think it is incredible that they have given part of their lives to us like that, and I know I will treasure it forever. And the way their faces lit up when they recognized it was something they'd said, or something they'd done, just made my heart melt.

The project provided a space for both young and old to meet, with the purpose of sharing and shaping their stories. It gave an impetus for talk, for action, and for the employment of memory. Although some seniors had expressed their concern about their declining memories, it became apparent their memories were stimulated and vibrant once they began to speak. Several even learnt their lines for the final song, singing alongside the young actors. Recent research into the benefits of drama on the brain have found numerous positive effects, including the improvement of memory, and relief from depression, because drama makes the brain work in different ways.[39]

The United Nations General Assembly recommends ensuring 'that the social integration of older persons' becomes, 'an integral part of the development agenda'.[40] In this project, the young people learnt from the seniors and then used their drama skills to provide an authentic and public showing of the stories, while the seniors were honoured and seen as knowledgeable with the presentation of their tales. In this way, there was a sharing of expertise, with the young students gaining insight into the social history of New Zealand, while the seniors became familiar with applied theatre techniques. Throughout the process, the seniors found a space for their voices to be heard and found them being valued.

At the start of the project, only half the residents said they might have told their stories to their own families and only one felt their grandchildren knew their story.

Nicholson[41] believes intergenerational storytelling is a project that is never complete, and one which looks to the future. Perhaps O'Connor's reflections in the emotionally charged conclusion to the project can be understood in these terms. Minchin's treacly lyrics and music hide the revolutionary power of words which suggest it is in the refusal to take it on the chin and bear it that we have the best chance to make a difference. It is in its own way a call to resistance, one which young and old in the performance space passionately advocate. Perhaps the power of the piece is in seeing older people still willing to resist, able if only briefly be part of something bigger than the individual, still seeing their lives as meaningful. Perhaps the power for the younger people was in seeing that their work 'reveals connections between people across social, cultural, temporal, and geographic divides'.[42] Young people and seniors can together 'build[s] mutual understanding and appreciation through joint creative activity', both 'life affirming' and 'life-changing'.[43]

Postscript

Two weeks after the final performance at Blockhouse Bay, the company performed in front of a large audience at The University of Auckland. Their audience was made up of professors, researchers, doctoral and postgraduate students in drama education and applied theatre. The seniors once again joined the young performers on stage to sing 'When I grow up'. The audience gave the performance a standing ovation, and afterwards met to mingle with the performers and the seniors. Cindy, one of the seniors, expressed her feelings late that night via Facebook:

> I'm trying to find the right words to describe tonight's *Capturing The tales*. It just about blew me away, the emotion in that room, was felt by everyone there, the intensity of the acting from your young actors, was so strong, and sincere. . . . Last night for me, and I guess for everyone else, will always be a very special moment in my life. I would like to thank you and your team very much for your patience and kindness during all those sessions we had. It has been an honour and a pleasure, sharing these wonderful fun moments. This is certainly not 'Good Bye'.

Cindy it seemed had finally had her moment on the stage. Earlier in her life she had won a scholarship to study acting in London. For a range of family reasons she never went. More important for her, however, was the nature of the affective response she felt in the room. Marginalized and forgotten, their stories rendered invisible, applied theatre as research that evening may not have changed anyone's lives. The power and the beauty of the performance touched deeply the audience and the performers. In this communal sharing more than stories were honoured, Human connections were rebuilt in a community where they had been lost. At the heart of the work were the relationships which developed between the young and old, and the recognition among the seniors of their importance – of their lives and of their stories. Cindy's comments portray a sense that drama has brought new excitement and value into her life as well as a sense of fun. As O'Connor reminds us,

> A world without play and without hope is a world devoid of humanity. Play is the beating heart of humanity, something to be cherished in children and to be joyfully retained into old age.[44]

Working Together: Collaborative Journeys in Cross-Cultural Research and Performance

Linden Wilkinson

First contact

In all my field trips to north-west New South Wales (NSW), I had never seen the country around Myall Creek look so lush. The statewide rains that had poured for a week had finally stopped; local towns scattered across the district were no longer threatened by floodwaters. By the time we climbed out of the hired Tarago, my six actor/co-researchers and I, it was late on a cloudless Saturday afternoon. Sydney was 8 hours behind us and we could stretch our legs, while strolling through the memorial to the Myall Creek massacre of 1838, the physical, emotional and spiritual centre of my research project.

The Aboriginal people, the Weraerai,[1] who were butchered on the slopes below this memorial on Sunday, 10 June 1838, were victims of a wave of genocidal violence. Perpetrated by convict and ex-convict stockmen, led certainly in this case by a free-born scion of a privileged pioneering family, such vigilantism was condoned by the labourers' powerful employers, the squatters. Drought and a crash in wool prices in the 1840s would curtail the squatters' expansionist zeal but from 1835, when the first flocks of sheep were herded on to these abundant grasslands, this country, if it mirrored then what we were seeing now, promised enormous wealth.

One of my research participants, 'Gerry', prioritizes the causal factors of the massacre this way:

> but those convicts . . . they were really in another sense scapegoats, because the people who were the really guilty ones were also the landholders like Dangar, who, who – and so it wasn't the Mum and Dad settlers who in this case, who were the drivers, it was the, if you like, the multi-nationals of their day. That was the driving force. You could argue it wasn't racism that was the key ingredient; it was greed.

Using Myall Creek as a case study, the massacre and the memorial erected to commemorate it in 2000 by a committee of Aboriginal and non-Aboriginal people coming together, I wanted to locate a reconciliation narrative as part of my doctoral research project. Over the preceding 5 months I had collected about 25 hours of interviews with nine Aboriginal and eleven non-Aboriginal participants; from those interviews I had distilled a performance ethnography, discussed later in this chapter, using verbatim theatre as a mode of delivery.

And this is what we were here for: to perform the text, a text we had yet to read together. I thought there would be plenty of time. There wasn't.

Bonding via bitumen and adrenalin

Entitled *Today We're Alive* the play now in its first draft form was to be read the following day by my three Aboriginal and three non-Aboriginal actors to an invited audience of research participants. Our long trip to Myall Creek had been rich in often hilarious anecdotes; we were already an adrenalin-pumped fledgling ensemble. All my actor/co-researchers were known to me as colleagues and as friends; Fred, Lily and Aunty Rhonda were all members of Moogahlin, an Aboriginal theatre company based in Sydney, with whom I was now developing a new theatre work. My three non-Aboriginal actors, Anna, Genevieve and Terry, had become friends through performances of plays that had occurred up to 30 years before. Each group knew each other but I was the only one, who knew everyone.

There had been no time for rehearsal and no budget. Because I had to wait for several key participants to become available, the first draft had been delayed to incorporate their narratives. Consequently, the first read-through had been scheduled to occur only days before we left Sydney and then at the last minute not all the actors could attend. The stroll through the memorial would be, I thought, a valuable orientation exercise; the actors could gain a sense of the physical place. But, as I would later find out, for all of them it was to be much more than that.

In my subsequent interviews with the actors this time at the memorial was critical to informing their performance practice for the next day's public reading. All of them became attuned to the spiritual dimension that emanates from this beautiful sheltered grove on Crown Land that overlooks undulating pasture and the supposed massacre site.

This chapter explores the nature of collaboration in the cross-cultural context. Through the experience of devising and presenting this first draft of the play, I discover cross-cultural collaboration is a multidimensional experience involving significant interactions over time; these interactions don't necessarily focus the crafting of text nor are these interactions linear. Moments of insight might only be revealed long after they have occurred and their importance only defined by a much later, seemingly unrelated event.

So on this Saturday afternoon what I thought represented the end of one phase of the research journey – going to the memorial – was actually the beginning of a whole new understanding of the play. Perhaps with rehearsal I would have pruned the draft but without a performance I doubt I would have understood what was redundant nor, more significantly, why.

Focusing on the research plan

The return to the research field addressed both ethical considerations, validating the journey participant narratives had taken from interviews to edited play text, and made my subjectivity, as the only arbiter of the play's content, 'accessible, transparent and vulnerable to judgement and evaluation'.[2] Because I had actors I trusted and respected with me, I had invited another level of critical support. Apart from the feedback I anticipated from the research participants, I would also have commentary on the play as an evolving work for performance. The reading was to take place in the memorial hall, a tin shed 500 metres from the massacre site on Sunday morning. Built in 1923 in remembrance of the local fallen in World War I, the tin shed serves as a community hall. It is also where all the public meetings were held as the decision-making process around the Myall Creek massacre memorial gained momentum and where the annual commemorative services to the massacre begin and end.

By the time we reached the memorial, the group dynamic no longer needed reinforcing. Everyone was ready to stand back, to be silent and alone. I, too, was conscious the research journey was now shifting. Now having devised the first draft, I was in the throes of renegotiating the relationship from an intense engagement with the story-tellers to the solitary rigour of objectivity. It is a period of transition narrative inquirers, Clandinen and Connelly recognize as having an emotional wrench:

> Inevitably, narrative inquirers experience this tension, for narrative inquiry is relational. They must become fully involved, must 'fall in love' with their participants, yet they must also step back and see their own stories in the inquiry, the stories of the participants, as well as the larger landscape on which they all live.[3]

Self-reflexive questions regarding my settler background, the ongoing privileges it delivers and the historical, social and political perspectives I had once unconsciously adopted as truths had ebbed in the full and satisfying flow of artistic pursuit. I had been able to immerse myself in stories without confronting the epistemological challenges integral to what Bhabha refers to as 'received wisdom', the incomplete knowledge embedded in colonial discourse.[4] Now these questions would return, when, after the performed reading I left the field to analyse my findings.

But even on this golden afternoon at the memorial site, when I was thinking about the script, it was the massacre not reconciliation that re-emerged as a presence.

Being on country

We were met at the memorial by Colin Isaacs and a young man he was mentoring. Colin is a memorial committee member and a participant in this study; he had also designed and drawn the art work that illustrates the massacre story on the plaques of the seven stones that line the pathway down to the large boulder that overlooks the massacre site. His being there was a possibility but not conformed, so very welcome; he wanted to take us on to the site in the proper way. He explained he wanted to perform a short smoking ceremony at the beginning of the winding path but the wood was too damp to start a fire. He didn't say it but that's how it was for the bodies of the Weraerai.

There are no eyewitness accounts of the actual massacre but it is assumed, as only two shots were heard, that most of 28 old men, women and children, tied to each other, were decapitated through repeated cavalry-like charges. The young men, the fathers, were away at the time of the attack. After the slaughter the perpetrators had dragged logs over the massed torsos and tried to light a funeral pyre. But the wood was too damp; two eyewitness accounts of the massacre site several days after the atrocity attest to severed heads of women and children and to partially burnt remains. Being winter, it was too wet for the fire to take.

The fact that this massacre was ever investigated is an historical accident; if six white men all of whom were out of step with colonial morality had not been on history's stage at the same time, it never would have gone to trial and never left its distinctive legacy through court records. The investigation began with an initiative from the top: Governor George Gipps, the new governor of the penal colony, had arrived only 3 months before with instructions from London to form better relationships with the blacks and to curb the squatters' massive grabs for land. Ultimately Gipps failed to fulfil either of these commands but, once the massacre had been reported by an outraged farmer, Frederick Foot, Gipps decided to set an example. He sent Police Magistrate Edward Denny Day out to the frontier to find those responsible and bring them in. Day succeeded in locating 11 of the perpetrators; the leader, John Henry Fleming, only 22 at the time, sought protection through his affluent and extended family. Fleming survived until the end of the century, a public figure, a married man, still with a price on his head that gathered dust for almost 60 years.

The perpetrators went on trial in November, 1838, their defence funded by their employers, Henry Dangar among them. The first trial produced a 'not guilty' verdict, the second indicted seven of the eleven accused; those seven were hanged in December 1838 and the colony was in an uproar. Gipps feared civil unrest, for all this happened at a time when in the words of one of the participants, 'Nathan':

Previous to [Myall Creek] they argued: why was it a crime to . . . um . . . to kill Aboriginal people? We could kill them like you would shoot a duck or shoot a dog. Something like that, because nobody was ever brought to trial for doing that up until then.

Non-Aboriginal participant 'Letitia' has another perspective:

It's so sad. It's so sad for the people and for the convicts themselves. They were so oppressed . . . they come out here, they had these horrible masters and overseers over them and I just feel for them. . . . They came from one country to another country and they end up dying and they didn't have a chance in the world. It was a horrific thing for both sides.

The four perpetrators remaining in jail were freed 2 months later in the furore that followed. But Myall Creek remains the only massacre in Australian history where some but not all of the perpetrators were punished. But it drove all other massacres underground. Manning Clark suggests that the executions of the Myall Creek perpetrators directly contributed to what became known as an 'actual war of extermination'.[5]

Most of the Myall Creek story is told on the memorial plaques in English, Kamilaroi and through Colin's art work. Being unable to perform a smoking ceremony, Colin's pupil using clap sticks sang us on. I stayed back with Colin and let the others go first. They took their time to walk down the winding path towards the final big boulder, moving with a reverence similar to that Batten had observed in her research participants, who came on to this site as if it were a pilgrimage.[6] But the reverence I was observing did not reflect inner calm, as their interviews later revealed. Genevieve said her hair stood up on the back of her neck; Aunty Rhonda heard screams but Anna, who was about to return to her native Poland, said she thought about Auschwitz:

> The only thing I felt very strongly, I suppose, was that I just kept thinking of Auschwitz when we were at the Memorial itself. . . . I saw how sad I looked in the photographs. Not just for these people for everybody who gets massacred by the people in charge. I had anticipated that but I was amazed how strongly I felt. . . . These feelings were related to the human psyche, how people treat each other. Just a reminder. How brutal we are to each other. . . . So I felt it wasn't just a particular story, it was a general story. A human story.

Lily, a strong culture woman, was initially troubled by the song Colin's pupil was singing:

> And then when we were going into the site, that was really uncomfortable . . . being sung into a site with a North Queensland song . . . and I knew that guy wasn't Aboriginal. . . . And so underneath

my own breath I was singing my own song, so I was going to bounce that energy back. Then cruising along the trail and the further in you got the more emotional. . . . Overlooking the valley you smell death. Noisy birds when we went in, then became still by the second rock. A warning or a welcome? Bit of both. It's alright for you to come here but be prepared for the sorrow. Be prepared to feel the spirits of your ancestors

I knew none of these stories; we didn't talk about the memorial after we left. However the time spent there profoundly impacted on all their performances for reasons investigated at the end of this chapter. And I wonder, if it hadn't been a research site for me, a place that needed to be assessed, analysed and logistically organized around, would it have brought with it a greater spiritual dimension? Would the first draft have been different?

A goodwill landmark

I didn't choose this site because of its colonial trauma, I chose it because something positive had happened there. The memorial is seen as a 'goodwill landmark in colonial and heritage history'.[7] It is a unique place, where in 1998 after 160 years a disparate group of people, led by Sue Blacklock, a descendant of a massacre survivor, in partnership with members of the Uniting Church, came together and invited others to join them 'in an act of reconciliation, and in acknowledgement of the truth of our shared history'.[8] I wanted to know about this act of reconciliation, how did it happen? How did the two groups of people come together and what could it tell us about the process?

My interest in cross-cultural research had been aroused not by a social justice agenda but through an awakened curiosity in the potential of cross-cultural performance to deliver new ways of being. I had approached this endeavour as an artist and teacher; it was my curiosity not my conscience driving the work. And this curiosity had been sparked by witnessing a haka in a cross-cultural New Zealand drama classroom in 2007; I wasn't even in Australia, when I began thinking about Aboriginal people – for a second time.

Enter New Zealand

The first time was in the 1980s in New Zealand, in a place so close to Australia geographically, so different culturally – or so it seemed. To be in New Zealand in the 1980s was to consciously occupy Homi Bhabha's liminal space, the space where the pedagogical or traditional narrative interplays with the performative, the enunciatory present.[9] In this liminal space counter-narratives of changing identity were epitomized, for me, by a visceral Māori cultural resurgence. It was this force that was a driving change that was, as Lo observes, theoretically contributing to a 'dismantl[ing of] dominant narratives of power and enable[s] alternative subjectivities ... to be articulated'.[10]

For over three decades from the early 1980s, I travelled to New Zealand from Australia for professional and personal reasons. As an actor and writer, as a partner and as a friend and colleague, I recognized and responded to the emotional energy being released, as cultural innovations interrupted the predictable rhythms of a British heritage. I thought then such interruptions were only of significance within the narrow confines of art and arts practice; I experienced these shifts as colleagues claiming a new confidence in national identity and at times felt quite alienated by this surge in pride. In Australia at the time, multiculturalism might have championed diversity but there was still a resistance to its rhetoric, 'a tendency to homogenise different responses to being Australian'.[11] In New Zealand I didn't distinguish between Māori and Pākehā; compared to Australia I saw New Zealand as an already inclusive arts community, I worked with Māori and Pacific Islander actors all the time. I didn't realize then that inclusivity did not equate to a celebration of diversity nor a recognition of hybridity. That came later through the development of relationships, which brought with them stories rather than appearances.

But I was not attuned then to the broader forces initiating cultural transition nor of the artistic community's position in both responding to them and simultaneously reflecting them back. I didn't understand that there was an interrelational dimension to arts practice; that that arts had the capacity to be, as McNiff suggests, 'a primary way of understanding and examining experience'[12]; or a way of showing us who we are and what we might become[13]; or a way of mapping our shifting identities, marked by 'the conjuncture of our past with the social, cultural and economic relations we live within.'[14]

How re-inventions and transformations occur is explored in the notion of Bhabha's third space, the aforementioned liminal or in-between space, where cutting edge translation and negotiation occurs.[15] Bhabha considers these liminal spaces to have within them a counter-hegemonic agency:

> At the point at which the coloniser presents a normalising, hegemonic practice, the hybrid strategy opens up a third space of/for rearticulation of negotiation and meaning.[16]

Both colonized and colonizers participate in interpretative, interrogative and enunciative third space exchanges and what emerges is entirely new.[17] For an outsider at this time in New Zealand, participation in this cultural shift, in my experience, came through reflection; renegotiations about one's notions of belonging and nationhood. I became conscious of the lack of Aboriginal participation in my own culture but no more than that; I was much more interested, like many Australians at the time, in being the first generation to embrace my convict heritage.[18] However, New Zealand raised questions I tried to answer decades later. By the time I did, the research question had evolved into one about Aboriginal and non-Aboriginal reconciliation and not about belonging.

The haka insight

In 2007, back in New Zealand, I had been teaching a group of acting students a week-long course in improvisation. To celebrate the conclusion of the week's work, the students, a multi-cultural second year, performed the drama school haka. In watching that dance of incredible power, I had a startling revelation that has propelled everything since: my doctoral study; my relationship with Aboriginal Performing Arts Company, Moogahlin; my interest in cross-cultural work.

I realized for a whole week I had watched Māori and Islander students shift effortlessly between cultures, as they investigated improvisational scenarios, but until the haka I had never seen Pākehā students do the same. Until the Pākehā students danced and sang in a Polynesian culture, I had never seen them reflect an identity other than the one grounded in their British heritage, one that I related to. But here they were making sounds and moving their bodies as one within a different culture. And I wondered, what would it be like in Australia, if we explored, through performance, Aboriginal and non-Aboriginal ways of being?

A random act

In 2008, before I decided to begin doctoral study, I initiated a series of meetings. I wrote a short film script about a random group of Aboriginal and non-Aboriginal people sheltering in a roadside diner during a storm. Through a friend I took the film script to a fledgling Aboriginal Performing Arts Company, Moogahlin, and for the first time I engaged with people, Fred and Lily, who identified as Aboriginal.

I discussed the project; Fred and Lily agreed to have a workshop on the draft, if I could locate funding. We received a small grant, enough to pay ten of us for a day's work; we had a reading. Before we began, Lily announced to the circle that everyone was going to make these blackfellas written by a whitefella sound like blackfellas – and laughed, it was, it seemed, something they all had done before – or had wanted to. We read the draft, then Fred got us on our feet and we improvised stories based on the script.

One of the stories we worked on for most of the afternoon concerned the three older women, who were on a road trip: two Aboriginal women, 'Toots' and 'Dolly', and one non-Aboriginal woman, 'Col'. Fred wanted to know why they were together; it wasn't enough for him that I, as the writer and as 'Col', explained that they were friends; all of the women were marginalized by poverty and long-term illness and they found themselves isolated in the inner-city fringes in supported accommodation and together. But for Fred the situation was so unusual, a friendship across cultures, it had to be investigated. And what remained unsaid between us was a recognition of colonial history and its 200-year legacy of violence and exclusion. It was the elephant in the room.

Exploring the unsaid

Read[19] considers the colonial narrative to be a narrative of avoidance. The manner of dispossession was never discussed, the massacres never mentioned, Indigenous culture was considered lost; it was, as Read suggests, for the colonists – then and now – 'a genuine attempt to foster emotional possession of the land'.[20]

Like some of my non-Aboriginal participants I had lived unquestioningly under successive Government policies of Assimilation and Integration, with their intergenerational policies of child removal, mission isolation and social exclusion. Perhaps 'Tom's' story best captures a shared history:

> I'd always had an interest in the past generally and including the Aboriginal past. There were no Aborigines in the area where I grew up. None. At all. At Dungog. There were none at the school. I don't think we ever saw an Aborigine. There were none at Hurlstone Agricultural high school, where I went for the last years of my secondary education

and the only references that were made really in the Primary school social studies book were things about how Aboriginals were hunters and gatherers and their houses were gunyahs and whatever and I think there was probably a mention of the Myall Creek massacre in those early studies but very general nature

W. E. H. Stanner called this systemic failure to question the brutal process of colonial dispossession 'the great Australian silence'.[21] Manne considers this notion of a national silence to profoundly contribute to a new understanding of the national character:

> In the anthropological exploration of non-indigenous Australia, Stanner's 'great Australian silence' was perhaps the most important discovery ever made. It provided the vital clue to the puzzle at the heart of Australian national identity.[22]

Two participant narratives, one from Tom and another from 'Uncle Roland' talk about the transformative role discovering this institutionalize silence had in their own lives:

> As a young teacher I was sent to the Nimbin central school . . . the Nimbin school a sporting excursion to another town up there near-by. . . . And I was the acting sports master on that trip, wasn't I, and anyone who knows me well will know what a joke that was. But the deputy principal of the school took me out for a drive in the afternoon and he took me out to the local Blacks' camp. On the side of a hill out from town and ah . . . old motor cars and housing with sheets of iron, you know, generally a marked step down in housing quality of several grades from the rest of the community and very much a ring, an outer fringe and I was you know, I felt the injustice of that . . . um . . . and he made some remarks how difficult it was to get the kids to do much at the school. And so on – the aboriginal kids.

> And the next day was this sporting carnival and there was this one name of this kid who was . . . who kept getting all the events. You know? And somewhere along the way I worked out or was told that he was an Aboriginal boy. And we . . . (*he cries*) and there was a dance that night and he was the only aboriginal child that came. (*He sobs*) and ah . . . he

hung about outside . . . I tried to get him to go in but he . . . hung his head and wouldn't . . . (*cries*). . . . Anyway that's a memory obviously that still moves me.

Uncle Roland's story is included in *Today We're Alive*:

> When I left home, when I left the mission, I had a hatred for white people. I hated especially white women until the time I was playing in bands all over Sydney. And during that time I met this one white man – he was there with me all the time; he was a fan, he liked my music. He did things for me that I didn't look at – and he opened my eyes up to, to humanity, I guess. He was what I call a sincere white person. Because he said he was white that's it, nothing else. But the one I grew up under, he said I'm white, I'm boss, I'm superior to you. That's the difference, that's what opened my eyes up. He didn't know how significant he was. I went to visit him in hospital, I shed a tear for him, when he passed away. I've got a picture of him here on my wall today.

> Same with Myall Creek, there were white people there, who did things, who reported investigated, who stood and supported those people.

Even attempts to introduce less paternalistic policies under a self-determination agenda have not yet manifested in greater social inclusion. As indicated by key statistics on disadvantage, Australia continues to lag behind the United States, New Zealand and Canada, countries that share similar concerns, are English-speaking and have similar social profiles.[23] Although Aboriginal and Torres Strait Islander people now make up to 3 per cent of the population, they represent 24 per cent of the total prison population and have life-expectancy gap 17 years lower than non-Indigenous Australians. Although terra nullius,[24] considered the first great fiction of British settlement, was abandoned as a legal principle in the courts in 1992, it continues as an insidious influence.[25] According to Reynolds:

> [it] still holds sway. It may have been expelled from the courts but it still resides securely in many hearts and minds. As a nation we find

it very hard to recognise our own distinctive forms of racism. They exist in . . . ways of thinking which are often taken as no more than common sense.[26]

There is no Treaty, no reparations for land that was taken and Aboriginal peoples are still not mentioned in the Constitution. Les Malezer, Co-chair of the First Peoples' Congress, is cautious in his expectation of Constitutional change:

At no time have . . . institutions and foundations taken account of the fact that a First peoples exist in the country – continue to exist and continue to exist with rights.[27]

Paradoxically in the current environment, although institutions might resist change the general public appears to be seeking a relational shift.

The business of show

In the world of arts and media an Aboriginal presence is both strong and acclaimed: Wayne Blair's *The Sapphires,* about a girl group going to Vietnam in the 1960s, was the highest-grossing domestic film in 2012; after a campaign of 25 years a dedicated television station, National Indigenous Television (NITV) began broadcasting in 2007, and the outstanding success of mainstream television dramas like *Redfern Now*[28] and biopic, *Mabo,*[29] continue to constructively address the former absence of Aboriginal and Torres Strait Islander representation. But the shift in visibility is slow in delivering relationship.

The Australian Reconciliation Barometer is a national research study that examines the relationship between Indigenous and non-Indigenous Australians every 2 years. It is specifically designed to measure changing perceptions and how they might impact on progress towards reconciliation. In 2011, Social Justice Commissioner Mick Gooda commented in his speech to the National Press Club on the fifth anniversary of the Close the Gap Campaign for Indigenous Health:

> Key findings of the 2010 Australian reconciliation barometer include some really good news: 87% of all Australian agree the relationship between black and white is important.... But we still don't trust each other. Just 9% of all Australians feel that trust between the two groups is good.[30]

In 2012, the importance of relationship remained static at 87 per cent, however trust had advanced by four percentage points. Reconciliation Australia considers that this continuing low level of trust indicates that relationships are less likely to begin and more likely to break down. Significantly for all artists Reconciliation Australia considers secondary sources, like the media and therefore the arts, play a greater role in shaping perspectives, when personal contact remains remote.

Perpetuation of negative myths and stereotypes in the media can profoundly influence public policy.[31] As Gail Wallace, Executive Officer of the Aboriginal Justice Advisory Committee, writes:

> The media should not underestimate its ability to inform and influence social opinion on race issues. It is not incorrect to state the stereotypical messages produced by media sources influence all facets of our community, including service provision in the private and public sectors.[32]

A media climate that disrupts stereotypes potentially magnifies its transformative intention through controversy. When these stereotypes are deconstructed, as is currently occurring through a stronger Aboriginal peoples' presence through the media, it opens the way to increased levels of participation in the public discourse. And in the case of the project with Moogahlin, deconstructing stereotypes opened the door to humour.

Investigating the elephant in the room back in 2007, when Fred wanted to explore the nature of the women's friendship, we played around with deceit, we played around with affection. Our many interactions developed into a narrative and that became a play over a 5-year period. Entitled *This Fella, My Memory*, the play was performed in 2013. Its journey from its first workshop to the mainstage concludes this chapter, as learnings gained from the research process involved in *Today We're Alive*, particularly re-drafting it for a subsequent tour to north-west NSW in 2013, were significant in the script development of *This Fella, My Memory*. Using a lot of storytelling and improvisation we discovered a kind of freedom that allowed us to be outrageous. In one of the early improvisations, I, as prickly 'Col', suggested that Lily and Aunty Rhonda, as 'Toots' and 'Dolly', didn't introduce themselves as Aboriginal to members of 'Col's' estranged family but if asked, they were to say they were – I pulled a nationality out of the air – Maltese. It caused great mirth in the rehearsal room and disappeared completely from every draft of the play, until it came to performance. Fred, as director, wanted the line back in.

I was apprehensive. We were to play to Aboriginal audiences. I, as a non-Aboriginal actor and blindly racist character, felt that I would create anger. Perhaps I did momentarily but it was brilliantly released by 'Toots'' timing. When 'Col' asks the other two Aunties not to reveal their Aboriginality but call themselves 'Cuban', 'Toots', now played by Elaine Crombie, stops, stares, waits and says dismissively, 'No'. And the audience erupted in laughter; later I asked Lily why that had been the response. She said, 'It happens all the time. We just don't worry about it.'

In her work in mental health Professor Helen Milroy alludes to the importance of valuing the great inner strength of Aboriginal and Torres Strait Islander people:

> What is often not understood is the incredible resilience of Aboriginal and Torres Strait Islander people in surviving such adversity. . . . Psychological strengths include narrative style, humour, creativity, visualisation and imagery, holistic understanding, capacity for acceptance of others, collaboration styles, and respect for life and ancestry.[33]

Performance builds on all these resources. It seems in our *This Fella* process, we found ways of accessing most of them over time. But as can be seen from above in the decolonizing space there are meanings embedded in both text and silence. Therefore performance is an appropriate practice through which to also investigate epistemological hegemonies in the dynamic intercultural context. And this was the context in which I particularly wanted to understand relationships.

Going back to that time, in 2008, so early in the play's development, I didn't know how or if we would proceed. So to investigate how Aboriginal/non-Aboriginal relationships might reconcile, I needed to go it alone. I chose to focus on research and hope my arts practice with Moogahlin would continue. If I separated the two experiences, I could be demanding of the research in one project but continue to preserve the freedom of arts practice in another.

Going alone

I began my doctoral thesis in 2008. I wanted to locate a reconciliation narrative and use performance ethnography as a methodological frame work.

Considered by Alexander to be 'the staged re-enactment of ethno-graphically derived notes',[34] the term, performance ethnography, as Sallis indicates, has many variations.[35] O'Toole mentions just three alternatives: 'performed ethnography, ethnographic performance and ethnodrama',[36] Sallis, p. 14. The differences between these terms might indicate differences in intentions and data or script development techniques but Sallis considers all of the terms indicate that the research

> originates from a study of real people and their culture ... that the text is written or devised to be performed and that is presentation re-performs the real life experiences and situations of the research participants.[37]

Performance ethnography has evolved from the understanding that 'cultures travel in the stories, practise and desires of those, who engage in it'.[38] In reworking the personal narrative through performance, the personal reveals the cultural and 'opens the intercultural and ethnographic dialogue to all'.[39]

Recognizing that 'bodies harbour knowledge about culture and that performance allows for the exchange of that knowledge across bodies',[40] researchers and participants are offered 'a body-centred method of knowing'.[41] It is the body that becomes the primary site in performed ethnographic research; it is the body that conveys 'information, transmission and transformation'.[42] Conquergood perceives culture and identity as constructed and relational, therefore performance demonstrates 'embodied experience grounded in historical process, contingency, and ideology'.[43] Through narratives, we can understand how we make sense of our own and others' worlds through performance, to borrow from Conquergood, we experience the struggle for meaning in the gaps between old certainties.[44]

Hearing narratives spoken – performed – as opposed to reading a written report creates the opportunity for performance to generate multiple truths, where what is said and not said, how it is heard and responded to offer new understandings of cultural interaction. Audience members can become attuned to different voices telling multiple narratives; through performance new sites of possible interrogations and interruptions of old interactions are demonstrated and challenged.[45]

The role of the audience is a key variant in performed ethnographic research. Some proponents like Mienczakowski invite audience participation as an extension of forum theatre; the script therefore is constantly updated and never has 'a definitive, authoritative set of "fixed" social meanings'.[46] Whether the audience participates or not, Alexander considers that:

> The power and potential of performance ethnography resides in the empathic and embodied engagement of other ways of knowing that heightens the possibility of acting upon the humanistic impulse to transform the world.[47]

Empathy in the drama context emanates from the audience and the actors' readiness to identify and engage with the characters/performers emotionally, to be able to walk in the characters' shoes, to relate to the characters' struggles as they 'reinvent their ways of being in the world'.[48] For transformative learning to occur, as Alexander suggests it can through performance ethnographic texts, Arnold recognizes that both emotional and cognitive stimuli need to be present in order to sustain empathy and therefore allow possibility of responding to new knowledge.[49] It is in sustaining engagement that performed ethnography practitioners benefit from a regard for the aesthetics inherent in the theatrical realization of mainstream drama like tension, momentum, stage craft, conflict, economic dialogue and humour. Researchers need to marry intent with the execution of craft.[50]

Of primary importance in this dynamic relationship is the choice of research site; from this all else evolves. Denzin maintains that performance ethnography, like any play, is most effective when it focuses on crises and moments of epiphany; this should be the place that the research seeks to explore: the space where culture lives, adapts and changes. Implicit therefore in the search for a reconciliation narrative is the necessity for conflict to precede it.[51]

The role of crisis – imagined and real

With a massacre and the building of a memorial to it as pivotal points in my elected case study, I hoped I had given the play at least two crises: the story of the massacre and the challenge of building a memorial, an exercise I assumed had invited dissent and compromise. Reconciliation had been on the national agenda since the 1990s but Myall Creek and its memorial was the only story I could locate with a beginning, a middle and an end. It was a story where a group of Aboriginal and non-Aboriginal people had come together to address their past; from a traumatic beginning, the event had been contained in an ending. My view of what constitutes 'an end' has changed since devising the play and experiencing the responses to it, from audiences, actors and research participants, but in the beginning I was looking for a three-act structure and so I found one.

However, from a theoretical point of view, ideas that there might be 'endings' are counterproductive. To locate new ways of knowing is central in decolonizing research, whose task it is not only to define a shared, equitable and sustainable future but also to find ways of confronting and addressing the wrongs of the past. Goals of the decolonizing process therefore include not only intellectual shifts but transformations in consciousness in order to 'honour difference and promote healing'[52]; 'to learn the ways that teach respect',[53] to value all relationships. Concerned with Indigenous peoples' emancipatory rights and autonomy, L. T. Smith links these two challenges – the importance of understanding the past in order to re-create the future:

> Decolonization is a process which engages with imperialism and colonialism at multiple levels. For researchers, one of these levels is concerned with have a more critical understanding of the underlying assumptions, motivations and values which inform research practices.[54]

The representational crisis[55] inherent in qualitative research is further heightened in this decolonizing sphere by issues of epistemological perspectives and the pervasive dominance of the Western tradition's insistence on its superiority.[56] In decolonizing research, focus shifts from confronting how the researcher's ideas are shaped, to how ideas, beliefs and values have shaped the researcher. Data, as L. T. Smith advises, needs to be continuously interrogated in order to accommodate multiple ways of knowing.[57]

To operate effectively across cultures, as well as within them, researchers therefore need the skills to be able to know themselves. Only by knowing the self politically, socially, morally and cognitively, Chilisa maintains, can a researcher be able equally to accommodate the researched ways of knowing.[58] L. T. Smith suggests that this makes movement across cultures inherently problematic because of 'the complex ways in which the pursuit of knowledge is deeply embedded in the multiple layers of imperial and colonial processes'.[59] Ladson-Billings contends that the dominant paradigm, the Euro-American epistemological tradition, is 'more than just another way to view the world – it claims to be the only legitimate way to view the world'.[60]

Therefore for those who come from the dominant paradigm, Canadian economist John Ralston Saul makes the demand explicit: 'Our challenge is to learn how to recognise what we have trained ourselves not to see.'[61] It is this resistance to other world views, which continues to obfuscate 'the links between globalization, poverty and human rights abuses'.[62]

Structuring the play

I thought at this early stage in the play's development that audience engagement would be greatest during the retelling of the arrest and trial story, an area of focus in the participant narratives. I would reinforce the difference between the historical narratives of then and now, I thought, with the inclusion of documentary material. The memorial story I imagined would be part of the resolution of the past; it would be Act 3.

With my participants' interviews in small piles of culled transcripts on the floor around my desk, I had a clear chronological structure to follow. Although I had sought participants' responses to a 2005 incidence of vandalism at the memorial as a stimulus for commentary about racism, the incident was quickly dismissed. Those I asked were surprised it hadn't occurred more often. So I could find little current conflict in this tale of murder, of retribution, of recognition. I had ultimately a happy story.

I suspected I had not located a reconciliation narrative but I still had more steps to go in my research plan. After the performed reading, there would be a feedback session; then interviews with my actor/co-researchers. The data weren't all in yet. But I was worried; as much as I was inspired by the participants' narratives, their reflections and their sense of purpose, I wanted more conflict. On the other hand I didn't want that to be only the barbarity of the massacre itself; I thought the material might be considered exploitative and offensive. The massacre was there in all the stories but so were other narratives. Of course, the massacre would be in the play but used as an impetus for action. However, there were no disputes in the reported reconciliation process and I had expected there to be some. An Aboriginal Elder, Sue Blacklock, put forward the idea for a memorial, it was accepted, everyone came on board, it all took 18 months; there was no conflict. This didn't feel like reconciliation. It was all too cheerful. What was I missing?

A clever encounter

Although I had not met Graham Hingangaroa Smith before our paths crossed at Sydney University in November 2011, I was aware of his influence and his significance as an outstanding scholar and educator, particularly in the Māori language revitalization movement that began in the late 1970s. I had witnessed major cultural shifts in New Zealand, as mentioned earlier in this chapter. Through his writings and those of his partner, Linda Tuiwhai Smith, now as a researcher rather than as an artist, I had become familiar with the fundamental imperatives of developing and implementing decolonizing research methodologies in order to acknowledge the primacy of Indigenous ways of knowing and thereby, as a non-Indigenous researcher, confront and adapt my own.

In 1990, Graham formally created the framework for Kaupapa Māori research theory, theory that validates the acquisition and dissemination of knowledge privileging the Māori world view; knowledge which is Māori owned and Māori controlled.[63] First to identify the six principles of Kaupapa Māori, these same principles underpin all Indigenous resistance to neo-colonial pedagogy:

> encouraging and empowering indigenous peoples to make colonizers confront and be accountable for the traumas of colonization . . . [they] honour difference and promote healing.[64]

The goal of all Kaupapa Māori research, Graham argues, is to achieve self-determination, located within 'the struggle for autonomy over our own cultural well-being'.[65]

If Graham was prepared to see me, I thought, I'd ask about a researcher's decolonizing process, how it could be supported for I felt that my own work was not yet delivering appropriate outcomes. A conversation around my own deconstruction might illuminate what I couldn't yet see. I accepted it might be time now to focus on what the play didn't say and why. My task as a researcher, I recognized, should be to concentrate on the history of marginalization and the miracle of survival in the face of over 200 years of oppression. I might now be encouraged to methodologically address colonization's hegemonic legacies and focus on the problems and not the possibilities of cross-cultural research in the Australian context.

For although I had elected to support my performance ethnography with a verbatim text, the authority of the authentic word still remains subject to researcher bias.[66] And, as Conquergood asserts, the hegemony of text may not reveal encrypted messages of resistance; 'transcription is not a transparent or politically innocent model for conceptualizing or engaging the world'.[67] Therefore it was not that I disregarded the epistemological challenge now I was developing a script; but self-reflexivity can only deliver insights, as awareness evolves and clearly mine was wanting.

So I was prepared to adopt other ethnographic performance models; ones, for example that included the ethnographer as an actor in the drama, so manifesting a symbolic reality that 'rehydrate the written word through embodied techniques'.[68] I couldn't afford to rehearse my actors, but I could open the text up to include myself. Perhaps I could use simultaneous contra-narratives to reinforce disenfranchisement; perhaps I could structure silence into the play text to emphasize oppression; perhaps I should be telling the meta-narrative of colonization in parallel with the participants' stories of resistance and counter-hegemony.

Innovative practices are encouraged in the evolving field of performance ethnography;[69] the challenge is to make the presentation of the research as complex as the research field but remain accessible and artistically satisfying. In terms of delivering decolonizing outcomes, I was ready to adopt whatever Graham might recommend.

It came as a complete surprise that Graham was immediately supportive of drama as a research methodology in the cross-cultural sphere. I think I expected to have to justify it. For drama brings with it the risk, being text based, that it could privilege dominant culture ways of knowing; furthermore I as a non-Aboriginal Australian was researching a site of Aboriginal trauma. Neither of the factors was of concern.

Graham was enthusiastic about drama, because of its potential to create transformative states, not in the researcher but in the audience. It allowed audience members, he recognized, the chance to 'hop into my shoes'.[70]

Although this was encouraging, it was the subsequent discussion about the four quadrants of the Canadian First Nations learning circle that delivered new as opposed to familiar knowledge. From this specific Indigenous perspective holistic learning can be seen as co-existing within four interdependent quadrants: spiritual and emotional in one quadrant, intellectual in another, physical in another and health in the final quadrant.

A doctoral student of Graham's, Lee Brown, argues that the colonization process involved the deliberate dismantling of the spiritual, emotional and for him, the moral domain.[71] The objectified other, Brown elaborates, inherits 'emotional pain . . . and a distorted, inaccurate negative view of the self and identity based on colonialism and oppression'.[72] Negativity creates a desensitized self, where learning on all levels becomes blocked: cognitively, psychologically and in terms of vision and self-determination.

Brown's work was permission to use drama techniques as a methodological tool for decolonizing research; not only was he concerned with the development of positive emotions around hope and thereby strengthening of one's relationship with oneself, but he was also aware of changing interpersonal dynamics through an increased emotional repertoire. He notes 'emotional skills such as the ability to forgive, were taught and encouraged'.[73] Furthermore storytelling was a safe environment; it released the pain of colonialism and released the energy that held it. Any concern I might have had about the appropriateness of my methodology evaporated. As a methodology, performance ethnography makes complex emotional responses accessible.

Performance enables us to seek affinity not justify objectivity and detachment; and affinity arcs across the emotional spectrum. Through the arts generally, we can perceive the human unity that lies beneath culture. The arts are able to reveal what makes us human, as Rosaldo observed, 'just as a tapestry's interconnections are revealed only if the embroidery is turned and viewed from its underside'.[74] I may not have conflict between representational characters but I could demonstrate a suppressed presence through the body, through placement of the actors for example. We could show pain, indifference, loss as embodied emotions.

Now with a clear understanding of the immediate task, I was ready to leave when Graham had a request. He asked for at least one third of the play to be about hope. He concluded:

> The story is sordid but offers bright hope by contrast. The story gives affect to what you really want to say. It's about the hope part, new ways of doing, learning from our history even though it's still here. But we can learn from it.[75]

But this was the play I already had. It was up-beat. This was however not the first time I had been made aware of the importance of positivity. I just hadn't really thought it should apply to me.

Hearing the message

Denzin considers the absence of hope sufficient to jeopardize the potential for the decolonizing research process to supplant the dominant discourse of the West. For Denzin hope's role 'as a form of pedagogy, confronts and interrogates cynicism, the belief that change is not possible or is too costly'.[76]

I remembered another occasion, when I had heard about the importance of laughter. It was in a research field, before I was conscious it *was* a research field. As part of my familiarization process after that first workshop with Moogahlin in 2008, so I could listen to more blackfellas, Lily had suggested I meet Dharug Elder, Uncle Greg Simms.

Most of the day I spent with Uncle Greg was in a cleared reserve in the foothills of the Blue Mountains. Uncle Greg needed to make a shield, a gift for a corporate benefactor. The reserve had suitable trees. While he hewed the wood with an axe, he asked me if I'd ever wondered why, when I saw Aboriginal people sitting together, they were always laughing. He assumed I would have thought they were drunk. I said nothing. And then he laughed. They were calling up spirit, he said. Not grog. Real spirit. It sits above them and keeps them strong. Perhaps those weren't his exact words but that's as I remember them.

Out in the bush with the shadows lengthening, listening to the steady rhythm of Uncle Greg's axe, it was possible to drift to another place, another time – foreign but not remote. We were reconnecting with the past, not through story but through the senses, through the imagination; an experience Pink recognizes as creating valid ethnographic data.[77] And it talked to that same spirit of resilience Professor Helen Milroy had identified noted earlier as being of great psychological strength in Aboriginal peoples.

Reinforcing the necessity of research to subvert models of persistent despair, Chilisa recognizes that hopelessness can be reinforced by methodologies that generate

> deficit-driven and damage-centred research and literature, which chronicle only the pain and hopelessness of the colonized and which entrench existing structures of domination.[78]

Confident in the play's content to tell a local story, I was not actually prepared for all the meanings generated by the performance in the memorial hall on the Sunday morning. The Myall Creek story grew rapidly to have national significance from the moment the actors introduced themselves; the Aboriginal actors identified themselves through country and clan; the non-Aboriginal actors through their places of residence. Survival and heritage, identity and perspective instantly through this introduction meant these themes were integral to the story's subtext. From the outset the play became political. As Jones argues: 'performance ethnography's attention to embodiment (and the attendant politics of embodiment) situate the practice deeply in a political frame.'[79] But I did not understand then how through the potency of emotional affinity, a shared purpose could overcome a political divide. That was all ahead.

The ticking clock – the alchemy of dramatic tension

Our first read-through of the play with all the cast was over breakfast on Sunday morning. Everything was rushed, muddied and apprehensive. The memorial hall was still 40 minutes up the road and word had come through that Uncle Roland was on his way but had to find an alternative route. There was floodwater on the road up-country.

Waiting for Uncle Roland, who failed to appear, we began the reading half an hour late; the audience was all non-Aboriginal and were mostly friends of actor/co-researcher Terry, who had recently been directing plays with the Bingara local theatre group. The play was to take 70 minutes and, as we were at floor level, the actors stood to read, moving slightly as scenes changed. Even Genevieve, who had broken her ankle two days before, managed to stand, script in one hand, crutch in the other. Uncle Roland, the only Aboriginal audience member, made a spectacular entrance halfway through the reading.

I had divided the text into 18 scenes, 12 focused on the events of 1838 and before, the history of first contact in the region, the massacre, the pursuit of the perpetrators and the trials that followed. Two scenes transitioned the text from 1838 to 1998 and four scenes told the memorial story.

I gave all my scenes a title, which I read, an intrusive voice from the side. But as all the actors were reading the words of composite characters, their lines were designated by their actual names. There were no 'characters'; I thought the scenes' headings would give the actors a chance to change gear. They were players on history's stage, I told them, and their speeches, not their characters, drove the play forward. It was a way of handling the data.

Although the text, I believe, was faithful to the narratives in the field, it did not adhere to its potential in terms of an emergent theatrical aesthetic. This I attribute to lack of time, lack of knowledge and surfeit of caution. The lack of time is easily attributable to the circumstances around completing the interviews and the booking of the memorial hall, which had been made months previously. The lack of knowledge refers to the potency of the body to tell history and to demonstrate its political and social consequences.

Through the performance I discovered that dates and deeds are incidental to the sweeping narrative of persecution, dispossession and injustice and it is within the sweeping narrative that the *Today We're Alive* story is situated. For that story to be told, I now understand, you need actors, Aboriginal and non-Aboriginal, on stage, together but their words don't tell the big picture, their physical isolation and their emotional responses do. *Today We're Alive* could not dwell too long on the massacre's aftermath, it could not slip into extolling the triumph of British justice – on this one occasion in November 1838. This was a discovery I might have made in rehearsal, had we had any.

But the surfeit of caution, however, was a new understanding that could not have come from rehearsal. It was a consequence of misplaced sensitivity and it was an insight Aunty Rhonda shared – through performance.

Although I felt I had accurately captured the tone of the narratives in the field and supported them with documentary material, I was concerned that by repeating the manner in which the Weraerai were slaughtered – decapitation by repeated cavalry-inspired charges – that the content may cause distress. Even though that particular story is told on the memorial itself, I wondered if in performance the images would become more vivid, more painful. So I buried it. I put 11 scenes before it.

Finally I read:

Scene 12: Re-imagining the massacre

In their own time the actors get to their feet (not Genevieve); they find a space to visualise the terror.

And halfway through the scene the truth is told:

Rhonda: And they came upon them and they never had a chance. When they came upon them they just never had a chance.

Gen: They captured them and tied them up and led them away with the convicts on horseback and the rest being tied to . . . to a leg rope . . . it's so called . . . and I imagine it's a rope used for restraining animals or tying them around their legs . . . and they were tied to this long rope and led away over a slight rise, so that Anderson, who was at the hut couldn't see what happened.

Fred: These guys only had three swords. And I mean that's – and Anderson only heard two shots. So I mean you know when you kill 28 people with just two shots you know and only 3 swords and those poor people had to wait a hell of a long time for their turn to be slaughtered. You know, tied to a rope . . . an absolutely horrific crime.

Rhonda: And then we know we have to forgive. And um it's hard.

Terry: And I don't think there was time for the sort of sports you know, the releasing of one person at a time and the so on . . . I've had it suggested to me that more than likely – the convicts rode at this tied-up group with their swords and ah . . . decapitated then from horseback. I think that's more . . . I don't know of course . . .

Terry sits.

Rhonda: What it actually would have been like? Just the fear and the terror that they would have experienced.

Lily: I s'pose, after they done it, all the pots would all still be boiling, the fires going but there would be no sound. And they made a bonfire of their bodies. Um. Must have been terrible, you know?

Rhonda: Yeah, . . . (*cries*) . . . just thinking what those people went through.

Fred: And then the men come home looking for their wives, their kids . . . (*Today We're Alive*, First draft, 2011).

I am not sure when Aunty Rhonda began to cry, I just knew that she did, because the play slowed right down. But as her story from her subsequent interview reveals her tears sprang from multiple stimuli:

> I was actually sobbing and I just kept trying to slow myself down and take some deep breaths and say my lines. . . . I guess it was because I was right there in that country. And it was almost like you could feel them, you know, you could feel the people; feel the mums and their children and that. Well, having ten grandchildren of my own, you know. . . . I guess it really, really hit me. It hit me hard. But what an honour it was to be there, with these amazing actors, professional actors, who cared enough to come and travel and we had that experience of travelling together and getting to know each other. . . . Because growing up in our day, you just wouldn't hear of these things, you know. Where non-Aboriginal people would come and do a play and then the ancestors of the people, who murdered the Aboriginal people were there in the audience and they cared to come and see the play and afterwards come up and talk with us, Aboriginal people. I mean that's a ceremony, you know. That's a healing ceremony. Can't put it in words, just so powerful and so spiritual.

None of the perpetrators' descendants were actually there on the day; however two descendants of Police Magistrate Edward Denny Day were. But the perpetrators' descendants presence at the anniversary services at the memorial were mentioned by all the Aboriginal participants in the study as being of enormous significance. And it was these testimonies I had waited for, those of the perpetrators' descendants, delaying the compilation of the first draft. And so for Aunty Rhonda, they were there, because their words were; their presence was significant for her, too.

What happened when Aunty Rhonda began to cry was like the low rumble of a deep shock wave. The cast hesitated, should they stop? Should they comfort her? Should they plough on? And as one rhythm snapped – the rhythm of an energized reading – another rhythm took its place – a rhythm that was broken by uncertainty and empathy but, because of the subject matter, reinterpreted by those hearing the play as incredulity and horror. The words were surrounded by a portentous silence and the silence made what was said resonate more strongly, because it seemed to come out of a conscious decision to speak. Silence could therefore be interpreted as hesitation; hesitation could be interpreted as defying a cultural imposition and speaking out, it could be seen as managing shock, it could be seen as expressing an unfamiliar empathy. It was at this point I noticed how powerfully the audience, too, were engaged. Aunty Rhonda wasn't the only one crying.

As a result of these few pages of intense uncertainty, the end of the play, the building of the memorial, became celebratory; a huge emotional release. The building became the heart of the play, sharing what was done about what was known. It was where the action was, the hope, the energy, the optimism. It was where the meaning of the play resided; the massacre might have dominated individual narratives but collectively the play's story, I discovered, was about community.

Consequences – learning outcomes for an evolving practice

Given all these insights, the second draft of *Today We're Alive*,[80] the draft that 18 months after the memorial hall performance, I was able to rehearse and then take on tour, is leaner, faster, has less history but is still verbatim theatre and still structured as a chronology, with a few variations. The history that had been edited out was not the massacre but the trial, the stories of the corruption, the attempts to pervert the course of justice, all the moral outrages of the time. The big story that remains is that the massacre had happened. Cast size has been reduced to four and running time to 55 minutes instead of 70. To support the emotional journey we were able to budget for a sound track, which continues underneath the entire play. The silences now structured into the script are not totally silent in performance.

Three key play-making tools utilized during this research process evolved further, when taken into the development of *This Fella, My Memory*. They include the role of storytelling to develop relationship and script content; the importance of being in the physical world to inform personal practice, to bring into the performance space a sense of country and the stories it holds; and the multiple meanings that might be held within silence. As we discovered in *This Fella, My Memory*, acts of forgiveness are not necessarily acts of healing, they might just be an invitation to move forward; it's what happens before and after silence that holds the meaning and the drama.

Collaborations in the cross-cultural performance, I suggest, are not confined to old ideas of shared input on a script. Collaborations in the performance space, for both researchers and dramatists, I believe, occur in all the quadrants of the Learning Circle: the intellectual quadrant through mentors, like Uncle Greg, like Graham Hingargaroa Smith; the spiritual and emotional quadrant through a shared engagement by all players with story; the physical quadrant through time spent in the physical world, experiencing its sensual, cultural and historical resonances; and the health quadrant through hope, through positivity, through shared grief, through laughter.

Millis in his authoritative account of the massacre at Myall Creek, notes that one of those murdered, named Daddy by the convicts, was a *wirrigan*, a clever man, one that held the knowledge for the clan.[81] I suggest that the word 'collaboration' needs to be reinterpreted in the decolonizing space. New relationships have a new dynamic;

researchers are embarking on a journey of encounters, a journey filled with clever conversations, where they are to look, listen and learn with respect, as well as question, challenging not the knowledge expressed but their own uncertainty. If it can be recognized that decolonizing narratives are new, then it might be possible to let go of preconceived ideas about their conclusion; not to begin, as I did in *Today We're Alive*, at the end, seeking a story that will reflect a neat three-act structure of a beginning, a middle and an end; not to begin at an end I knew, a middle I hoped to find and a beginning I could contrive.

Further reflections on collaboration

The search for proof to support a predetermined structure as a foothold for research further demonstrates for me a colonized mindset; if I had found any participant who had been upset by the graffiti incident of 2005, the play would have been different. But there was no one; I had to deal with the more distant past. So I discovered through performance that with my focus on the convicts, on the trial, that I had tried another way to obfuscate the truth, however I called it being sensitive, being politically correct. But this first performance of *Today We're Alive* had one more lesson for me: through interaction with the audience afterwards, my final collaborators, the play demonstrated the potency of Read's narrative of avoidance, mentioned earlier in this chapter.

Performance as a research methodology recognizes that meanings are co-created, that authority and knowledge shifts between participants. During the feedback session after the performed reading the historians in the audience gradually dominated. They emphasized the need for accuracy – massacres needed to be reported in 'the right order'; properties needed to be named 'how locals would understand them'. Even though the play text is verbatim and therefore edited transcripts, it felt completely normal to be instructed this way, to be challenged and I dutifully took notes.

I quickly became completely unaware of how these demands were diffusing the shared emotional response; how the value of the shared experience was evaporating. It was my actor/co-researchers, Terry and Fred, who brought the discussion back to sharing how we felt, back to the performance. Authority shifted from the intellectual back to the emotional; validation of the experience returned to the collective and audience members once more told personal stories of gratitude and transformation before the feedback session ended. Their position of emotional disempowerment, caused by the hierarchical demands for accuracy in a field of knowledge based on hearsay, shifted. And old way of knowing, in this case disengagement, receded in the wake of a new energized focus on change. We talked about grief, we talked about hope, we talked about the relief of being able to share stories about both emotions.

In decolonizing research performance, through action and reaction, offers us all a way of understanding 'how culture operates pedagogically to produce and reproduce victims'.[82] As can be seen from above, a colonial culture can make victims of us all. Applied Theatre as a decolonizing research methodology prioritizes new understandings through interaction with each other and with the self; as it is embodied, it offers new ways of being; as it offers flexibility, it honours receptivity to insight; as it strives for respectful relationships, it recognizes that authority is a negotiated site. In a recent speech at the Australian Performing Arts Market, 2014, Rachel Maza, Artistic Director of Ilbijerri, an Aboriginal Theatre company based in Melbourne, suggested that it was time for non-Aboriginal Australians to walk two paths, to walk in two cultures, just as 'blackfellas have been doing for over two hundred years'. Performance offers us a way of feeling how to do this – to move forward on two paths, not as separate but in parallel.

And have I, as an Australian, found a reconciliation narrative? Not yet. Through Myall Creek I've located an acknowledgement story.

The Myall Creek Committee seek a national apology for the massacres, they want to raise $15 million to build a National Cultural and Education Centre that will tell the truth about first contact. Acknowledging a shared history has brought all parties to the table; but no one knows yet what the future will be. That's another story. But we do have a beginning.

It's a Tricky Business:
Performing Poetry with the Ghost

Esther Fitzpatrick

For George Belliveau who showed me
how to be an a/r/trographer

(In a Piratey voice)
'Tis a half blood that I be,
The Muggles world rejecteth me.
I can't think strayt I never shall,
Kant can't Kant me with his spell.
I swerves and leaps then turns around
And sometimes soars to higher ground,
Where misteries and angels thrive
And songs and colours come alive.
I feast on dreams and then I sup
On imaginations' freedom cup.
I stare into my looking glass
And see an echo of the past.
Refracted fragments of a ghost
Speak to me and gives me hope.

It is a tricky business talking to ghosts. They can snare you with their tantalizing world of secrets. You can find yourself on a journey to worlds, imagining their families and histories, and chasing mere fragments of information into the early hours of the next day. But how does one – as Derrida[1] implores researchers' to do – speak to the ghost? Derrida's theory of hauntology as a method of deconstruction provides no articulate way of pursuing such an objective. This chapter posits that critical art-based methods, such as a/r/tography and ekphrasis, and performance can provide a medium to speak to the ghost.

George Belliveau's keynote presentation[2] at the first International Critical Research Symposium on applied theatre at the University of Auckland in 2010 on a/r/tography changed the way I now see, understand, and practice research. It was fortuitous, as I was busy deciding what methodology I would use to explore my tentative research question: What is a Pākehā educator? I was already an Eisner[3] convert and believed that arts research should be able to exist without constantly having to justify itself to more dominant research methodologies. Belliveau's performance exemplified an arts-based methodology that wove in narrative, drama and visual methods. The poem I begin this chapter with is a celebration of my position as an a/r/tographer; straddling the restrictions imposed in my current world of being a university researcher, and the desire to imagine new ways of exploring and making sense of important questions in society. This fits with Denzin's directive that 'as researchers we need to find new ways of connecting persons and their personal troubles with social justice methodologies'.[4] The broader project this study sits inside is to further develop a methodology that enables empathetic capabilities, for adults and children, breaking the persistence of stereotypes in our postcolonial societies.[5]

This chapter is also in response to, and a continuation of the conversation given by Gauntlett and Holzwarth.[6] In this conversation they responded to the puzzlement of other academics about issues with the use of creative artefacts within the research process: For instance, 'how researchers can use and interpret such visual artefacts'[7] Gauntlett and Holzwarth posit that researchers should be developing visual creative methods. They are convinced that creative methods are a 'good way of building sociological knowledge, and offer a positive challenge to the taken-for-granted idea that you can explore the social world just by asking people questions, in language'.[8] Rather, they insist that creative methods are an enabling methodology that provides a way for participants to express what they feel about the issue or question, and to express their embodied experience within the study.

The business of talking to ghosts took place in an autoethnographic study. Through the autoethnographic study I was personally interested in Pākehā identity; Pākehā refers to the descendants of the white colonial settlers of New Zealand. Cognizant of Gauntlett and Holzwarth's conversation, I speculated that using a range of arts-based processes in an autoethnographic work would provide a method for me, as the researcher, to have a 'deeper and more reflective engagement . . . a bodily engagement'[9]; when exploring issues of ethnic identity in multi-ethnic and postcolonial settings. Using arts-based methods in an autoethnographic study responds to Gauntlett and Holzwarth's statement that:

> we need research which is able to get a full sense of how people think about their own lives and identities, and what influences them and what tools they use in that thinking, because those things are the building blocks of social change.[10]

A/r/tography, ekphrasis and performance

A/r/tography values the three intersecting roles of *a*rtist, *r*esearcher and *t*eacher. Throughout this study I applied the arts-based method of a/r/tography as a form of critical self-reflection and analysis. A/r/tography provided a critically reflective way for me as researcher to engage in a creative activity, to explore and imagine future possibilities, through reimagining our histories. Dwelling in in-between spaces I used the arts to explore multiple identities, complexity, difference and similarity.[11] The objective of the researcher-artist is to understand more deeply who I am and what I believe. . . .[12]

As a researcher I was interested in using my art making as a medium to talk to the ghost. Gina Wall[13] describes the medium of photography as 'Ghost Writing' making explicit links to Derrida's notion of hauntology and différance. The visual image of the photograph conjures up questions of 'what is?' that are haunted by questions of 'what is not'. 'Between the [visual] image and the subject is a gap, and in this in-between is the play of the spatial and the temporal . . .'.[14] The visual work creates a gap between the real and the image, a distance which disrupts temporality and provides a space for the ghost to speak. Are not all art works haunted by the trace of otherness? As Derrida[15] suggested the essence of photography is the spectral. Does not all art work like a 'medium', providing space for the spectre to return? I propose that the arts in this study is like ghost writing, 'a medium which writes the present into an archive enabling it to repeat and repeat again and that the 'past is never completely finished with . . . the ghost returns again . . . demanding we anticipate our possible futures'.[16]

Throughout this study data was generated as I responded to the historical archives I was exploring. I took photos, drew sketches, told stories, wrote poems, painted ancestors (or illusions of them) created a wire Pākehā, and wrote more poems. I then started performing my poems and stories. Playing with data, such as writing poetry, enabled me to 'interrogate the self, within the social and political'.[17] Poetry as an art form provided a different way to develop understanding, to explore and analyse the story. Rinehart[18] also explores the use of poetry in research urging us to 'creatively apply our own imagination and memory to profound problems that both touch on and are implicit within . . . [my study]'. The playful and imaginative approach of art making also provides a more sophisticated way of responding to more complex issues and questions such as identity.

Through my journaling, using a selection of arts-based methods, I began to use ekphrasis[19] where I would use one art form to respond to another art form to reveal, communicate and illuminate the message. I used the ekphrasis process to disrupt traditional readings of visual and textual art, and to analyse these art works providing additional layers of meaning. The creation of my artwork was in response to my own original art works. Ekphrasis was then used as interplay between visual, textual and performative works. Hence, a cyclic interplay was used to disrupt any privileging of one art form over another. Rather, ekphrasis was used to problematize the work and provide an interpretative framework[20] drawing out and transforming the essence of the arts work to evoke further interpretation. Prendergast[21] highlights five important categories from Bruhn[22] on the use of ekphrasis in inquiry. First, the potential for ekphrasis to recreate through other art forms in response to an original art work (transposition). Second, the potential for ekphrasis to add non-spatial, for example sensory, dimensions (supplementation). Third, it provides a stimulus to trigger memories (association). Fourth, it provides the researcher with a critical eye (interpretation). Last, ekphrasis has the potential for playfulness in the crafting of the new art work.

Tim Ingold's 'Ways of mind-walking'[23] enabled me to consider ekphrasis further as the interplay between the forms of art work. He suggests that the reader consider the visual . . . 'as a node in a matrix of trails to be followed by observant eyes'. Ingold describes two instances of one art responding to another art form, which I liken here to the process of ekphrasis as defined above by Pendergast. First is the essay by Kandinsky on the Spiritual in Art, inspired by an art exhibition where the essay questions the ability of the observer to experience a painting.[24] Second is the description of a musical composition (*Pictures at an Exhibition*) written by Mussorsky in response to the paintings of his late friend Russian artist Victor Hartmann. Each piece of music responded to an art piece he imagined hanging in a gallery. Ingold suggested that '[t]ogether [the painting and the music] open the mind to inner truths that are ontologically prior to the outward forms of things . . . directly touch the soul and set it in motion'.[25]

Performance of an ekphratic poem enhances the potential to generate an embodied experience of the subject of inquiry for both the researcher and reader/audience. Spry describes the process of performance as a continuation of the writing process where the body is moved from the 'page to the stage'.[26] The performance of autoethnographic text is understood as a method of inquiry and analysis that engages the body with the text, and further works to create more text. Embodying the text through performance provokes the researcher to become vulnerable to critical reflection, where they can then continue to work through and understand the self. The performance also invites the audience to engage in the story:

> Dialogic performance . . . is the interpretation of the complex interaction between performer (self), text [poem], and sociocultural context; it is what allows/invites/motivates an audience to engage the performance, to communicate with the persona, to exist in the world of the story.[27]

My use of ekphrasis is most apparent when I perform poetry and fictional scripts in response to stories, photos and other visual art forms. I have also created visual work in response to a textual work. Performing the work has further transformed the work into an 'utterance'. Utterance is, defined by Bakhtin, as an 'expression embedded in a history of expressions by others in a chain of ongoing cultural and political moments' . . . 'thus fundamentally *dialogic* and historically *contingent*'.[28] The process of ekphrasis moving to performance has involved me expressing not just my findings but also my feelings – an embodied experience of being Pākehā. Taking me 'deeply down into [my] subject'.[29] It is through these art forms I am able to speak to the ghost. When I am deep down into my subject of inquiry I embody my ghosts. As Avery Gordon states:

> Haunting is a constituent element of social life . . . [Being] haunted draws us affectively, sometimes against our will and always a bit magically, into the structure of feeling of a reality we come to experience, not as cold knowledge, but as transformative recognition.[30]

Hauntology and Pākehā

'In learning to live – between life and death – one *must* talk with or about some ghost'.[31]

Hauntology is a methodology of deconstruction that works to problematize particular narratives. Originally coined by Derrida, hauntology restored speaking to ghosts as a respectable subject of enquiry. Hauntology involves interrogating our relationships with our dead to 'examine the elusive identities of the living, and to explore the boundaries between the thought and the unthought'.[32] As Bell[33] and others insist, Pākehā need not be ignorant about their ancestors, but rather come to an understanding of their colonial heritage; and all the guilt that might come with it. Similarly Wells[34] argues that Pākehā need to acknowledge their colonial heritage and also celebrate its positive aspects, not drown in colonial guilt. Hauntology provides a method for remembering our past and interrogating how it speaks to our present. As Ruitenberg states:

> Ghosts unsettle us, make us feel uncomfortable . . . those parts of our histories that we – or some of us – would rather not acknowledge and that, when we do, threaten to disrupt the comfort of our everyday assumptions and make our moral hair stand on end.[35]

I also liken hauntology to Traue's[36] metaphor of 'Whakapapa of the mind'. In his essay 'Ancestors of the mind – a Pākehā whakapapa', Traue illustrates his Pākehā identity through using the Māori claim to identity of 'Whakapapa' and recited his own genealogy. The term Whakapapa refers to the layered Māori genealogy which includes spiritual, mythological and human stories, including ancestors. Significant to this discussion is where Traue included his ontological ancestors in his Whakapapa, making reference to the many different ideas of ancient to modern day writers and thinkers. Traue's Whakapapa resonates with hauntology where Davis[37] (2005) argues that all stories are haunted by ghosts and owe a debt to the literary ghost, that 'ghosts [are the] ungrounded grounding of representation and a key to all forms of storytelling'. Traue argued that Pākehā need to recognize their ancestors of the mind and be proud of their inheritance.

Other works, by Maddison-MacFadyen[38] and O'Loughlin[39] describe how we are haunted by our pasts and in particular 'our childhood touchstone stories, those stories that live deeply within us and inform our perspectives of the world'. Maddison-MacFadyen also argued the importance of analysing our touchstone stories, which often provide a colonial meta-narrative, and the need to engage with 'counter stories' to be involved in the process of decolonization. In a similar vein, Gramsci earlier describes how our identity is the 'product of the historical processes to date which [have] deposited in [us] an infinity of traces, without leaving an inventory'.[40] Bell further described how our sense of identity is not constructed out of thin air but rather 'out of the ways of thinking and relating that we inherit from the past'.[41]

I now have several networks of family all over the world chasing down our ghosts. We scroll through Census records, transcribe wills, visit cemeteries, pore over ancient church records, and sit in the hushed rooms of library special collections. What happens when I summon up a ghost? I give them permission to speak. I invoke a memory. The ghost only exists when it is given permission to speak. In summoning up the ghost I have remembered them, I have named them and given them voice. Gye speaks of the dependent existence of ghosts on the evoker by explaining

> the ghost as revenant, that which exists only by virtue of its return, reminds us that past and present cannot be neatly separated from one another, as any idea of the present is always constituted through the difference and deferral of the past, as well as anticipations of the future.[42]

The insubstantial Pākehā: Setting the scene

The term Pākehā is fraught with contentious meanings and sentiments. Pākehā are usually understood as the white European partner in New Zealand's bicultural relationship with Māori – the Indigenous people of New Zealand. Understanding the development of such an identity in New Zealand is a significant undertaking since it is complicated by recent globalization, polyethnic communities and a bicultural relationship between two founding peoples, Indigenous Māori and Pākehā settler. The development of an identity for Pākehā is even more complicated by a history as colonists, their hegemonic position in society, and for some, their ignorance of white privilege.[43]

To make sense of our colonial traces Ruitenberg suggests we need to speak to these ghosts. She describes the impact of colonialism on our present where:

> Our world or culture bears the marks of Christian and colonialist inheritances . . . Denying the traces of these inheritances in the world today, or trying to bury these traces as deeply as possible, does not stop their influence . . . we should aim to come to (speaking) terms with them.[44]

Pākehā denial of their turbulent histories caused a 'gap at the heart of the construction of Pākehā identity narratives'.[45] Through denying their history and divorcing themselves from their colonial past, she argues that Pākehā exist as a people without a history. Bell argues that such a denial of history results in a 'repressed cultural psyche'. She claims that to deny history 'is not to know oneself'. She, furthermore, warns that Pākehā will continue to be chained to a colonial relationship with Māori unless they can engage with their colonial history.[46] Other researchers have described Pākehā as having no culture,[47] or that what culture they do have is appropriated from Māori,[48] and that Pākehā are situated in a place of internal exile.[49] Pākehā, however, understood as an emerging identity, resonates with Hall who argues that 'cultural identity . . . is a matter of "becoming" as well as "being". . . . Far from being eternally fixed in some essentialised past [Pākehā are] subject to the continuous play of history, culture and power'.[50]

Pertinent to my study is the argument that many Pākehā encounter significant problems with 'belonging'.[51] Bell argues that Pākehā struggle with belonging because of inherited guilt and a lack of knowledge of their ancestral stories. Belonging is described as the most important marker of ethnic identity and is associated with ideas of commitment and attachment to place.[52] In order to achieve a secure sense of belonging, people need to be involved in a process of exploration, where individuals experience, seek information and reflect on aspects of their own ethnic identity.[53] Further, an achieved, secure sense of belonging is demonstrated by feelings of comfort, and positive feelings, about one's ethnic group. A positive ethnic identity enables the individual to reject negative perspectives of others founded on stereotypes.[54]

Autoethnography: A method of speaking to the ghosts

For the purpose of this study I required a methodological approach that would enable me to construct an in-depth exploration of becoming

Pākehā. I needed to choose the 'right tool[s] for the right job'[55] to generate, slice, stitch and create something new. I therefore applied a postcritical ethnographic approach, drawing on Kincheloe's[56] notion of Bricolage. As a critical, multidisciplinary approach, bricolage accommodates a wide range of theoretical and philosophical ideas that are inherent in the various aspects of the research act Becker likens the Bricoleur to a 'maker of quilts'[57] where aesthetic and material tools available are employed in the process. As the Bricoleur in this study I drew on a range of textual and critical strategies to interpret and deconstruct the phenomenon of my own Pākehā identity.

As a form of critical social research it has the potential for moral effect through disrupting sociopolitical structures that are unjust and unfair. Through its 'relentless nudging against the world of traditional science [it] holds wonderful, symbolic, emancipatory promise', where it says that the knowledge I have (and those less privileged than me) matters.[58] Transformative potential is obtained through a process of critical engagement, involving a cyclic in-depth analysis of the lived experience of being Pākehā.[59]

Pivotal to the autoethnography was the adoption of an ongoing reflexive and recursive approach that was applicable throughout all phases of the study. An ongoing reflective dialogue was established through the use of a research journal to document my embodied experience as researcher. This involved reflective conversations with *self* about the data – the choices being made, the patterns being identified and the process of questioning and unravelling the deeper and more complex meanings the data evoked. The research journal provided a place to be creative and play with the data through writing poems, recording anecdotal stories, memos to self, visual texts and metaphor.

Haunting tales

Each example of ekphrasis presented tells me something different about my becoming Pākehā. The first example is my making the Wire Pākehā (Figure 15) and my response during the process of making. A poem

Figure 15 Wire Pākehā.

was birthed as I manipulated the wire. I remember being on the deck at home with all my wire and wire tools, playing with the wire and having to rush back inside to get a pen and paper.

Wire

I am drawing out the wire
It is neatly bound like my Grandma's yarn of wool
I am imagining how I will weave my wire Pākehā
I draw out the wire carefully
Knitting, weaving, tukutuku koru
I draw more wire and remember
An ancestor who drew wire
In Thurgoland
An ancestor who used wire
In Sheffield
An ancestor who manipulated wire
In Auckland
To make my Poppa's crib

And then I think of number eight fencing wire
And remember
An ancestor who won a bet
Building fences
In Christchurch New Zealand
My mother's chicken wire
Chinese bantams, Rhode island red
And then I remember running a race
Across the paddocks
Dodging the cow pats
Smeared with paspalum
ZAP
My first electric fence.
(December 2012)

It was through the act of playing, of drawing out the wire, that I felt my ancestors speak to me of their various relationships with wire. In New Zealand we take pride and sometimes have a bit of a laugh at ourselves about how important 'wire' has been in our emergence as a culture – specifically number eight wire. This is both a Māori and Pākehā experience. It is part of our culture that, cognizant of we celebrate our ingenuity, our 'make do-ness'.[60] We live on the edge of the world where we 'give it a go!' The wire poem spoke to me of my connectedness with one world I never knew much of – an industrial Yorkshire, England. I now have a photo taken on a recent visit to my ancestor's wire mill in Thurgoland, Yorkshire, built in 1624. It is pinned to the wall in my office, a spectral image of something speaking to me, disrupting the fabric of time. It conjures up an image of people . . . workers . . . working with wire to create something new. Coming to New Zealand as early settlers they brought their skills, their strengths and their desire to forge something new.

The second example of ekphrasis is of the painting: 'Before arrival – a haunting past' (Figure 16) and the poem entitled 'A Pākehā Haunting – Part I.' The painting is something I played at for many months. It represents my responses to my own genealogical huntings as I scrolled

Figure 16 Painting 1. Before arrival: A haunting past.

through census records, read ancient family stories and began to make sense of this very distant and not so distant past.

A Pākehā Haunting – Part I

What if you were blind?
How would you see me then?
How would you read my actions?
How would you hear my words?
If you touched my skin
Would it be soft and warm?
Sweaty from the summer sun,
Salty from the sea,
Smokey from the hangi?
If you shared my meal
Would you taste my love,
My invitation for friendship?
If we had time to share our stories
Would we talk of our arrivals,
The waka and the ships,
Our whakapapa stretching back in time.

I believe we would love and cry,
Argue and agree.
And you would see my Pākehā bricolage:
My Jewish bones,
My Viking skin,
My Sami cheek bones,
My Danish eyes,
My German hair,
My Cornish courage,
My Yorkshire creativity,
And my Welsh love of singing.
(January 2013)

I started the painting with a yellow base, to signify the struggle for a better future. The face at the top of the painting looms large, pale and ghostly over the rest. This was to represent my embodied experience of being so white, a throwback to some Nordic Viking or Sami (Sápmi) ancestry, that influenced me all of my life as a child growing up in the rural town of Opotiki, as someone different. The mother with the baby wrapped in her shawl represents all of my Jewish mothers who have fled, suffered and survived to bring me, eventually, safe to this land. I have borrowed 'The Scream' and have sewn a Star of David onto his garments to represent the horrors my ancestors experienced. The rubbing up against each other of the Jewish and Christian religion is demonstrated in the Ten Commandments and the burial ground. The poppies in the middle of the painting drip the blood of those who died back in the Nile, from whence they first fled with Moses. But there is more there to contemplate. In painting this work I realized it would always be an unfinished piece, just like me. These ghosts that arrived on the canvas spoke to me of survival, of struggle and love, of war and hate, but most of all of courage.

The poem 'A Pākehā haunting 1' began to take shape after I first started painting. My embodied experience of being labelled white, and Pākehā, had silenced my story of being many. I began to see while painting, my many stories of becoming. It was a complex bricolage of bits, fragments of becoming, entangled and juxtaposed against each other. My being

Pākehā would have different meanings depending on the context I was in, and was forever emergent, 'subject to the continuous play of history, culture and power'.[61] It is a poem also for others to juxtapose their own unique stories against of becoming Pākehā, to begin to draw on their own diverse histories of becoming. It is a poem to enable others to begin to tell their stories of arrival and of their Whakapapa stretching back in time. It is a poem to disrupt the standard story of being Pākehā that Pākehā are not a homogenous group but a complex and diverse group of people who call Aotearoa New Zealand home.

The last example of ekphrasis is different again. This time it began with a poem. I suppose this poem has been in process of becoming since my childhood. It eventually made its way to paper when Whakaari, Ruapehu and Tongariro (three volcanic mountains) started rumbling in 2012. The poem 'In memory of a Ringatu Prophecy from my childhood' was written in response to a 'touchstone' story from my childhood that represented a significant part of my upbringing.

In memory of a Ringatu Prophecy from my childhood

White Island – Whakaari – is troubled.
Ruapehu shudders in anticipation.
Tongariro shouts out a warning.
Queen Victoria's great great great granddaughter still sits on the throne.
Aging, her eyes dimming, reaching for the night.
A premonition, a prophecy in waiting:
'Evacuate the shore, stay away from the rivers
At her death the great wave will come'.
(December 2012)

The green hill painting grew from the poem as I imagined all these stories, the names of places and people that informed my childhood and the many hills I would run up to imagine their lives and mine. I carved their names into the vivid green hill to reveal the blood of those

Figure 17 In memory of a Ringatu Prophecy from my childhood.

ancestors of my mind who speak to me. Both the poem and the painting demonstrate the two worlds I straddled as a child. In the poem we have the Māori prophecy I grew up with about the British Queen who we were told ruled our world. The painting gives the names of significant places, people and stories revealing the Māori Hauhau movement: A political and religious uprising during the New Zealand wars between the settlers and the Indigenous Māori, and how it touched our lives in the Waioeka valley. The language is both Māori and English.

The poem and painting resonate with Said's[62] musical metaphor of entanglement. Said likened the relationship between colonizer and colonized to two (or more melodies) that coexist in a complex relationship. This entangled relationship could contribute to a 'richer musical form' as it progressed through both 'discordant and harmonious moments'.[63] My becoming Pākehā is forever in response to my relationship with Māori. My touchstone stories come from the myths and legends of Waioeka, from the Bible, and from my experiences as a child both on the Marae and in the Church. As I show in the painting, this relationship for Pākehā summons up memories that are enriching and painful. It was on top of the green hill at Matawai, confiscated land, that I would look down over the Waioeka valley and the hills of the Ureweras and visualize Māori warriors being pursued by the British soldiers and the burning of the bush to reveal their hiding places. The dead trees stood like crosses in the graveyard. If I looked harder, toward the ocean, I could see the peach tree that once belonged to my Great Grandfather, where Carl Volkner was hanged by the Hauhau's who accused him of being a spy for the British army. These were the stories of my childhood.

It is always with trepidation that I step out onto the stage to present my work. I position myself in a place of vulnerability, by opening up my stories, and my art for critique. The performing of my stories, my works of art for others, has been another level of interpreting and opening up of self. I have drawn out the wire, I have embodied the experience of the labour as I have recited the poem 'Wire', with the Wire Pākehā hanging in the background – taking me deep down into my subject. I scripted the poem 'A Pākehā haunting 1' and performed it with my sister. During the performance, with the painting as a backdrop we evoked a deeper level of emotions, perhaps as Ingold[64] (2010) describes, directly touching the soul and setting it in motion. In performing 'In memory of a Ringatu Prophecy from my childhood' I found myself chanting the words, reminiscent of my experiences with prophecy on the Marae. It is here, in being haunted, that we begin to feel, to experience and to recognize ourselves.

'Kia Kaha' they whisper
'Be strong' they say as they push me on the stage
'Take courage'.

In this study I have been able to spend time playing and art making, immersing my whole self in the process. And it took time. The wire Pākehā uncoiled itself slowly from my imagination; it's beginning a three strand woven spine. Through each art making I summoned up my ghosts. Their complex complicated stories transformed by paint on canvas; creating a collage of colour. Through the use of ekphrasis I wrote poems to give a richer and deeper understanding of the issue being explored. Drawing the reader closer to the work to evoke an embodied response through the engagement with the visual and poetic.[65] Through adopting ekphrasis as an approach I speculate that the researcher employs a critical gaze at their first work of art, providing a deeper engagement with the complexities of the issue through another interpretation of the work.

With a world increasingly shrinking through globalization many postcolonial/multiethnic societies are grappling with making sense of new and in-between identities. The importance of being able to articulate a positive identity and develop respect for others is essential to combat stereotypical behaviour and racism. This is particularly relevant for most white identity groups in postcolonial societies. Descendants of European settlers often lack any coherent sense of ethnicity and rather blindly persist in an imagined national identity, perceiving themselves as the 'norm'. Many researchers insist that it is important to know our histories to understand our present. With this in mind I postulated that arts-based methods would provide me with a strategy to speak to my ghosts. I found a way to draw on historical archives and stories to make a sense of my own becoming Pākehā. Through speaking to my ghosts I was able to develop a sense of an ethnic identity that is constantly in the process of becoming. The complex and multilayered history of my becoming is especially evident where my 'touchstone' stories drew from more than one cultural experience.

Through the making and performing of art I embodied the experience of examining global issues of in-between and emerging identities at a personal level. By adopting the process of ekphrasis I was able to critically analyse my own stories through a thoughtful reflective reinterpretation. This work supports the use of arts-based processes to tap into embodied knowledge and provide a richer, fuller description of the issue/question being explored. I anticipate that in sharing these stories, it is possible for the reader/audience to engage with the issue and make sense of the work for themselves. Further, that in the sharing of these visual and textual stories, the reader/audience is provoked to analyse their own histories, to make sense of their own becoming, and in doing so develop empathetic capabilities.

Life Drama Applied Theatre in Papua New Guinea: 'It may be performative, but is it performative research?'

Brad Haseman

Over the past decade researchers across applied theatre, arts education and the creative arts have challenged many of the established protocols of organized research by introducing a number of radical methodological innovations into their research practice. These include placing a primacy on professional and creative practice in the research process and proposing alternative forms for reporting research outcomes. However, rather than merely disrupting traditional protocols, many see their innovations as signals of an emerging third paradigm of research, one which is separate to, but complementary with, the quantitative and qualitative traditions. In the quest to identify alternative research frameworks, various different, but not dissimilar approaches have been proposed.[1] They include Creative Practice as Research (most commonly in the United Kingdom) and Artistic Research (in Scandinavia and Europe in particular). My writings on this matter[2] argue that we stand at a pivotal moment in the history of research, and based on the achievements of both arts-based and practice-led researchers, we can now claim a third space, a new paradigm of research, called Performative Research.[3]

In summary my proposal is that

> when research findings are presented as performative utterances,
> there is a double articulation with practice that brings into being
> what, for want of a better word, it names. The research process
> inaugurates movement and transformation. It is performative. It
> is not qualitative research: it is itself – a new paradigm of rese-
> arch with its own distinctive protocols, principles and validation
> procedures.[4]

Of course this assertion demands elaboration and challenge. While
Barbara Bolt, for instance perceives that 'a performative paradigm
potentially offers the creative arts a radical new vision and a way of
distinguishing its research from the dominant models of knowledge',
she goes on to observe that to be convincing and credible 'it must
establish criteria whereby it can interpret and validate its research
within a broader research arena'.[5]

This is an essential task. Not to meet the established criteria demanded
by research in the 'broader research arena' relegates performative
research to a term worthy of Humpty Dumpty who, in Alice and
Wonderland, rather scornfully declared, 'When I use a word it means
just what I choose it to mean – neither more or less'. Researchers in
applied theatre or any of the creative arts are not free to simply choose
what we want the word 'research' to mean. Instead, exactly as Bolt says,
we must craft our argument for any new form of research using the
criteria whereby the claim can be validated and interpreted 'within the
broader research arena'.

In this chapter I will seek to address this challenge by drawing on
four criteria proposed by Biggs and Buchler in 2008 'that form the
core model that also characterizes traditional and dominant models of
academic research, and as such are comparable to scholarship about
research in other areas'.[6] To demonstrate how these four criteria play
out in action, the chapter is grounded in an existing and lived piece
of performative research, in this instance research using the principles

and dynamics of applied theatre. The applied theatre research project to be discussed is *Life Drama*, conducted in Papua New Guinea from 2008 to 2013.

Life Drama in Papua New Guinea: An HIV and AIDS Education Program

Papua New Guinea (PNG) is the largest low-income country in the Pacific, with some of the worst health and education statistics in the region.[7] Political, social and economic instability contribute to the spread of diseases, particularly HIV. Violence occurs at all levels of society in PNG and increased mining activity accelerates the transition from subsistence living to a cash economy in ways that are often culturally insensitive. The *Life Drama* Project, funded by an Australian Research Council[8] (ARC) Linkage Grant, focuses on sexual health promotion in Papua New Guinea through community capacity building, using Applied Theatre.[9] The *Life Drama* model aims to mobilize and train trainers with the capacity to lead the training and promulgate the programme throughout the country.

Life Drama 'trains the trainers' to act as change agents inside their culture, and to extend their skills and capacities in addressing sexual health issues along with destigmatization, transmission and prevention of STIs and HIV prevention. Combining techniques from drama in education, improvisational drama and theatre of the oppressed with non-drama activities such as condom demonstrations and gathering information on local knowledge and customs, *Life Drama* is a practical and experiential workshop-based approach to HIV and AIDS Education. Underpinning the work is a commitment to the belief that change needs to be sustained at a grass-roots level in community and by community.

The arc of the project moved through three distinct stages: a pilot project in Tari, Hela Province; an Intercultural Theatre Exchange

Laboratory bringing together a number of Australian, British and Papua New Guinean theatre practitioners in Madang, Madang Province; and a final trial on Karkar Island, Madang Province. Local theatre and cultural workers were engaged as co-researchers and co-artists in the development of the *Life Drama* methodology and the training materials. At each site in PNG, a local Research Advisory group counselled the team on the cultural dynamics at play. This included all important understandings on matters such as culturally specific gender and local sexual taboos, spirituality and kinship structures.

Stage I: Pilot workshops in Tari

After appropriate invitation protocols were observed the *Life Drama* team began its development work in 2009. Two workshops were held, each lasting 1 week and with a 3 month gap between them. Participants included community leaders and workers from Barrick Gold, church leaders and health and education providers in the remote highland town. Workshop sessions were structured around key issues related to HIV and AIDS education (e.g. voluntary testing and counselling, stigma and acceptance) and incorporated well-known techniques and conventions from process drama, drama in education and theatre of the oppressed. Reaction to these workshop games and exercises was extremely positive. Participants engaged enthusiastically and were especially thrilled and delighted by any activity driven by the tension of surprise or deception. For instance, the well-known game of 'Grandmother's Footsteps' was frequently called to a halt while students laughed wildly, struggling to hold a frozen image as they deceptively crept up on their fellow player. Concentration games such as Boal's Columbian Hypnosis were also popular (Figure 18).

All activities were drawn from the established applied theatre toolbox and the group securely worked from games and activities to simple hot-seat role-plays to more complex open stories which began to feel like rudimentary process dramas. One of the most telling open stories came

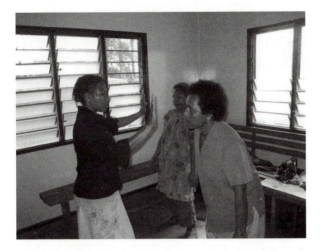

Figure 18 Concentration games – Boal's Columbian Hypnosis.

from improvisations around Sam, a truck driver, his wife Alungi and his daughter Onpain. After a series of belief-building activities the open story was built from a pretext which has Alungi accidentally reading the following text messages on her husband's mobile phone:

> **Lucy:** Sam mi wetim yu long kona junction we u save pikup long mi long em yu yu stap long wei nau?. (**Sam, I am waiting for you at the corner junction where you normally pick me up, where are you?**)
>
> **Sam:** Wetim mi stap – Mi kam (**I'm coming, why are you rushing me? relax, I'm coming**), yu sikirap ya (**you are really asking for it**)

Not surprisingly this aroused the suspicions of everyone. Who was Lucy? Was she a highway meri? (A prostitute who travels the highlands highway for truck drivers.) Could Sam be having unprotected sex with Lucy? If so was he at risk of HIV infection? What might this discovery mean for Alungi? For their daughter Onpain? After further improvisations and discussion one course of action emerged: Sam needed to visit the clinic and take an HIV test. But would he go? Participants were unequivocal that high male status and pride, continually affirmed in

Figure 19 Mask work in movement activities investigating ways the HIV could 'invade' communities.

a culture of polygamy and 'bride price', would prevent most men from presenting for HIV testing. What then would be necessary for Sam to reconsider his position and make that all important visit to the clinic for testing?

In spite of the success of the work we struggled to find points of connection between our 'Western' approach and the deeply embedded Indigenous performance practices of PNG communities. For instance, we tried a number of times to incorporate mask work in movement activities investigating ways the HIV virus could 'invade' communities. This is illustrated in Figure 19 which shows Martin Tonny, a choreographer working in mask and leading such an exercise.

Stage II: Intercultural theatre exchange laboratory (Madang)

It was clear that, while our attempts were well meaning, they were little more than clumsy gestures at building intercultural practices and by November 2009, our initial findings from the pilot workshops in Tari demonstrated that *Life Drama* was not yet adequately connecting with, or being enriched by, Indigenous PNG performance practices. In response, an intercultural theatre exchange laboratory was arranged, bringing together the *Life Drama* team and PNG theatre artists to develop a stronger intercultural performance practice which would in turn inform *Life Drama's* existing applied theatre strategies and hopefully lead to a more culturally appropriate set of new strategies. This theatre laboratory deliberately followed Bharucha's belief[10] that, 'for any breakthroughs in forms or idioms of acting, . . . we need institutions where alternatives can be explored and sustained'.[11] The challenge for *Life Drama* was to connect with and enrich its emerging practice with aspects of traditional performance forms.

In researching the theatre and performance forms developed by PNG theatre and cultural workers, the *Life Drama* team encountered the work of Raun Raun Theatre. Active in Goroka between 1978 and 1983, Raun Raun had developed a particular form of Indigenous theatre called folk operas. Originally drawn from postcolonial performance theory from Nigeria and Africa, Greg Murphy, the founder of Raun Raun describes folk operas as drawing on local origin stories from across PNG and Greek theatre traditions while retaining 'the feeling force of dance, the picture force of mime and the story form of speech'.[12] As we worked together participants at the intercultural theatre exchange laboratory began to feel that a deeper knowledge of folk operas could inform and more effectively shape the design and delivery of *Life Drama's* training regime. Perhaps folk operas could serve as the bridge to link existing *Life Drama* techniques with the potent existential performative practices of PNG communities? And if this was the case could *Life Drama* in turn be transformed and enriched by embracing such practices? Consequently it became a priority to investigate whether folk opera could become 'a narrative mode, a dramatic structure . . . themes or metaphors, indexes on the reality of stereotypes, a structure of feeling'[13] and incorporated into the *Life Drama* approach.

Consequently over a 2-week period in February 2010, the laboratory members collaborated using traditional PNG songs and dances, examples of *Life Drama's* applied theatre techniques, and excerpts from folk operas and village plays devised by Raun Raun Theatre some 20 years earlier. Participants then embarked on creating contemporary folk opera forms to be used as part of *Life Drama*. The former Raun Raun Theatre members present at the laboratory, who had been co-authors of the original folk operas and village plays, became 'conduits of their culture',[14] helping the investigators consider how elements of folk operas could be applied within *Life Drama*.

Stage III: Applying the folk opera form (Karkar Island)

The final stage of research took the discoveries from the intercultural theatre exchange laboratory and, through another stage of creative development, sought to apply them to the *Life Drama* programme. This was done on Karkar Island, a small volcanic island in the Bismarck Sea, a 2-hour boat ride from Madang. *Life Drama* was invited to work on the island by local Member of Parliament Ken Fairweather (MP) and hosted by the local village community of Patilo.

The *Life Drama* team travelled to Karkar Island twice during this stage of the project so that by June 2010, two levels of *Life Drama* Training had been established and the first *Life Drama* Handbooks drafted. Most excitingly, the innovations involving the inclusion of folk opera forms were successfully incorporated into the team's suite of applied theatre forms. This was done by seeing whether a folk opera could be developed based on the Tari story of Sam, Alungi and Mary. The Karkar participants were enthusiastic about creating this heightened form of improvisation and performance which explored the same key issue identified in Tari – what would be required to motivate Sam to visit the clinic and take an HIV test. What would influence and change his attitudes and behaviours with regard to HIV testing? Consequently, the 'HIV testing folk opera' was created and a full account of it can be found in Haseman et al.[15]

So the approach developed during the intercultural theatre exchange laboratory was followed with the Karkar participants. They moved through the creative development stages easily although adapted the Tari narrative and the folk opera structure to include their own worldview and beliefs. For instance the daughter, Onpain, was seen as a pivotal influence on Sam, her father. They framed the folk opera and played out Sam's dilemma within a dream which invoked one of the Karkar Island gods who shared his daughter's name, Onpain. Over a full day of workshopping and performance the HIV testing folk opera was prepared, played out and discussed. It was generally felt by participants that the folk opera introduced a larger and shared cosmological order which would drive Sam to seek testing and confirmation of his condition. The whole folk opera was created and performed in their normal street clothes. When the discussion was over and we were about to conclude for the day, the group, quietly but strongly, said they would like to perform the folk opera a second time, but now in *bilas*. *Bilas* refers to traditional island dress and body adornment. The next morning, wearing their traditional dress of vibrant pink grass skirts and adorned with elaborate shell jewellery, participants performed their folk opera once again. This time the level of intensity and conviction in the playing out of this challenge to the culturally dominant male practice of simply refusing to undergo HIV testing was heightened and deeply significant for all players. Figure 20 captures the beginning of the folk opera with Alungi coming to Sam as he falls asleep and calling on him to go for testing. In his dream Sam was visited by forces (Figure 21) which reinforced the social and moral orders which insist he undertook testing.

One final point is important here. As this performance unfolded, it quickly became clear that the intensity and authenticity of the scenario/folk opera played out by the group in *bilas* could not have been effectively

Figure 20 Alungi coming to Sam and calling on him to go for HIV testing.

Figure 21 Dream sequence of forces insisting on HIV testing.

reported using the quantitative or qualitative research paradigms alone. Text-based descriptions (as well as the black-and-white still images used above) fail to capture fully the dynamism and significance this folk opera-infused form of applied theatre had on participants.

This brief outline of the research design that gave rise to the *Life Drama* programme for PNG can now be used to illustrate how its methodological innovations strained the recognized protocols of traditional research practice. Can the *Life Drama* project stand as legitimate research within a broader research arena as Bolt has challenged? To answer this question, it is helpful to test *Life Drama* against four criteria set down by Biggs and Buchler as 'definite terms that we think are essential and that are characteristic of research in all academic areas'.[16] These four criteria are Methods, Questions and Answers, Knowledge and Audiences.

1 Methods

Biggs and Buchler make it clear that, no matter the field of research, all researchers must accept that 'if one is interested in this particular question, then a particular route would be appropriate in order to find out something or develop the interpretation of this issue and precipitate a meaningful outcome'.[17] The 'particular route' a researcher follows refers to his or her methodology.

Following Denzin and Lincoln, the challenge for researchers is to design their methodology with appropriate research strategies and methods of data collection and analysis.[18] Together this establishes an articulated process of research, one which fellow researchers can scrutinize, along with final research findings. Of course decisions about methodology are not made capriciously. Biggs and Buchler remind researchers that their 'proposal for determining the appropriateness of method is based on how the answer is a consequence of, and relevant to, the question, in the context of the needs of the audience'.[19]

In the case of *Life Drama*, the methodology needed to develop in response to the promising opportunities and fresh possibilities which emerged from the needs of practice in the field. As this happened, the research questions evolved. Because of the emergent nature of the work, the team selected practice-led research as its principal research strategy. Carol Gray was among the first to define practice-led research as 'research which is initiated in practice, where questions, problems, challenges are identified and formed by the needs of practice and practitioners'.[20] Admitting such openness into the research design and process was essential for the integrity of the work itself. As white Western researchers from countries with a colonizing past, we were acutely aware of what we did not know about the PNG context, and to simply follow a neat and tidy research plan established in air-conditioned offices in Australia would have been not only irresponsible but also dangerous. Our use of practice-led research was supported by our use of the inquiry cycle from participatory action research, reflective practice and recent developments in visual and sensual ethnography.

The methods of data collection and analysis we used incorporated well-established techniques from both the quantitative and the qualitative traditions. Once again these methods were selected on 'best fit for purpose' criteria. As we were seeking to assess attitude and behaviour change we needed to undertake questionnaires, focus groups and interviews with participants of *Life Drama* workshops, including pre- and post-programme interviews with participants on Karkar Island. Researchers kept fieldwork journals, documented sessions with video and photographic records, and assembled handbooks based on the efficacy of the activities tested in the field. While these processes gave the research team valuable data, the quantitative and qualitative data failed to provide a complete picture of the full workings of the research, including the emerging forms of *Life Drama*, effects for participants and impacts on the researchers.

Once again the research team took the lead from Carol Gray who elaborated upon her definition of practice-led research by proposing that it 'is carried out through practice using predominately methodologies and specific methods familiar to us as practitioners'.[21] This is a game-changing idea: that creative practice researchers, including those from applied theatre, can draw on our own established methods of practice and repurpose them as research methods to address our research questions. Following this lead the research team actively used the conventions and techniques of improvised drama to generate data upon which we could monitor the reception of the activities and review their use. For example, tableaux were used to gain data on the affective impact of particular activities, and the development and application of the folk opera form was documented and treated as data to track the ethical integrity of this cross-cultural invention. In that case, recording on-the-floor action on video was essential and these records were used for review and reflection during the period of fieldwork and subsequently as evidence of the quality of the research outcomes.

Any discussion on methods must address matters of ethics. Before we travelled to PNG for the first time, we understood we had to be respectful when it came to access and collaboration. We worked by invitation only, quickly enlisted cultural consultants (three of whom went on to undertake research degrees in Australia) and established advisory groups of respected local leaders. Over the first months we formulated eight principles of *Life Drama* built around reciprocity and exchange. In country, the research team needed to be highly self-reflexive; we watched each other and our interactions closely and questioned each other's easy and habituated assumptions about PNG and our work there. We also needed to question many of the accepted ways of undertaking research. Securing informed consent, for example, required fresh protocols. Consent had to be obtained in translation, using either the local language or Pidgin, the lingua franca of PNG. Because participants did not live in the Western mediasphere and had little experience of being filmed or photographed, it was a particular challenge to help them understand the ways in which their work might be displayed and used internationally. Ensuring this understanding occurred, and that genuinely informed consent was given, was a matter of great ethical importance to the research team.

Finally, credible research investigations must be located within, and built upon, relevant fields of inquiry. Effective research builds upon (or challenges) the discoveries of others. *Life Drama* was informed by practices, perspectives and debates from the following conceptual domains: Process Drama, Theatre for Development, Theatre of the Oppressed, Intra-Cultural Theatre, Theories of Human Development, Experiential Learning, Post-colonialism, Performance Practice, and Adaptation Theory.

2 Questions and answers

> It is unavoidable that research has explicit questions. . . . The reason it is unavoidable that research has a central question, issue or focus is that it is essential that the researcher come up with an answer or some kind of response in order to make a contribution.[22]

This assertion by Biggs and Buchler is a fair and proper challenge to all applied theatre and creative arts researchers, and is a necessary requirement for all organized and funded research.

Life Drama was funded with a clear statement of focus and intent

> to establish a sustainable infrastructure for the implementation and evaluation of experiential learning programs for young people in PNG, addressing sexual health issues, particularly safer sexual behaviours . . . , adapted for the cultural environments and developmental contexts of the project.[23]

Quoting Balkema and Slager,[24] Biggs and Buchler also acknowledge '. . . it is common that artists, for example, become uncomfortable when they are asked to name the central question in their investigation'. There are reasonable grounds for artists to be cautious about this requirement for all research, because of the contingent and emergent nature of creative practice. While creative practitioners may start off with an initial focus, often that focus is redirected or transformed as they encounter resistances or opportunities with the materials and content of their enquiry. This is exactly what happened in *Life Drama* as the research agenda, which was 'led' from and by the practice, altered over time.

As researchers working in the performative paradigm our work began predictably enough by focusing on experiential learning using improvised forms of drama with the Tari community and with an instrumental focus on HIV and AIDS awareness. However, by reflecting on and learning from that practice, the research focus shifted, moving into a more poetic and artistic enquiry engaging with Indigenous performativity, intercultural performance and folk opera. While there remained a broad research focus on the use of applied theatre to promote sexual health, the study did shift in unanticipated directions and produce unforeseen outcomes.

Applied theatre researchers do meet the second credibility test of posing specific questions to which answers are sought, but both the posing and the seeking occur in distinctive ways. Final research questions may emerge late in the study, as the most potent and important questions arise. The more traditional pathway, by which research questions arise from a gap in the field identified after a substantial literature review, seldom applies for the practice-led and applied theatre researcher.

3 Knowledge

The third test of research lies in the requirement that all researchers are expected to share their knowledge claims or findings. This ensures that research adds to the stocks and flows of human knowledge and also allows for fellow scholars to peer review the research and its claims. Biggs and Buchler remind us that 'Knowledge can be of different kinds, and depending on the nature that is attributed to it, there are different expectations as to the contribution that it will make'.[25]

This is a fundamental issue and early career researchers are quickly schooled on the power and efficacy of the widely accepted forms of knowledge representation which flow from the quantitative and qualitative research paradigms. In his Sage Dictionary of Qualitative Inquiry, Thomas A. Schwandt proposes that 'Perhaps the clearest use of the adjective [qualitative] is to distinguish between qualitative data – nonnumeric data in the form of words – and quantitative data – numeric data'.[26] The *Life Drama* research drew on both of these research traditions. From a quantitative point of view, we collected statistics on workshop participation, as well as some surveillance data on HIV prevalence in Tari. However, other quantitative techniques (such as the use of numerical scales on questionnaires) were found to be culturally inappropriate and not useful, given the low level of numeracy among the participants. Qualitative techniques were more readily accepted and yielded a more extensive range of useful data. For example, the team undertook interviews before and after the workshops to gather data on destigmatization. Answers to the question 'Should a female teacher with HIV be allowed to continue teaching?' enabled the team to monitor attitudinal changes as demonstrated in the follow table.

Table 7.1 Qualitative attitude change, Tari 2010

	Pre-Training	Post-Training
Man, 18	Don't know.	Yes – the sik is in her blood, it can't pass by talking.
Man, 50	No. She's sick, she won't teach the children well. She won't attend class.	Yes. She can teach until AIDS develops, then stop.
Man, 25	No, it will affect the students.	Yes. She won't spread HIV to others.
Woman, 40	No. It's her own fault.	Yes. It's her duty to teach so she must be allowed to teach.

However, reporting on the outcomes of *Life Drama* in numbers and words alone amounts to a serious diminution of the impact of this research. One of the most significant questions to be thrown up by the research was this: *How may indigenous PNG folk opera forms be a driver of behaviour change to seek voluntary counselling and treatment for HIV?* This question can only be answered by addressing the dynamics of the folk opera form used and the affect it had on participants. The execution of the folk opera, particularly the group's reprisal of it in *bilas*, is actually a performative utterance which brings into being a research outcome which answers that particular question. The playing out of the folk opera provides researchers with performative evidence to sit alongside the quantitative and qualitative evidence and give a full and rounded account of the merit of the study. Performative evidence identifies knowledge of a different kind and represents it through rich media rather than the words and numbers of other kinds of research evidence.

Clearly performative researchers do address knowledge claims but in a way that expands the epistemological foundations upon which human knowledge claims can be made and tested.

4 Audiences

Research findings have always been placed under scrutiny by the scholarly community to assess the quality of their contribution to knowledge and this is done through a sophisticated and global network of academic journals. In a real sense the system of journals, article selection through double- or single-blind peer reviewing and scholarly publication constitutes a key piece of infrastructure for all researchers. Typically these journals are read by a 'Specialist academic audience that is in a position to decide about relevance and appropriateness of the question and method and so on'.[27] However, Biggs and Buchler note that there is a general academic audience who will also consume the research. Such audiences include specialists from other disciplines and those from industry and government bodies.

As noted above, performative researchers are constrained in claiming what they know when they are bound to publish findings using words and numbers alone. The established protocols of text-based publishing, established in the early eighteenth century, are problematic not only for the *Life Drama* team but also for arts-based researchers generally. This can be illustrated in the case of this current chapter. It was recognized that to report on *Life Drama* using words alone seriously constrains a reader's capacity to understand the complexity of what actually happened. Four images were then included which provide readers with visual representations of action from the familiar and shared drama workshop (Figure 18), to our first stuttering attempts to use mask (Figure 19) and then to the rich and complex execution of the folk opera performed in bilas (Figures 20 and 21).

This is not simply a matter of illustration. Rather our contemporary moment which calls on researchers to demonstrate the impact of their research only highlights the fact that many aspects of our current systems for research reporting are antiquated and in dire need of renovation. Indeed researchers from many fields, including those from eScience managing vast quantities of big data,[28] are now turning to rich media to present the complexities and dynamics of their findings. In seeking answers to the question *How do we capture the expressive forms of artistic outcomes and creative practice and present them as reliable research evidence?*, performative researchers have begun to develop useful protocols for the multi-modal presentation of research evidence.

As the *Life Drama* team assembled rich media and video representations of our research, it was necessary to develop and apply a set of principles for the construction of such research statements for without these principles and constraints, the would-be researcher could edit and manipulate the moving images in ways which misrepresent the research design and deceive peer reviewers.

The first challenge for the *Life Drama* team was to make sure the data being presented acts as evidence and not advocacy for the research or its findings. The onus is on all researchers, no matter the form of publication, to apply the tests of validity and reliability to their claims and the same rigour applies in the composition of rich media documents. At the simplest level, all footage needs to be tagged and time-coded as it is recorded so that viewers can be reassured that the chronologies and sequences of images they are witnessing actually happened in the order presented. Such legitimacy protocols, which track the providence or evidence trail of the research, may not be applied with such astringency when the purpose is to advocate for and promote the research, to funding bodies for example.

Our next concern was to ensure that in the editing room we made choices which would deepen the criticality of the viewer. This meant, for instance that we were careful not to amplify practices which unnecessarily displayed exoticism or strangeness. PNG is an extraordinarily fascinating non-Western country but as researchers our task was not to accentuate that exoticism and so disarm viewers with pyrotechnics of strange and surprising display. Similarly we were careful not to deliberately intensify the likely viewers empathetic response to what was being presented on screen. As *Life Drama* worked in sites characterized by financial hardship and gender-based violence, it was not uncommon for those stories to dominate our emotional and conceptual understandings of the research. There is a fine line that we had to walk around as researchers, for while we did not want viewers to be overwhelmed by the emotional force of a situation, we hoped to engage aesthetically with the affective and tacit dimensions of the work shown on screen. This involved a comprehensive questioning of our decisions at every stage of the editing process to ensure that we demonstrated a trail of evidence to support the claims made. We were particularly aware, for example, not to construct 'victory narratives' for either the research participants or the members of the research team showing how those involved triumphed against the odds to deliver exceptional research results.

Conclusion

Over the last decade researchers in the arts have questioned whether the traditional research methodologies are able to address their particular and distinctive needs. This challenge is not a cry of special pleading; that arts researchers are 'special' and should not, and cannot, be forced to conform to the expectations which other researchers face. Instead, as this chapter has argued, researchers in fields like creative arts and applied theatre are able to meet those challenges but in productive ways which are serviceable for the performatives of their practice. It can be also argued that, rather than being seen as a quirky and marginal set of research approaches, these researchers are making methodological innovations and breakthroughs aligned with governments and funding bodies who expect to see the impact of research clearly communicated to their publics.

Acknowledgements

I wish to acknowledge Andrea Baldwin, Hayley Linthwaite and Jackie Kauli, colleagues in *Life Drama*, for their contribution to this chapter. Sections of this chapter were first presented in a keynote address to the third Colloquium on Artistic Research in Performing Arts, University of the Arts, Helsinki, Finland, March 2013.

Afterword

Peter O'Connor and Michael Anderson

The series of cases provided in this book point to a new way of considering and realizing research. In considering what they might have to offer, we argue that they separately and collectively describe a radical departure from the notion that research can continue in a business as usual fashion.

We have suggested that the post-normal times we live in demand a different form of research that deliberately and consciously aligns itself with the interests and needs of the marginalized and the silenced. Research can no longer be constricted to merely describing or analysing the world as it is, but it must also provide hope that life might be different and better. Research that attempts to merely synthesize the best evidence for something misses the point. The best evidence we currently have suggests only too clearly that the world is ordered and constructed so as to make radical change impossible. Best evidence suggests we can only learn from what exists already rather than from what we might imagine. We argue that applied theatre provides vital tools for a re-visioning of research centred in critical hope. This vision constructs research as a political activity that resists and challenges the neo-liberal forces that continue to dehumanize and oppress millions at the behest of globalized capitalism.

The cases in this book all represent ways researchers have attempted to work with marginalized and disenfranchised communities, not to transform them, but in ways which provide for the aesthetic expression of possibility and hope. We can see in these examples how applied theatre as research can humanize communities through the telling and sharing of stories through fictional frames. The separate cases for example show us how elderly people in New Zealand and children living in care in England found ways to explore and make sense of their lives through very different aesthetic processes. In both cases possibilities were opened through the relationships that were fostered as part of the research processes. We should not underestimate how deeply, politically confronting and challenging this form of research is within a post-normal context.

This book also celebrates the power of beauty in research. The deliberately haunting quality of Esther Fitzpatrick's poetry and its engagement with questions of her own and others' identity in a postcolonial nation speaks way beyond the cognitive and affective domains, into a deliberate connection with the spiritual. Although we cannot hear the singing at the end of the *Capturing the Tales* performance, we can, through Jane Luton's colourful writing, imagine its power. Tears welled in our eyes as we read these pages of her chapter for the first time. Tears came too in reading the story of the massacre of Aboriginal people at Myall Creek. There is no pretence in this story of seeking for objective truths, the pain of cavalry-like charges on children and adults chained together so that they can be decapitated, demands a side be taken. Yet Wilkinson takes us beyond the pain and the politics of this history. In sharing the beauty of the theatre made in this sacred place we can hope for a world where such things belong to the past.

We trusted that these cases of Applied Theatre as Research will have moved and disturbed, unsettled and troubled. That they will have created an affective as well as cognitive response in you, the reader. We have imagined that at times that response will be embodied. We believe that accounts of research should make us at various times angry, curious, happy, sad, fearful, outraged or bemused. They should force us out of our seats and make us engage in debate with our partners, our children, our friends and colleagues. The power of the beauty in these cases should not act in a cathartic way to purge us of our emotional engagement with the issues at hand, but should act as a spur to action, as a challenge to the passivity of the traditional detached academic worldview.

The case studies also clearly remind us that practice does not always match the rhetoric of the claims that researchers and applied theatre practitioners make for their work. Life is far too messy, far too ambiguous and murky for straight lines. In each of the cases we can recognize missteps, chances and opportunities not taken, an unwilling and unconscious falling back into the old ways of doing research. The principles that underpin Applied Theatre as Research are ethically demanding in ways far beyond the constraints of ethic committees in universities. Living up to principles is always a difficult and demanding task. It requires a deep and personal commitment to the ideals of democratic and decolonizing forms of research, recognizing that this is not an exact science, but rather something to move hesitantly towards. One danger in principled action is to decry the work done by others based on their different principles. We recognize that the history of research has been marked by work which has seriously and negatively impacted on the lives of those who have been the victims of that research. In particular, it has reinforced and recolonized Indigenous groups in a way that has caused immeasurable damage. However, we are also pragmatic enough to understand that the quality of our lives has been immeasurably enhanced by the work of, for example, science and technology researchers who understand research in completely different terms. In the social sciences however, we recognize the grievous harm that research has caused and the need for careful and hopeful decolonizing methods to inform applied theatre research.

This book also moves beyond the dichotomy of quantitative and qualitative methodologies in research. We argue for a third paradigm, that builds on the pioneering work of arts-based research, Participatory Action Research and Community-based research that has re-conceptualized the way research can be undertaken. We argue that applied theatre can synthesize an approach where the generation of story, its analysis, representation and presentation can be done through the participation of researchers and co-researchers in theatre making. This is about more than using the arts piece-meal, or using aspects of arts approaches in the presentation of findings. Applied Theatre as Research is an umbrella term that defines a politicized and principled approach to research that has at its heart the making of theatre with non-actors in non-traditional theatre spaces so as to re-imagine the world.

The University Research Committees we talked about at the beginning of this book cannot morally continue to base their funding and decisions on the value and merit of research for the enhancement of career prospects of the researcher. Such an approach perpetuates a neo-liberal discourse that further marginalizes and disempowers the communities universities might be expected to serve. It is way past time to leave these self-serving notions of research behind. Applied Theatre as Research is offered as the much needed radical departure point.

Endnotes

Chapter 1

1 Smith, L., *Decolonizing Methodologies: Research and Indigenous Peoples*, 2nd edn. London and New York: Zed Books, 1999, p. 176.

2 Brown, L. and S. Strega (eds), *Research as Resistance: Critical, Indigenous, and Anti-oppressive Approaches*. Toronto, ON: Canadian Scholars Press, 2005, p. 106.

3 Denzin, N., *Performance Ethnography: Critical Pedagogy and the Politics of Culture*. USA: Sage Publications, 2003, p. 225.

4 Brown and Strega (eds), *Research as Resistance*, 2005, p. 11.

5 Zinn, H., *Declarations of Independence: Cross-Examining American Ideology*, New York: HarperCollins Publishers, 1991.

6 Smith, *Decolonizing Methodologies*, 1999, p. 177.

7 Anderson, M., 'The challenge of post-normality to drama education and applied theatre'. *Research in Drama Education* 19, 1 (2014): 110–20.

8 Yeats, W. B. and Richard J. Finneran (ed.), *The Collected Works of W.B Yeats*, New York: Macmillan, 1990.

9 Sardar, Z., 'Welcome to postnormal times'. *Futures* 42, 5 (June 2010): 435–44 (436).

10 Ibid.

11 Wilkinson and Pickett, *The Spirit Level*. New York: Bloomsbury Press, 2009; Stiglitz, J., *The Price of Inequality*. New York: W.W. Norton and Company, 2012.

12 Silvio Funcowitz and Jerome Ravetz (1993).

13 Sardar, *Futures*, pp. 435–44.

14 Ibid.

15 Ibid.

16 Giuliani, R., Speech to the United Nations, 2001. Retrieved 9 January 2013, from http://www.washingtonpost.com/wpsrv/nation/specials/attacked/transcripts/giulianitext_100101.html.

17 *Sunday Star Times*, 30 January 2005.

18 *Herald Scotland*, 9 January 2011.

19 Sardar, *Futures*, pp. 435–44.

20 *The Guardian*, accessed 2 August 2013 at http:/www.theguardian.com/
    environment/2007/aug/31/climatechange.food.

21 Martin Luther King, http://www.cbsnews.com/news/mlk-a-riot-is-the-
    language-of-the-unheard, 1968. Retrieved 13 March 2014.

22 Wilkinson and Pickett, *The Spirit Level*, 2009.

23 Wade, R., 'Inequality and the west', in M. Rashbrooke (eds), *Inequality:
    A New Zealand Crisis*. Wellington: Bridget Williams Books, 2013,
    p. 40.

24 Ibid.

25 Ibid.

26 Ibid., p. 43.

27 Sardar, *Futures*, pp. 435–44.

28 Griffin, D., 'Teacher Pay, Performance and Leadership', in *Education
    Reform: The Unwinding of Intelligence and Creativity*. Springer
    International Publishing, 2014, pp. 135–51; Muijs, D., C. Chapman and
    P. Armstrong, 'Can Early Careers Teachers Be Teacher Leaders? A Study
    of Second-year Trainees in the Teach First Alternative Certification
    Programme'. *Educational Management Administration & Leadership* 41,
    6 (2013): 767–81; Vasquez Heilig, J. and S. J. Jez 'Teach For America: A
    Return to the Evidence'. Boulder, CO: National Education Policy Center.
    Retrieved 1 September 2014 from http://nepc.colorado.edu/publication/
    teach-for-america-return.

29 Heilig, J. V. and S. J. Jez, *Teach for America: A Review of the Evidence*.
    Arizona State University: Education Policy Research Unit, 2010.

30 Luke, A. and A. F. Woods, 'Accountability as testing: Are there lessons
    about assessment and outcomes to be learnt from No Child Left
    Behind?' *Literacy Learning: The Middle Years* 16, 3 (2008): 11–19.

31 Giroux, H., *Public Time and Educated Hope: Educational Leadership
    and the War against Youth*, 2003. www.ciconline.com/wo4-democracy,
    May 2004.

32 Freire, P., *Pedagogy of Hope*. London: Bloomsbury, 2005.

33 Denzin, *Performance Ethnography*, 2003.

34 Rossatto, C., *Engaging Paulo Freire's Pedagogy of Possibility*. Toronto: Rowan and Littlefield Publishers, 2005, p. 81.

35 Dewey, J., *Democracy and Education: An Introduction to the Philosophy of Education*. New York: MacMillan, 1916.

36 Kemmis, S. and R. McTaggart, 'Communicative action and the public sphere', in N. K. Denzin and Y. S. Lincoln (eds), *The Sage Handbook of Qualitative Research*, vol. 3. London: Sage Publications, 2005, pp. 559–603.

37 Bergold, J. and S. Thomas, 'Participatory research methods: A methodological approach in motion'. *Forum Qualitative Sozialforschung/ Forum: Qualitative Social Research* 13, 1 (January 2012): 25.

38 Ibid.

39 Minkler, M. and N. Wallerstein, 'Introduction to community based participatory research'. *Community-based Participatory Research for Health* 3–26 (2003): 4.

40 Israel, B. A., A. J. Schulz, E. A. Parker, A. B. Becker, A. J. Allen and J. R. Guzman, 'Critical issues in developing and following community-based participatory research principles'. *Community-based Participatory Research for Health* 1 (2003): 53–76.

41 Freire, P., *Pedagogy of the Oppressed*. Harmondsworth: Penguin Books, 1972.

42 Israel, B. A., et al. *Community-based Participatory Research for Health*, pp. 53–76.

43 Dixon, M. and K. Senior, 'Traversing theory and transgressing academic discourses: Arts-based research in teacher education'. *International Journal of Education & the Arts* 10, 24 (2009). Retrieved 15 March 2014 from http://www.ijea.org/v10n24/, p. 6.

44 McNiff, S., *Art-Based Research*. London: Jessica Kingsley Publishers, 1998, p. 29.

45 Ibid., p. 30.

46 Ibid., p. 37.

47 Eisner, E. (2013), *Does Arts-Based Research have a Future? Inaugural Lecture for the First European Conference on Arts-Based Research*. Belfast, Northern Ireland, June 2005. Retrieved 19 November 2013 from http://

www.jstor.org/stable/pdfplus/25475802.pdf?acceptTC=true&acceptTC=
true&jpdConfirm=true, p. 29.

48   Brecht, B. (1950), 'The Modern Theatre Is the Epic Theatre: Notes to
     the Opera *Aufstieg und Fall der Stadt Mahagonny*'. *Brecht on Theatre:
     The Development of an Aesthetic*. Ed. and trans. John Willett. London:
     Methuen (1964).

49   Leavy, P., *Method Meets Art: Arts-Based Research Practice*. New York:
     The Guilford Press, 2009.

50   Haseman, B. and D. Mafe, 'Acquiring know-how: Research training
     for practice – led research', in H. Smith and R. T. Dean (eds), *Practice –
     Led Research, Research Led Practice in the Creative Arts*. Edinburgh:
     Edinburgh University Press, 2009, pp. 211–29.

51   Rolling, J. H., 'Standing up beneath the imposed ceiling: The art
     education classroom as a site of resistance', in K. Tavin and C. Ballengee-
     Morris (eds), *Standing Up, for a Change: Voices of Arts Educators*. Reston,
     VA: National Art Education Association, 2013, pp. 199–206 (p. 205).

52   Herising, F., 'Interrupting positions: Critical thresholds and queer pro/
     positions'. in Brown, L. and Strega S. (eds), *Research as Resistance:
     Critical, Indigenous, and Anti-oppressive Approaches*. Toronto, ON:
     Canadian Scholar's Press; Women's Press, (2005): pp. 127–52.

53   Rolling, J. H., 'Standing up beneath the imposed ceiling: The art
     education classroom as a site of resistance', in Tavin and Ballengee-
     Morris (eds), *Standing Up, for a Change*, pp. 199–206 (146).

54   Haseman, B. and D. Mafe, 'Acquiring know-how: Research training for
     practice – led research', in Smith and Dean (eds), *Practice – Led Research,
     Research Led Practice in the Creative Arts*, pp. 211–29.

55   Conrad, J., *Nigger of the Narcissus*. New York: Harper and Row, 1897, p. 58.

56   Leavy, *Method Meets Art*, 2009, p. 12.

57   Bordo, S., *Unbearable Weight: Feminism, Western Culture, and the Body*.
     California: University of California Press, 2004, p. 3.

58   Butler, J., *Bodies That Matter: On the Discursive Limits of Sex*. New York:
     Routledge, 2011, p. 93.

59   Grosz, E., *Volatile Bodies: Toward a Corporeal Feminism*. Indiana:
     Indiana University Press, 1994, p. 10.

60 Dixon and Senior, *International Journal of Education & the Arts* 10, 24 (2009). Retrieved 15 March 2014 from http://www.ijea.org/v10n24/.

61 Denzin, *Performance Ethnography*, 2003.

62 Eisner, E., 'On the differences between scientific and artistic approaches to qualitative research'. *Educational Researcher* 10, 4 (April 1981): 5–9 (6).

63 Donmoyer, R. and J. Yennie-Donmoyer, 'Data as drama: Reflections on the use of readers theatre as a mode of qualitative data display'. *Qualitative Inquiry* 1, 4 (1995): 402–28 (416).

64 Goffman, E., *The Presentation of Self in Everyday Life*. London: Allen Lane, 1969.

65 Thompson, J., *Performance Affects*. London: Palgrave Macmillan, 2009, p. 2.

66 Belliveau, G. and G. W. Lea, 'Research-based theatre in education', in S. Shonmann (ed.), *Key Concepts in Drama Education*. Rotterdam, Holland: Sense Publishers, 2011, pp. 333–8.

67 Ackroyd, J. and J. O'Toole, *Performing Research: Tensions, Triumphs and Trade-offs of Ethnodrama*. Stoke-on-Trent: Trentham, 2010, p. 5.

68 Denzin, *Performance Ethnography*, 2003.

69 Ibid., p. 239.

70 Ibid.

71 Smith, *Decolonizing Methodologies*, 1999, p. 158.

72 Rolling, J. H., 'Standing up beneath the imposed ceiling: The art education classroom as a site of resistance', in Tavin and Ballengee-Morris (eds), *Standing Up, for a Change*, pp. 199–206 (p. 200).

73 (Ben Okri).

74 Denzin, *Performance Ethnography*, 2003, p. 209.

75 'Applied theatre/drama: An e-debate in *Research in Drama Education*, 2004', 2006, p. 90.

76 Pitman, W. cited in Gallagher, K. and D. Booth (eds), *How Theatre Educates: Convergences & Counterpoints*. Toronto: University of Toronto Press, 2003, p. 171.

77 Ibid.

78 Ibid.

79 Stinson, S., *The Passionate Mind of Maxine Greene: Maxine Greene and Arts Education*. New York: Falmer Press, 1998.

80 Balfour, M., 'The politics of intention: Looking for a theatre of little changes'. *Research in Drama Education* 14, 3 (2009): 347–59.

81 O'Connor, P., 'Applied theatre: Pure of heart-naively complicit'. *Caribbean Quarterly* 53, 1 and 2 (2007): 23–37.

82 Ackroyd, J., 'Applied theatre: Problems and possibilities'. *Applied Theatre Research Journal* [on line serial], 1999. Available at http:www.gu.edu/centre/atr.

83 Conrad, *Nigger of the Narcissus*, 1897, p. 59.

84 Thompson, J., 'The ends of applied Theatre', in Sheila Preston and Tim Prentki (eds), *The Applied Theatre Reader*. London: Routledge, 2008, pp. 116–24.

85 Thompson, *Performance Affects*, 2009, p. 2.

86 Ibid.

87 Winston, J., *Beauty and Education*. New York: Routledge, 2010, p. 139.

88 Ibid.

89 Maxine Greene as cited in Stinson and Pinar 2003, p. 226.

90 Dewey, *Democracy and Education*, 1916.

91 Dewey, J., 'Democracy and educational administration'. *School and Society* 45 (3 April 1937): 457–67, http://wolfweb.unr.edu/homepage/lafer/dewey%20dewey.htm.

92 Lankshear, C. and M. Lawler, *Literacy, Schooling and Revolution*. London: Falmer Press, 1987, p. 74.

93 Freire, *Pedagogy of the Oppressed*.

94 Henry, M., 'Drama's ways of learning'. *Research in Drama Education: The Journal of Applied Theatre and Performance* 5, 1 (2000): 45–62 (51).

95 Cahill, H., 'Research acts: Using the drama workshop as a site for conducting participatory action research'. *NJ* 30, 2 (2006): 61–72.

96 Conrad, D., 'Exploring risky youth experiences: Popular theatre as a participatory, performative research method'. *International Journal of Qualitative Methods* 3, 1 (2004): 12–25.

97 Cahill, *NJ*, 2006, pp. 61–72 (62).

98 Belliveau, G. and G. W. Lea, 'Research-based theatre in education', in Shonmann (ed.), *Key Concepts in Drama Education*, pp. 333–8.

99   Gallagher, K., 'Theatre as methodology or, what experimentation
     affords us', in S. Shonmann (ed.), *Key Concepts in Theatre/Drama
     Education*. Rotterdam, Netherlands: Sense Publishers, 2011, pp. 327–31
     (p. 328).

100 Ibid.

101 Fels, L. and G. Belliveau, *Exploring Curriculum: Performative Inquiry,
     Role Drama, and Learning*. Vancouver, British Colombia: Pacific
     Educational Press, 2008.

102 Brown and Strega (eds), *Research as Resistance*, 2005, p. 120.

103 Smith, *Decolonizing Methodologies*, 1999, p. 1.

104 Brown and Strega (eds), *Research as Resistance*, 2005, p. 7.

105 Smith, *Decolonizing Methodologies*, 1999.

106 Brown and Strega (eds), *Research as Resistance*, 2005, p. 121.

107 Smith, *Decolonizing Methodologies*, 1999, p. 176.

108 Denzin, N. K., 'The politics and ethics of performance pedagogy', in
     D. S. Madison and J. Hamera (eds), *The SAGE Handbook of Performance
     Studies*. London: SAGE Publications, 2005, pp. 325–36 (p. 334).

109 Conquerwood, D., 'Performing as a moral act: Ethical dimensions of
     the ethnography of performance'. *Literature in Performance* 5, 2 (1985):
     1–13 (10).

110 Kovach, M., 'Conversational method in indigenous research'. *First People
     Child & Family Review* 5, 1 (2010): 40.

111 Conrad, *The Nigger of the Narcissus*, 1897, p. 57.

112 Denzin, *Performance Ethnography*, 2003, p. 237.

113 Yates 2004, p. 134.

114 Baños Smith, H., 'International NGOs and impact assessment. Can we
     know we are making a difference?' *Research in Drama Education* 11, 2
     (June 2006): 157–74 (158).

115 Etherton, M. and T. Prentki, Editorial in *Research in Drama Education,
     Vol 11, Issue 2. June 2006*. United Kingdom: Taylor & Francis, 2006,
     p. 206.

116 Baños Smith, *Research in Drama Education*, 2006, pp. 157–74 (170).

117 Ibid., pp. 157–74.

118 Ibid., pp. 157–74 (158–9).

119 Balfour, *Research in Drama Education*, 2009, pp. 347–59.

120 Etherton and Prentki, *Research in Drama Education, Vol 11, Issue 2. June 2006*, 2006, p. 147.

121 Ibid., p. 144.

122 Osterland, E., 'Evaluation of theatre for social change: What counts and what is being counted?', in *Applied Theatre Research*, vol. 1, no. 1. United Kingdom: Intellect Journals, 2013.

123 Ibid.

124 Saldaña, J., *Longitudinal Qualitative Research: Analyzing Change through Time*. Lanham, MD: Rowman Altamira, 2003.

125 Etherton and Prentki, *Research in Drama Education, Vol 11, Issue 2. June 2006*, 2006, p. 140.

126 Osterland, 'Evaluation of theatre for social change: What counts and what is being counted?', in *Applied Theatre Research*, 2013, p. 104.

127 Anderson, M. and P. O'Connor, 'Applied theatre as research: Provoking the possibilities'. *Applied Theatre Research* 1, 2 (2013): 189–202.

128 Dixon and Senior, *International Journal of Education & the Arts* 10, 24 (2009). Retrieved 15 March 2014 from http://www.ijea.org/v10n24/, p. 325.

129 Barone, T. and E. Eisner, *Arts based Research*. Thousand Oaks, CA: Sage, 2001, p. 13.

130 Denzin, *Performance Ethnography*, 2003, p. 9.

131 Conquerwood, *Literature in Performance*, 1985, pp. 1–13 (8).

132 Ibid., pp. 1–13 (13).

133 Haseman, B., 'A manifesto for performative research'. *Media International Australia Incorporating Culture and Policy* 118 (2006): 98–106; Norris, J., *Playbuilding as Qualitative Research: A Participatory Arts-based Approach*. Walnut Creek, CA: Left Coast Press, 2009; Sallis, R., 'From data to drama – the construction of an ethnographic performance'. *NJ* 31, 2 (2008): 7–20; Springgay, S., R. L. Irwin, C. Leggo and P. Gouzouasis (eds), *Being with a/r/tography*. Rotterdam: Sense Publishers, 2008.

134 Gallagher, K., 'Theatre as methodology or, what experimentation affords us', in Shonmann (ed.), *Key Concepts in Theatre/Drama Education*, pp. 327–31.

135 McNiff, *Art-Based Research*, 1998, pp. 33–4.

136 Ibid., p. 36.

137 Leavy, *Method Meets Art*, 2009, p. 1.

138 Kovach, *First People Child & Family Review*, pp. 46–7.

139 Leavy, *Method Meets Art*, 2009, p. 14.

140 Ibid.

141 Chilton, G., *Altered Inquiry: Discovering Arts-Based Research Through an Altered Book* in *International Journal of Qualitative Methods*. University of Alberta, 2013, p. 469.

142 Richardson, L., (1994), 'Writing: A method of inquiry', in N. K. Denzin and Y. S. Lincoln (eds), *The Sage Handbook of Qualitative Research* 3 (2005): 516–29.

143 Janesick 1994, p. 214.

144 Richardson 1994, p. 522.

145 O'Toole, J., *The Process of Drama, Negotiating Art and Meaning*. London: Routledge, 1992.

146 Bowell, P. and B. Heap, *Planning Process Drama*. London: David Fulton Press, 2001.

147 Carroll, J., 'Framing drama: Some strategies'. *NADIE Journal* 10, 2 (1986): 5–7.

148 Carroll, J., 'Point of view: Linking applied drama and digital games', in M. Anderson, J. Carroll and D. Cameron (eds), *Drama Education with Digital Technology*. London: Continuum International Publishing Group, 2009, pp. 81–97.

149 Boal, A., *Theatre of the Oppressed*. New York: Urizen Books, 1979.

150 Vygotsky, L., 'Play and its role in the mental development of the child', in J. Bruner (ed.), *Play: A Reader*. London: Penguin Books, 1933 orig., trans. 1976.

151 Boal, *Theatre of the Oppressed*, 1979.

152 Bolton, G., *Towards a Theory of Drama in Education*. Longman: Harlow, 1979.

153 Boal, A., *The Rainbow of Desire: The Boal Method of Theatre and Therapy*, trans. A. Jackson. London: Routledge, 1995, p. 44.

154 Ibid., pp. 45–6.

155 Leavy, *Method Meets Art*, 2009, p. 14.

156　Boal, *Theatre of the Oppressed*, 1979.

157　Carroll, J., M. Anderson and D. Cameron, *Real Players?
Drama, Technology and Education.* Stoke on Trent: Trentham
Book, 2006.

158　Saldaña, *Ethnotheatre*, 2011.

159　Denzin, *Performance Ethnography*, 2003, p. 237.

160　Eisner, *Educational Researcher*, April 1981, pp. 5–9 (7).

161　Freire, P., *Pedagogy of Hope*. New York: Continuum, 2004.

162　Prendergast, M., 'Misperformance ethnography'. *Applied Theatre Research*
2, 1 (2014): 86.

163　Freire, P., *Pedagogy of Hope*. London: Continuum, 1992, p. 2.

Chapter 2

1　All names of institutions and participants have been changed.

2　O'Toole, *The Process of Drama*, 1992, pp. 1–17.

3　This technique is described by Boal as 'photo-voice' in Boal, A., *Theatre
of the Oppressed*, trans. C. McBride and M.-O. Leal. London: Pluto Press,
2000, pp. 120–42.

4　Smith, *Decolonizing Methodologies*, 1999, p. 28.

5　Ted, a residential social worker at Mainplace. Extract from his written
feedback after the project.

6　After-show conversation between a senior manager and a participant.

7　Nixon, Paul Commissioning Officer, Children and Families extract from
his written feedback, after the performance event.

8　Simon Love, assistant director of Social Services Children and Families,
extract from his written feedback, after the performance event.

9　Etherton, M., 'West African child rights theatre for development, stories
as theatre, theatre as a strategy for change', in M. Etherton (ed.), *African
Theatre Youth*. Oxford: James Curry, 2006, p. 115.

10　Ethnographic techniques in the form of photography, video footage,
semi-structured interviews, questionnaires, letters and cards helped
to capture the work and the voices in each setting. I examined these

counter-narratives in juxtaposition with the policy and theory that framed each site of practice. I used a range of reflexive techniques to make sense of the emerging intricacies and trends revealed through the work. Often sculpture and sketches helped me to deconstruct patterns and paradigms I was unable to articulate immediately in written form.

11 As outlined in: Cohen, L., L. Manion and K. Morrison, *Research Methods in Education*, 5th edn. London and New York: Routledge, 2000, ch. 13.

12 Ibid., pp. 229–30.

13 Thompson, J., *Applied Theatre, Bewilderment and Beyond*. Oxford and New York: Peter Lang, 2003, pp. 147–8.

14 Etherton, M., 'Child rights theatre for development with disadvantaged and excluded children in South Asia and Africa', in Prentki and Preston (eds), *The Applied Theatre Reader*, 2008, p. 355.

15 O'Toole, *The Process of Drama*, 1992, p. 58.

16 O'Toole, *The Process of Drama*, 1992; Carroll, *NADIE Journal*, p. 5.

17 Foucault, M., *Discipline and Punish: The Birth of the Prison*, trans. A. Sheridan. Harmondsworth: Penguin Books, 1979, p. 142; Hendrick, H., *Child Welfare, Historical Dimensions, Contemporary Debate*. Great Britain: The Policy Press, 2003, pp. 9–48.

18 Muncie, J., *Youth & Crime*, 3rd edn. London and California: Sage Publications, 2009, p. 177.

19 Hendrick, *Child Welfare, Historical*, 2003, pp. 22–47; Dekker, J., *The Will to Change the Child: Re-education Homes for Children at Risk in Nineteenth Century Western Europe*. Frankfurt am Main: Peter Lang, 2000, pp. 104–16.

20 In the 1900s a number of child savers, and most notably, Dr Barnardo, discovered a viable opportunity in exporting 'the waifs and strays' they had rescued to work on colonies in Canada, South Africa and New Zealand. These children were seen as 'investments – human capital in its most elemental form' and were sent out to defend the nation's colours and work on agricultural colonies. Young people were utilised as the *sub-oppressors* of others in the expansion of the Great British Empire. Harry Hendrick states: 'we can only speculate as to the misery endured

by these boys and girls, taken from their parents, brothers and sisters, families, communities and friends, and put to work in often Spartan environments where they were subjected to exploitation and violence'. Hendrick, H., *Child Welfare, England 1872-1989*. London and New York: Routledge, 1994, pp. 80–2; Hendrick, *Child Welfare, Historical*, 2003, p. 47.

21 Samuel Smith, writing in 1885, cited by: Hendrick, *Child Welfare, Historical*, 2003, p. 48.

22 Foucault, M., *Discipline and Punish: The Birth of the Prison*, trans. A. Sheridan. London: Penguin Books, 1991.

23 Freire, P., *The Politics of Education: Culture, Power and Liberation*, trans. D. Macedo. Westport, USA: Greenwood Publishing Group, 1985, p. 72.

24 Smith, *Decolonizing Methodologies*, 1999, p. 29.

25 Ibid., p. 82.

26 Goffman, E., *Asylums: Essays on the Social Situation of Mental Patients and Other Inmates*. London and New York: Penguin Books, 1968, p. 11.

27 Foucault, *Discipline and Punish*, 1979, p. 43.

28 Goffman, E., *Stigma: Notes on the Management of Spoiled Identity*. New York: Simon and Schuster, 1963; Wolfensberger, W. and S. Tullman, 'A brief Outline of the Principle of Normalization'. *Rehabilitation Psychology* 27, 3 (1982): 139.

29 Dixon, J., 'Young people leaving care: Health wellbeing and outcomes', *Child and Family Social Work* 13, 2 (2008): 207–17; 'The cycle of deprivation' is discussed by Hendrick, *Child Welfare, Historical*, 2003, p. 242.

30 Department for Education and Skills. *National Statistics*, 2005.

31 The Centre for Social Justice, 'Breakthrough Britain: Couldn't Care Less, A Report from the Children in Care Working Group'. September 2008, p. 11.

32 Ibid., pp. 16–17.

33 Young people leaving local authority care are 50 times more likely to spend time in prison and 60 times more likely to homeless and 88 times more likely to be involved in drug abuse than other young people. *Our Children, their Future: A Manifesto*. London: NSPCC, 2000, pp. 7–23.

34 Katherine, verbal communication during on going work with Mainplace, after the first project.

35 Smith, *Decolonizing Methodologies*, 1999.

36 Freire, *The Politics of Education*, 1985, p. 72.

37 Smith, *Decolonizing Methodologies*, 1999, p. 37.

38 Balfour, M., *The Use of Drama in the Rehabilitation of Violent Male Offenders*. England: The Edwin Mellen Press, 2003, p. 8.

39 Prentki, T. and J. Selman, *Popular Theatre in Political Culture*. Britain and Canada in Focus. Bristol, Portland: Intellect, 2000, p. 158.

40 Kershaw, B., *The Radical in Performance, Between Brecht and Baudrillard*. London and New York: Routledge, 1999.

41 Heathcote cited by O'Toole, *The Process of Drama*, 1992, p. 233.

42 O'Toole, *The Process of Drama*, 1992, pp. 51–2.

43 Bundy, P., 'The Performance of Trauma', in Prentki and Preston (eds), *The Applied Theatre Reader*, 2008, pp. 238–40.

44 Nicholson, H., *Applied Drama, the Gift of Theatre*. Basingstoke and New York: Palgrave, 2005, p. 129.

45 Hooks, B., *Teaching to Transgress, Education as the Practice of Freedom*. New York and London: Routledge, 1994, pp. 25–7.

46 Preston, S., *Theatre for Development in Context, Exploring the Possibilities and Contradictions of Visions of Theatre and Development within the Action of Community*. King Alfred's College: Unpublished thesis, 2000, p. 122.

47 Extract from Aaron's *Individual Piece*. Mainplace Children's Home, 1999.

48 Foucault cited in Bouchard, D. F. (ed.), *Language, Counter-Memory, Practice: Selected Interviews and Essays*, trans. D. F. Bouchard and S. Simon. Oxford: Basil Blackwell, 1977, p. 209.

49 Feedback from a member of staff at Mainplace after seeing Julie's *individual piece*.

50 de Castella, T., *The Guardian Weekend*. 24 November 2007, pp. 27–34.

51 Etherton, M., 'West African child rights theatre for development, stories as theatre, theatre as a strategy for change', in Etherton (ed.), *African*

Theatre Youth, 2006, p. 117; Way, B., *Development through Drama*. London: Longmans, 1967, p. 5; Boal, A., *The Aesthetics of the Oppressed*, trans. A. Jackson. New York and Oxon: Routledge, 2006, p. 117.

52 Thompson states: 'I had spent many years condemning a theatre of mindless escapism and suddenly it became the radical counterpart to physical incarceration', in Thompson, *Applied Theatre, Bewilderment and Beyond*, 2003, p. 30.

53 Kershaw, *The Radical in Performance*, 1999, p. 26.

54 Mead, M., 'Children and ritual in Bali', in M. Mead and M. Wolfenstein (eds), *Childhood in Contemporary Cultures*. Chicago and London: Phoenix Books, 1963, pp. 40–4.

Chapter 3

1 Found poem from Maximus, the robot tutor created in the research workshop.

2 Campbell, A., *Educating New Zealand*. Wellington: Department of Internal Affairs, 1941, p. 12.

3 Summerhill School, A. S. Neill's Summerhill. 2004, from http://www.summerhillschool.co.uk/, accessed 30 October 2011.

4 Neumann, R. A., 'A report from the 23rd international conference on alternative education'. *Phi Delta Kappan* 75.7 (1994): 547–9.

5 Gerritsen, J., 'Creating a learning link'. *New Zealand Education Gazette* 14 (1999a).

6 Nairn, K. and K. Higgins, 'The emotional geographies of neoliberal school reforms: Spaces of refuge and containment'. *Emotion, Space and Society* 4 (2011): 180–6.

7 Vaughan, K., *Beyond the Age of Aquarius: Reframing Alternative Education*. Wellington: New Zealand Council for Educational Research, 2004, p. 81.

8 Gerritsen, J., 'An educated alternative'. *New Zealand Education Gazette* 14 (1999b).

9 Ibid., para. 14.

10 Clark, T. C., et al. *Youth'09: The Health and Wellbeing of Young People in Alternative Education. A Report on the Needs of Alternative Education Students in Auckland and Northland.* Auckland: University of Auckland, 2010.

11 Ibid., p. 75.

12 Brooking, K., B. Gardiner and S. Calvert, *Background of Students in Alternative Education: Interviews with a Selected 2008 Cohort.* Wellington: Ministry of Education, 2009.

13 Ibid., p. viii.

14 Found poem from recorded research interview, 14 December 2013.

15 Giroux, H., *Teachers as Intellectuals: Toward a Critical Pedagogy of Learning.* Massachusetts: Bergin & Garvey Publishers, Inc., 1988, p. xxx.

16 Langley, J., 'Submissions from the youth justice independent advisory group: Alternative education'. *Court in the Act: A regular newsletter for the entire Youth Justice community* 42 (2009): 6–7 (6).

17 Willis, P., 'Don't call it poetry'. *The Indo-Pacific Journal of Phenomenology* 2.1 (2002): 1–14 (2).

18 Heidegger, M., *The Question Concerning Technology and Other Essays,* trans. W. Lovitt. New York: Harper and Row, 1977.

19 Moorfield, J., 'Iwi'. 2014, http://www.maoridictionary.co.nz/search?id iom=&phrase=&proverb=&loan=&keywords=iwi&search=, accessed 30 January 2014.

20 Prendergast, M., C. Leggo and P. Sameshima (eds), *Poetic Inquiry: Vibrant Voices in the Social Sciences.* Rotterdam: Sense Publishers, 2009.

21 Richardson, L., 'The consequences of poetic representation: Writing the other, rewriting the self', in C. Ellis and M. Flaherty (eds), *Investigating Subjectivity: Research on Lived Experience.* Newbury Park: Sage Publications, 1992, pp. 125–37.

22 Ibid., p. 126.

23 Heidegger, M., *Poetry, Language and Thought,* trans. A. Hofstadter. New York: Harper and Row, 1971.

24 Neelands, J., '11/09 – the space in our hearts'. *2nd International Theatre and Drama Education Conference.* Athens, 2001.

25 Heathecote, D. and P. Herbert, 'A drama of learning: Mantle of the expert'. *Theory into Practice* 24.3 (1985): 173–80.

26 Thrupp, M. and M. White, *Final Report: National Standards and the Damage Done*. Hamilton: The University of Waikato, 2013.

27 Cayley, David, *The Rivers North of the Future: The Testament of Ivan Illich*. Toronto: House of Anasi Press Inc, 2005, p. 222.

28 Momaday, N. Scott, *The Names: A Memoir*. New York: Harper and Row, 1976.

29 Rousseau, J., *Emile*, trans. W. Boyd. London: Heinemann, 1956, p. 17.

30 Heidegger, *Poetry, Language and Thought*, 1971, p. 71.

31 Freire, P., *Pedagogy of the Oppressed*. London: Penguin Books, 1970. p. 69.

32 Geertz, C., *The Interpretation of Cultures*. New York: Basic Books, 1973, p. 363.

33 Merleau-Ponty, M., *The Prose of the World*, trans. J. O'Neill, ed. C. Lefort. Evanston: Northwestern University Press, 1973, p. 6.

34 Merleau-Ponty, M., *Phenomenology of Perception*. London: Routledge & Kegan Paul, 1962, p. 183.

35 Oxford Dictionaries, 'Tutor'. 2013, http://www.oxforddictionaries.com/definition/english/tutor?q=tutor, accessed 16 October 2013.

36 Noddings, N., *The Challenge to Care in Schools: An Alternative Approach to Education*, 2nd edn. New York: Teachers College Press, 2005.

37 Found poem from recorded interview with tutor research participant, 27 March 2013.

38 Ibid., 27 November 2012.

39 van Manen, M. *The Tact of Teaching: The Meaning of pedagogical Thoughtfulness*. Albany: State University of New York Press, 1991, pp. 3, 6.

40 Boal, *The Rainbow of Desire*, 1995, p. 43.

41 Ibid., p. 44.

42 Austin, J. L., *How to do Things with Words*, 2nd edn. Cambridge, MA: Harvard University Press, 1975, pp. 6–7.

43 Boal, *The Rainbow of Desire*, 1995, p. 45.

44 Brooking, Gardiner and Calvert, *Background of Students in Alternative Education*, 2009.

45 Buber, M., *I and Thou*, 3rd edn. trans, W. Kaufmann. Edinburgh: T. and T. Clark, 1970, p. 178.

46 Buber, M., *Between Man and Man*, trans. R. Gregor-Smith. London: Routledge, 2002, p. 126.

47 Oxford Dictionaries, 'Anoint'. 2014, http://www.oxforddictionaries.com/definition/english/anoint?q=anoint, accessed 30 January 2014.

48 Oxford Dictionaries, 'Vocation'. 2014, http://www.oxforddictionaries.com/definition/english/vocation?q=vocation, accessed 30 January 2014.

49 Education Review Office, *Alternative Education: Schools and Providers*. Wellington: Education Review Office, 2011, p. 70.

50 te Riele, K., 'Educational innovation for young people', in K. te Riele (ed.), *Making School Different: Alternative Approaches to Educating Young People*. London: Sage Publications, 2009, pp. 1–9.

51 Oxford Dictionaries, 'Instil'. 2014, http://www.oxforddictionaries.com/definition/english/instil?q=instil, accessed 30 January 2014.

52 Found poem from recorded interview with tutor research participant, 27 November 2012.

53 Found poem from recorded interview, 21 February 2013.

54 Rousseau, *Emile*, 1956, p. 17.

55 Beiser, F., Novalis and F. von Schlegel, *The Early Political Writings of the German Romantics*, trans. and ed. F. Beiser. Cambridge: Cambridge University Press, 1996, p. 85.

56 Ibid.

57 Ibid.

Chapter 4

1 Minchin, Tim, *When I Grow Up*. London: Royal Shakespeare Company, 2010.

2 O'Connor, Peter, *Address to Audience on the Final Night of Capturing the Tales*, 1 October 2013.

3 Dallow, Stephen, Interview with Jane Luton, Auckland, 21 September 2012.

4 Norris, *Playbuilding as Qualitative Research*, 2009, p. 272.

5 Nicholson, Helen, 'The performance of memory: Drama, reminiscence and autobiography'. *NJ (Drama Australia Journal)* 27, 2 (2003): 79–92.

6 Schweitzer, Pam, *Reminiscence Theatre: Making Theatre from Memories*. London: Jessica Kingsley Publishers, 2006.

7 Nicholson, *NJ (Drama Australia Journal)* 2003, pp. 79–92.

8 Schweitzer, *Reminiscence Theatre*, 2006.

9 Ibid.

10 Ketko, Raoul, *Waitakere Gardens Newsletter*, November 2013.

11 Myerhoff, Barbara, *Remembered Lives: The Work of Ritual, Storytelling, and Growing Older*. Ann Arbor, MI: University of Michigan Press, 1992.

12 Hough, Brian H. and Sigmund Hough, 'The play was always the things: Drama's effect on brain function'. *Psychology* 3, 6 (2012): 454–6.

13 Myerhoff, *Remembered Lives*, 1992.

14 Ibid.

15 Ibid.

16 Nicholson, *NJ (Drama Australia Journal)*, 2003, pp. 79–92.

17 Mackey, Sally, 'Of lofts, evidence and mobile times: The school play as a site of memory'. *Research in Drama Education: The Journal of Applied Theatre and Performance,* 17, 1 (2012): 35–52.

18 Nixon, Dena, *Poem*, January 1954.

19 Saldaña, Johnny, *Ethnotheatre: Research From Page to Stage*. Walnut Creek, CA: Left Coast Press, 2011.

20 Applied Theatre Consultants, programme note, Applied Theatre Consultants Ltd., *Capturing the Tales: Programme*, 2013.

21 Saldaña, *Ethnotheatre*, 2011.

22 Applied Theatre Consultants, programme note, Applied Theatre Consultants Ltd., *Capturing the Tales: Programme*, 2013.

23 Nicholson, *NJ (Drama Australia Journal)*, 2003, pp. 79–92.

24 Schweitzer, *Reminiscence Theatre*, 2006.

25 Myerhoff, *Remembered Lives*, 1992.

26 van Dijk, Bert, *Devised Theatre: A Practical Guide to the Devising Process*. Wellington, New Zealand: Toiora, 2011.

27 Dallow, Stephen, Advice to workshop participants, Auckland, 2013.

28 Mackey, *Research in Drama Education*, 2012, pp. 35–52.

29 Ibid.

30 Stanislavski, Constantin, *An Actor's Handbook: An Alphabetical Arrangement of Concise Statements on Aspects of Acting*. London: Methuen Random House, 1997.

31 Schweitzer, *Reminiscence Theatre*, 2006.

32 Ibid.

33 Bill, interview with Jane Luton, 1 October 2013.

34 Sally, interview with Jane Luton, 1 October 2013.

35 Ketko, Raoul, *Post Performance Speech Delivered at Capturing the Tales*, 1 October 2013.

36 O'Connor, Peter, 'Importance of play'. *UniNews: University of Auckland News for Staff* 43, 8 (2013): 8.

37 Myerhoff, *Remembered Lives*, 1992.

38 Ketko, Raoul, 'Capturing the Tales'. *Metlife* (2013): 28.

39 Hough and Hough, *Psychology*, 2012, pp. 454–6.

40 United Nations General Assembly, *Follow-up to the International Year of Older Persons: Second World Assembly on Ageing, Report of the Secretary-General*. New York: United Nations, 2013, pp. 1–12.

41 Nicholson, *NJ (Drama Australia Journal)*, 2003, pp. 79–92.

42 Julie Faulkner, *New Zealand Herald*, 4 April 2013.

43 Schweitzer, *Reminiscence Theatre*, 2006.

44 O'Connor, *UniNews*, 2013.

Chapter 5

1   The Weraerai people were a clan group of the Kamilaroi nation. Spelt as 'Wirrayaraay' on the Myall Creek Memorial plaques, 'Weraerai' is the spelling Millis (1994) uses and to my mind is closer to the received pronunciation.

2 Jones, Joni, 'Performance and ethnography, performing ethnography, performance ethnography', in Madison and Hamera (eds), *The SAGE Handbook of Performance Studies*, 2005, pp. 339–45.

3 Clandinen, Jean and Michael Connelly, *Narrative Inquiry, Experience and Story in Qualitative Research*. San Francisco: Jossey-Bass Publishers, 2000, p. 81.

4 Bhabha, Homi, 'The third space', in Jonathan Rutherford (ed.), *Identity – Community, Culture, Difference*. London: Lawrence & Wishart Ltd, 1990, p. 211.

5 Manning Clark cited in Marsh, Hayden, *Native Tears: Conflict on the Colonial Frontier and R vKilmeister (no. 2)*, https://eview.anu.edu.au/anuuj/vol3_11/pdf4/ch08.pdf, p. 102, accessed 13 March 2013.

6 Batten, Bronwyn, 'The Myall Creek Memorial – History, identity and reconciliation', in William Logan and Keir Reeves (eds), *Places of Pain and Shame: Dealing with 'Difficult' Heritage*. New York: Routledge, 2009.

7 Harris, Jennifer, *Memorials and Trauma, Pinjarra,1834*, http://wwwmcc.murdoch.edu.au/trauma/docs/JenniferHarris-paper.pdf, 2009, p. 7, accessed 25 February 2014.

8 Inscription on the eighth and final plaque of the memorial, fixed to the large boulder overlooking the massacre site.

9 Op. cit., Bhabha, 1990.

10 Lo, Jacqueline, *Staging Nation – English Language Theatre in Malaysia and Singapore*. Aberdeen: Hong Kong University Press, 2004, p. 2.

11 Grehan, Helena, *Mapping Cultural Identity in Contemporary Australian Performance*. Bruxelles: P.I.E. – Peter Lang, 2001, p. 20.

12 McNiff, Shaun, 'Arts-based research', in Gary Knowles and Ardra Cole (eds), *Handbook of the Arts in Qualitative Research*. Thousand Oaks: Sage Publications Inc, 2008, p. 29.

13 Tabrett, Leigh, *Vital Signs: Cultural Indications for Australia*, http://cmc.arts.gov.au/sites/www.cmc.gov.au/files/vitalsigns.pdf, p. 6, accessed 3 February 2014.

14 Rutherford, Jonathan, 'A place called home: Identity and the cultural politics of difference', in Rutherford (ed.), *Identity*, 1990, p. 19.

15 Op. cit., Bhabha, 1990.

16 Meredith, Paul, *Hybridity in the Third Space: Rethinking Bi-cultural Politics in Aotearoa/New Zealand*, Paper Presented to Te Oru Rangahau Maori Research and Development Conference, 7–9 July 1998. http:// lianz.waikato.ac.nz/PAPERS/paul/hybridity.pdf, p. 3, accessed 28 March 2014.

17 Bhabha, Homi, *The Location of Culture*. London: Routledge, 1994.

18 Tranter, Bruce and Jed Donoghue, 'Convict ancestry: A neglected aspect of Australian identity', *Nations and Nationalism* 9, 4, http://onlinelibrary.wiley.com/doi/10.1111/1469-8219.00127/ abstract;jsessionid î EC3C0943F1A33D06EB, accessed 1 October 2013.

19 Read, Peter, *Belonging – Australians, Place and Aboriginal Ownership*. Cambridge: Cambridge University Press, 2000.

20 Ibid., p. 180.

21 W. E. H. Stanner, 'The great Australian silence', in Robert Manne (ed.), *W. E. H. Stanner, The Dreaming and Other Essays*. Melbourne: Black Inc. Agenda, 2009, pp. 182–93.

22 Ibid., p. 14.

23 Kauffman, Paul, 'Diversity and indigenous policy outcomes – Comparisons between four nations', in Mary Kalantzis and Paul James (eds), *International Journal of Diversity in Organisations, Communities and Nations* 3 (2003): 159–80, http://tracker.org.au/wp-content/uploads/ downloads/2011/10/Diversity-and-Indigenous-Policy-Outcomes.pdf, accessed 21 November 2013.

24 Terra nullius is the doctrine under which Australia was claimed by the British in 1770; literally empty land or land belonging to no one. Despite having seen Aboriginal people all the way up the coast, because the then Lieutenant, later Captain, James Cook could see no identifiable signs of agriculture, under Enlightenment principles the land might have been occupied but it was not owned.

25 Eklund, Eric, *Terra Nullius and Australian Colonialism*, 2001, http:// treatyrepublic.newt/content/terra-nullius-0, accessed 28 May 2013.

26 Reynolds, Henry, *Why Weren't We Told?* Camberwell: Penguin Books, 1999, p. 222.

27 Malezer, Les, 'The hunting grounds of the imagination', *Encounter* (Radio
    Series) ABC National Radio, 15 December 2012, p. 6, http://www.abc.
    net.au/radionational/oprograms/encounter/the-hunting-grounds-of-
    the-imagination, accessed 26 December 2012.

28 *Redfern Now* is the first drama series to be written, directed and
    featuring Indigenous artists. It was produced by Blackfella Films and was
    screened on ABC National Television in 2012; a second series went to air
    in 2013.

29 *Mabo*, a docudrama about the life of Edie Mabo was screened on ABC
    National Television; it was produced by Blackfella Films and ABC.

30 Gooda, Mick (with Calma, Tom), *Their Speech to the National Press
    Club Celebrating the Fifth Anniversary of the Closing the Gap Campaign
    for Aboriginal and Torres Strait Islander Health Equity*, http://blogs.
    crikey.com.ay/croakey/2011/03/10/tom-calma-and-mick-gooda-their-
    spoeech-to-thenational-press-club-today, accessed 23 June 2013.

31 Conquergood, Dwight, 'Ethnography, rhetoric, and performance'.
    Quarterly Journal of Speech 78 (1992), 80–123.

32 Wallace, Gail, *The Race Hatred Act: Case Study 2*, pp. 1–2, https://www.
    humanrights.gov.ay/publications/racial-hatred-act-case-study-2-1,
    accessed 1 December 2013.

33 Milroy, Helen, 'The health model', in Louise Nash (ed.), *An Introduction
    to Indigenous Mental Health DRAFT*. NSW Institute of Psychiatry, 2011,
    p. 29.

34 Alexander, Bryant K., 'Performing ethnography: The re-enacting
    and inciting of culture', in Norman K. Denzin and Yvonna S. Lincoln
    (eds), *Handbook of Qualitative Research*, 3rd edn. Thousand Oaks:
    Sage Publications, Inc. 2005, p. 411.

35 Sallis, Richard, *The Drama of Boys – An Ethnographic Study and
    Performance*. Unpublished doctoral thesis, Melbourne Graduate School
    of Education, University of Melbourne, 2010.

36 O'Toole, John and the Drama Australia Research Community, *Doing
    Drama Research – Stepping into Enquiry in Drama, Theatre and
    Education*. City East: Drama Australia, 2006, p. 42.

37 Op. cit., Sallis, p. 72.

38 Op. cit., Alexander, p. 11.

39 Fortier, Brad, *On the Road to a New Ethnography: Anthropology,
    Improvisation and Performance,* http://bradfortier.com/2011/01/12/
    on-the-road-to-a-new-ethnography-anthropology-improvisations-and-
    performance, 2011, p. 1, accessed 22 June 2013.

40 Op. cit., Jones, p. 339.

41 Op. cit., Alexander, p. 411.

42 Op. cit., Jones, p. 340.

43 Conquergood, Dwight, 'Rethinking ethnography: Towards a critical
    cultural politics'. *Communication Monographs* 58, 2 (1991): 187.

44 Ibid.

45 Nicholson, Helen, 'Research as confession'. *Research in Drama Education*
    4, 1, Abingdon: Carfax, 1999: 100–3.

46 Mienczakowski, Jim, 'The theatre of ethnography: The reconstruction of
    ethnography in theatre with emancipatory potential', in Norman Denzin
    and Yvonna Lincoln (eds), *Turning Points in Qualitative Research, Tying
    Knots in the Handkerchief.* Walnut Creek: Altamira Press, 2003, p. 422.

47 Op. cit., Alexander, p. 412.

48 Madison, D. Soyini and Judith Hamera, 'Performance studies at the
    intersections', in Madison and Hamera (eds), *The Sage Handbook of
    Performance Studies,* 2005, p. xii.

49 Arnold, Roslyn, *Empathic Intelligence: Teaching, Learning, Relating.*
    Sydney: University of New South Wales Press Ltd, 2005.

50 Saldaña, Johnny, *The Essence of Ethnographic Performance.* Unpublished
    paper, Drama Victoria conference, 2005. Melbourne, 2005.

51 Denzin, *Performance Ethnography,* 2003.

52 Denzin, Norman K. and Yvonna Lincoln, 'Introduction: Critical
    methodologies and indigenous inquiry', in N. Denzin, Y. Lincoln and
    L. T. Smith (eds), *Handbook of Critical and Indigenous Methodologies.*
    Thousand Oaks: SAGE Publications, 2008, p. 12.

53 McCaslin, Wanda and Denise Breton, 'Justice as Healing: Going Outside
    the Colonizers' Cage', in Denzin, Lincoln and Smith (eds), *Handbook of
    Critical and Indigenous Methodologies,* 2008, p. 511.

54 Smith, *Decolonizing Methodologies,* 1999, p. 20.

55 Denzin, Norman and Yvonna Lincoln (eds), *The Sage Handbook of Qualitative Research*, 3rd edn. Thousand Oaks: SAGE Publications, 2005.

56 Op. cit., L. T. Smith.

57 Ibid., L. T. Smith.

58 Chilisa, Bagele, *Indigenous Research Methodologies*. Thousand Oaks: SAGE Publications Inc, 2012.

59 Op. cit., Smith, p. 2.

60 Ladson-Billings, Gloria, 'Radicalized discourses and ethnic epistemologies', in Norman K. Denzin and Yvonna S. Lincoln (eds), *The Sage Handbook of Qualitative Research*, 2nd edn. Thousand Oaks: Sage Publications, 2000, p. 258.

61 Saul, John Ralston, *A Fair Country – Telling Truths About Canada*. Ontario: Penguin Group, 2008, p. 35.

62 Madison, D. Soyini, 'Staging fieldwork/performing human rights', in Madison and Hamera (eds), *The SAGE Handbook of Performance Studies*, 2005, p. 400.

63 He Whakamārama, Kaupapa Māori, http://www.kaupapamaori.com/theory/6/, accessed 6 February 2014.

64 Op. cit., Denzin and Lincoln 2008, p. 12.

65 Smith, G. H. cited in op. cit. Smith, L. T., p. 185.

66 Bottoms, Stephen, 'Putting the document into documentary'. *The Drama Review* 50, 3 (2006): 56–68.

67 Conquergood, Dwight, 'Performance studies – Interventions and radical research', in E. P. Johnson (ed.), *Dwight Conquergood – Cultural Struggles: Performance, Ethnography, Praxis*. Ann Arbor: University of Michigan Press, 2013, p. 35.

68 Op. cit., Madison, p. 404.

69 Behar, Ruth, 'Anthropology: Ethnography and the book that was lost', in Knowles and Cole (eds), *Handbook of the Arts in Qualitative Research*, 2008, pp. 529–45.

70 Interview with Graham H. Smith, Sydney, 3 November 2011.

71 Brown, Francis Lee, *Making the Classroom a Healthy Place: The Development of Affective Competency in Aboriginal Pedagogy*. Unpublished Doctoral Thesis, University of British Columbia, 2004.

72 Ibid., Brown, p. 205.

73 Ibid., Brown, p. 206.

74 Rosaldo, Renato, cited in Davies, James, Introduction, in James Davies and Dimitrina Spencer (eds), *Emotions in the Field – the Psychology and Anthropology of Fieldwork Experience*. Stanford: Stanford University Press, 2010, p. 10.

75 Op. cit, Smith, G. H., 2011.

76 Denzin, Norman K., 'The politics and ethics of performance pedagogy – Toward a pedagogy of hope', in Madison and Hamera (eds), *The SAGE Handbook of Performance Studies*, 2005, p. 332.

77 Pink, Sarah, *Doing Sensory Ethnography*. London: SAGE Publications Ltd., 2009.

78 Op. cit., Chilisa, p. 160.

79 Op. cit., Jones, p. 343.

80 For a Youtube link to short excerpts from the touring draft, see http://www.youtube.com/watch?v=lOlYr1ORUMY&feature=youtu.be.

81 Millis, Roger, *Waterloo Creek – The Australia Day Massacre of 1838, George Gipps and the British Conquest of New South Wales*. Sydney: University of New South Wales Press Ltd, 1994, p. 283.

82 Op. cit., Denzin 2005, p. 334.

Chapter 6

1 Derrida, J., *Spectres of Marx: The State of the Debt, the Work of Mourning, and the New International*, trans. P. Kamuf. New York, NY: Routledge, 1994.

2 Belliveau, G., Shakespeare in the primary classroom. Keynote address at the Critical studies in drama in Education International Symposium. Hosted by the Critical Research Unit in Applied Theatre, Faculty of Education, Auckland University, 26–27 October 2010. Published on 4 December 2012, http://www.youtube.com/watch?v=SKWUYBlq-Y0.

3 Eisner, E. W., *The Arts and the Creation of the Mind*. New Haven, CT: Yale University Press, 2002.

4   Denzin, N. K. and Y. S. Lincoln (eds), *The SAGE Handbook of Qualitative Research*, 4th edn. Thousand Oaks, CA: SAGE publications, 2011, p. xl.

5   Fitzpatrick, E., 'How to get along with others: Children exploring issues of racial-ethnic identity in multicultural and multiethnic communities through drama'. *NJ Drama Australia Journal* 35 (2011): 90–104; Fitzpatrick, E., 'A conversation with Steinbeck: Finding my way to postcritical ethnography', in C. Mutch and J. Rath (eds), *Emerging Critical Scholarship in Education: Navigating the Doctoral Journey*. Cambridge, UK: Cambridge Scholar Press, 2014.

6   Gauntlett, D. and P. Holzwarth, 'Creative and visual methods for exploring identities'. *Visual Studies* 21, 1 (2006): 82–91.

7   Ibid., pp. 82–91 (89).

8   Ibid., pp. 82–91 (83).

9   Ibid., pp. 82–91 (89).

10 Ibid.

11 Springgay, Irwin, Leggo and Gouzouasis (eds), *Being with A/r/tography*, 2008.

12 Lymburner, J., 'Interwoven threads: Theory, practice, and research coming together', in R. L. Irwin and A. de Cosson (eds), *A/r/tography: Rendering Self through Arts-Based Inquiry*. Vancouver, Canada: Pacific Educational Press, 2004.

13 Wall, G., 'Ghost writing: Photographing (the) spectral north'. *Visual Studies* 28, 3 (2013): 238–48.

14 Ibid., pp. 238–48 (240).

15 Derrida, J., *Right of Inspection*, trans. D. Wills. New York, NY: Monacelli Press, 1998.

16 Wall, *Visual Studies*, 2013, pp. 238–48 (248).

17 Fitzpatrick, K., '"That's how the light gets in": Poetry, self, and representation in ethnographic research'. *Cultural Studies <=> Critical Methodologies* 12, 8 (2012): 8–14 (12).

18 Rinehart, R. E., 'Poetic sensibilities, humanities, and wonder: Toward an E/Affective sociology of sport'. *Quest* 62 (2012): 184–201 (191).

19 Maddison-MacFayden, M., 'This white women has journeyed far: Serendipity, counter-stories, hauntings, and ekphrasis as a type of poetic inquiry'. *Morning Watch Journal of Educational and Social Analysis, Special Edition: Narratives of Becoming a Researcher* 40 (2013): 1–15.

20 Watson, C., 'Picturing validity: Autoethnography and the representation of self?' *Qualitative Inquiry* 15, 3 (2009): 526–44.

21 Prendergast, M., *Ekphrasis and Inquiry: Artful Writing on Arts-Based Topics in Educational Research.* Paper presented at the meeting of Second International Imagination in Education Research Group Conference, Simon Fraser University, Vancouver, British Columbia, Canada. http://www.ierg.net/pub_conf2004.php, July 2004.

22 Bruhn, S., *Musical Ekphrasis: Composers Responding to Poetry and Painting.* Hillsdale, NY: Pendragon Press, 2000.

23 Ingold, T., 'Ways of min-walking: Reading, writing, painting'. *Visual Studies* 25, 1 (2010): 15–23.

24 Ibid., pp. 15–23 (20–1).

25 Ibid., pp. 15–23 (22).

26 Spry, T., *Body, Paper, Stage: Writing and Performing Autoethnography.* Walnut Creek, CA: Left Coast, 2011.

27 Ibid., p. 188.

28 Irvine, M., 'Bakhtin: Main theories. Dialogism, polyphony, heteroglossia, open interpretation'. *A Student's Guide.* Retrieved from http://www9.georgetown.edu/faculty/irvinem/theory.bakhtin-maintheory.html, 2013.

29 Maddison-MacFayden, *Morning Watch Journal of Educational and Social Analysis, Special Edition,* 2013, p. 7.

30 Ibid., p. 1.

31 Derrida, *Spectres of Marx,* 1994.

32 Davis, C., 'Hauntology, spectres and phantoms'. *French Studies* 59 (2005): 373–9 (375).

33 Bell, A., 'Authenticity and the project of settler identity in New Zealand'. *Social Analysis* 43 (1999): 122–43.

34 Wells, P., 'A song for Pakeha: Feeling bad about the past is no way to deal with the future'. *Metro*, Issue 362 (April 2012): 102–3.

35 Ruitenberg, C., 'Education as Se'ance: Specters, spirits, and the expansion of memory'. *Interchange* 40, 3 (2009): 295–308 (297).

36 Traue, J., 'Ancestors of the mind: A Pakeha Whakapapa'. Retrieved from http://www.recreationaccess.org.nz/files/traue_ancestors.pdf, 1990.

37 Davis, *French Studies*, 2005, pp. 373–9 (375).

38 Maddison-MacFayden, *Morning Watch Journal of Educational and Social Analysis, Special Edition*, 2013.

39 O'Loughlin, M., 'The curious subject of the child', *The Subject of Childhood*. New York, NY: Peter Lang, 2009.

40 Gramsci, A., *Selections from the Prison Notebooks of Antonio Gramsci*, trans. Q. Hoare and G. Nowell-Smith. New York, NY: International Publishers, 1971.

41 Bell, A., '"Half-castes" and "white natives": The politics of Maori-Pakeha hybrid identities', in C. Bell and S. Matthewman (eds), *Cultural Studies in Aotearoa New Zealand: Identity, Space and Place*. Melbourne, Australia: Oxford University Press, 2005, p. 122.

42 Gye, L., 'Halflives, a mystory: Writing hypertext to learn'. *Fibreculture Journal* 2 (New media, new worlds?) (2003): 5.

43 Addy, N., 'White privilege and cultural racism: Effects on the counselling process'. *New Zealand Journal of Counselling* 28, 1 (2008): 10–23.

44 Ruitenberg, *Interchange*, 2009, pp. 295–308 (299).

45 Bell, A., '"Cultural vandalisim" and Pakeha politics of guilt and responsibility', in P. Spoonely, C. Macpherson and D. Pearson (eds), *Tangata Tangata: The Changing Ethnic Contours of New Zealand*. Palmerston North: Dunmore Press, 2004, p. 12.

46 Ibid., p. 93.

47 Awatere, D., *Maori Sovereignty*. Auckland: Broadsheet, 1984.

48 Hoey, D., 'Chapter 12: There will always be a Taupo: Some reflections on Pākehā culture', in C. Bell and S. Matthewman (eds), *Cultural Studies in Aotearoa New Zealand*. New York, NY: Oxford, 2004.

49 Turner, S., 'Colonialsim continued: Producing the self for export', in J. Docker and G. Fischer (eds), *Race, Colour and Identity in Australia*

and New Zealand. Sydney, Australia: University of New South Wales, 2000.

50 Hall, S., 'Cultural identity and diaspora', in Rutherford (ed.), *Identity*, 1990, pp. 223–37.

51 Bell, A., 'Dilemmas of settler belonging: Roots, routes and redemption in New Zealand national identity claims'. *Sociological Review* 57 (2009): 145–62.

52 Ashmore, R. D., K. Deaux and T. McLaughlin-Volpe, 'An organizing framework for collective identity: Articulation and significance of multidimensionality'. *Psychological Bulletin* 130, 1 (2004): 80–114.

53 Webber, M., *What I Am or Who I Am? Adolescent Racial-ethnic Identity Behaviors, Perceptions and Challenges*. Unpublished doctoral thesis, Research. The University of Auckland, Auckland, 2011.

54 Phinney, J. S. and A. Ong, 'Conceptualization and measurement of ethnic identity: Current status and future directions'. *Journal of Counseling Psychology: Measurement of Ethnic Identity* 54, 3 (2007): 47.

55 Saldana, J., *The Coding Manual for Qualitative Researchers*. Thousand Oaks, CA: Sage, 2009.

56 Kincheloe, J. L., P. McLaren and S. R. Steinberg, 'Critical pedagogy, and qualitative research: Moving to the bricolage', in Denzin and Lincoln (eds), *The SAGE Handbook of Qualitative Research*, 4th edn, 2011.

57 Becker cited in Denzin and Lincoln (eds), *The SAGE Handbook of Qualitative Research*, 4th edn, 2011, p. 4.

58 Wall, S., 'An autoethnography on learning about autoethnography'. *International Journal of Qualitative Methods* 5, 2 (2006).

59 Starr, L. J., 'The use of autoethnography in educational research: Locating who we are in what we do'. *Canadian Journal for New Scholars in Education/Revue Canadienne des jeunes chercheur(e)s en education* 3, 1 (2010).

60 Wells, *Metro*, April 2012, pp. 102–3.

61 Hall, S., 'Cultural identity and diaspora', in Rutherford (ed.), *Identity*, 1990, pp. 223–37, 394.

62 Said, E., *Culture and Imperialism*. London, UK: Vintage Press, 1993.

63 Bell, A., 'Bifurcation or entanglement? Settler identity and biculturalism in Aotearoa New Zealand'. *Continuum: Journal of Media and Cultural Studies* 20 (2006): 253–68.

64 Ingold, *Visual Studies*, 2010, pp. 15–23.

65 Butler-Kisber, L. and M. Stewart, 'The use of poetry clusters in poetic inquiry', in Prendergast, Leggo and Sameshima (eds), *Poetic Inquiry*, 2009, pp. 3–12.

Chapter 7

1 Eisner, Elliot, 'Does Arts based research Have a Future? Inaugural Lecture for the First European Conference on Arts based research: Belfast, Northern Ireland, June 2005'. *Studies in Art Education* 48, 1, Arts based research in Art Education (Fall 2006): 9–18; Haseman, Bradley, 'A manifesto for performative research'. *Media International Australia Incorporating Culture and Policy Journal* 118 (2006): 98; Bolt, Barbara, 'A Performative Paradigm for the Creative Arts?' *Working Papers in Art and Design* 5 (2008). http://www.herts.ac.uk/_data/assets/pdf_file/0015/12417/WPIAAD_vol5_bolt.pdf; Jones, Simon, 'The Courage of Complementarity: Practice-as-Research as a Paradigm shift in Performance Studies', in Ludivine Allegue, Simaon Jones, Baz Kershaw and Angela Piccini (eds), *Practice-as-Research: In Performance and Screen*. Great Britain: Palgrave Macmillan, 2009, pp. 18–33; Coessens, Kathleen, Anne Douglas and Darla Crispin, *The Artistic Turn: A Manifesto*. Belgium: Orpheus Institute and Leuven University Press, 2009; Nelson, Robin, *Practice as Research in the Arts: Principles, Protocols, Pedagogies, Resistance*. http://qut.eblib.com.au.ezp01.library.qut.edu.au/patron/FullRecord.aspx?p=1209462, accessed 30 September 2013.

2 Haseman, *Media International Australia Incorporating Culture and Policy Journal*, p. 98.

3 Haseman, Bradley, 'Rupture and Recognition: Identifying the Performative Research Paradigm', in Estelle Barrett and Barbara Bolt (eds), *Practice as Research*, LB. London: I.B.Tauris & Co. Ltd, 2007.

4   Haseman, *Practice as Research*, 2007.

5   Bolt, *Working Papers in Art and Design*, http://www.herts.ac.uk/_data/
    assets/pdf_file/0015/12417/WPIAAD_vol5_bolt.pdf.

6   Biggs, Michael and Daniela Buchler, 'Eight criteria for practice-
    based research in the creative and cultural industries'. *Art Design and
    Communication in HE* 7, 1 (2008): 5–18.

7   Rosling, Hans, 'The New Health Gap: Science for Emerging Economies
    vs the Bottom Billion', http://videocast.nih.gov/launch.asp?15636,
    accessed 27 June 2011.

8   The ARC is a statutory authority within the Australian Government's
    Innovation, Industry, Science and Research portfolio. The ARC advises
    the Government on research matters, manages the National Competitive
    Grants Program, a significant component of Australia's investment in
    research and development, and has responsibility for the Excellence in
    Research for Australia (ERA) initiative. http://www.arc.gov.au/about_
    arc/default.htm.

9   This linkage research grant was a partnership between QUT, the ARC
    and the National AIDS Council Secretariat (NACS) PNG; Porgera Joint
    Venture/Barrick Gold; University of Goroka (UOG); and Marie Stopes
    International PNG and associate partnership with University of Papua
    New Guinea.

10 Bharucha, Rustom, *Theatre and the World: Performance and the Politics
    of Culture*. London and New York: Routledge, 1993, p. 7.

11 Bharucha, *Theatre and the World*, 1993, p. 7.

12 Murphy, Greg, *Fears of Loss, Tears of Joy*. Port Moresby: University of
    PNG Press and Bookshop, 2010, p. 58–69.

13 Pavis, Patrice, *Analyzing Performance*, trans. David Williams. Ann
    Arbor: University of Michigan Press, 1996, p. 16.

14 Murphy, *Fears of Loss, Tears of Joy*, 2010, p. 212.

15 Haseman, Bradley, Andrea Baldwin and Hayley Linthwaite, 'Folk Opera:
    Stories crossing borders in Papua New Guinea'. *Research in Drama
    Education* 19, 1 (2014): 98–109.

16 Biggs and Buchler, *Art Design and Communication in HE*, p. 8.

17 Ibid., p. 10.

18   Denzin, Norman K. and Yvonna S. Lincoln (eds), *The Sage Handbook of Qualitative Research*. California: Sage Publications, 2005, pp. 22–6.

19   Biggs and Buchler, *Art Design and Communication in HE*, p. 11.

20   Gray, Carol, 'Inquiry through practice: Developing appropriate research Strategies', 1996. http://www2.rgu.ac.uk/criad/cgpapers/ngnm/ngnm. htm (accessed 12 January 2005), p. 3.

21   Ibid.

22   Biggs and Buchler, *Art Design and Communication in HE*, p. 9.

23   Australian Research Council, *Life Drama – Sexual health promotion in Papua New Guinea: A Community Capacity-Building Approach using Drama-Based Experiential Learning Methods*. Linkage Projects Scheme LP0882458.

24   Balkema, Annette and Hank Slager, *Artistic Research, Lier en Boog Series of Philosophy of Art and Art Theory*. Amsterdam: Rodopi, 2004, pp. 157–79.

25   Biggs and Buchler, *Art Design and Communication in HE*, p. 10.

26   Schwandt, Thomas A., *Dictionary of Qualitative Inquiry*. London: Paul Chapman, 2001, p. 248.

27   Biggs and Buchler, *Art Design and Communication in HE*, p. 12.

28   Lynch, Clifford, 'Jim Gray's Fourth Paradigm and the Construction of the Scientific Record', in Tony Hey, Stewart Tansley and Kristin Tolle (eds), *The Fourth Paradigm: Data-Intensive Scientific Discovery*. Washington: Microsoft Research, 2009, pp. 177–83.

Select Bibliography

Ackroyd, J. (1999). 'Applied theatre: Problems and possibilities'. *Applied Theatre Research Journal* [online serial]. Available at http:www.gu.edu/centre/atr.

Ackroyd, J. and O'Toole, J. (2010). *Performing Research : Tensions, Triumphs and Trade-offs of Ethnodrama*. Stoke-on-Trent: Trentham.

Anderson, M. (2014). 'The challenge of post-normality to drama education and applied theatre'. *Research in Drama Education*, 19(1), 110–20.

Anderson, M. and O'Connor, P. (2013). 'Applied theatre as research: Provoking the possibilities'. *Applied Theatre Research*, 1(2), 189–202.

Balfour, M. (2009). 'The politics of intention: Looking for a theatre of little changes'. *Research in Drama Education*, 14(3), 347–59.

Barone, T. and Eisner, E. (2001). *Arts Based Research*. Thousand Oaks, CA: Sage.

Belliveau, G. and Lea, G. W. (2011). 'Research-based theatre in education'. In S. Shonmann (Ed.), *Key Concepts in Drama Education*. Rotterdam, Holland: Sense Publishers, pp. 333–8.

Bergold, J. and Thomas, S. (January 2012). 'Participatory research methods: A methodological approach in motion'. In Forum Qualitative Sozialforschung/Forum: *Qualitative Social Research*, 13(1).

Boal, A. (1979). *Theatre of the Oppressed*. New York: Urizen Books.

—(1995). *The Rainbow of Desire*. London: Routledge.

Bolton, G. (1979). *Towards a Theory of Drama in Education*. Harlow: Longman.

Brown, L. and Strega, S. (Eds) (2005). *Research as Resistance: Critical, Indigenous, and Anti-Oppressive Approaches*. Toronto, ON: Canadian Scholars Press.

Cahill, H. (2006). 'Research acts: Using the drama workshop as a site for conducting participatory action research'. *NJ*, 30(2), 61–72.

Carroll, J. (1986). 'Framing drama: Some strategies'. *NADIE Journal*, 10(2), 5–7.

—(2009). 'Point of view: Linking applied drama and digital games'. In M. Anderson, J. Carroll and D. Cameron (Eds), *Drama Education with Digital Technology*. London: Continuum International Publishing Group, pp. 81–97.

Carroll, J., Anderson, M. and Cameron, D. (2006). *Real Players? Drama, Technology and Education*. Trentham Book: Stoke on Trent.

Conquerwood, D. (1985). 'Performing as a moral act: Ethical dimensions of the ethnography of performance'. *Literature in Performance*, 5(2), 1–13.

Denzin, N. (2003). *Performance Ethnography: Critical Pedagogy and the Politics of Culture*. USA: Sage Publications.

—(2006). 'The politics and ethics of performance pedagogy'. In D. S. Madison and J. Hamera (Eds), *The SAGE Handbook of Performance Studies*. London, UK: SAGE, pp. 325–36 (334).

Dewey, J. (1916). *Democracy and Education: An Introduction to the Philosophy of Education*. New York: MacMillan.

Dixon, M. and Senior, K. (2009). 'Traversing theory and transgressing academic discourses: Arts-based research in teacher education'. *International Journal of Education & the Arts*, 10(24). Retrieved 15 March 2014 from http://www.ijea.org/v10n24/, p. 6.

Donmoyer, R. and Yennie-Donmoyer, J. (1995). 'Data as drama: Reflections on the use of readers theatre as a mode of qualitative data display'. *Qualitative Inquiry*, 1(4), 402–28 (416).

Eisner, E. (April 1981). 'On the differences between scientific and artistic approaches to qualitative research'. *Educational Researcher*, 10(4), 5–9 (6).

—(2013). 'Does arts-based research have a future?' Inagural Lecture for the First European Conference on Arts-Based Research: Belfast, Northern Ireland, June 2005. Retrieved 19 November 2013 from http://www.jstor.org/stable/pdfplus/25475802.pdf?acceptTC=true&acceptTC=true&jpdConfirm=true, p. 29.

Etherton, M. and Prentki, T. (June 2006). Editorial in *Research in Drama Education*, 11(2). Taylor & Francis: United Kingdom.

Fels, L. and Belliveau, G. (2008). *Exploring Curriculum: Performative Inquiry, Role Drama, and Learning*. Vancouver, British Colombia: Pacific Educational Press.

Freire, P. (1972). *Pedagogy of the Oppressed*. Harmondsworth: Penguin Books.

—(2005). *Pedagogy of Hope*. London: Bloomsbury.

Gallagher, K. (2011). 'Theatre as methodology or, what experimentation affords us'. In S. Shonmann (Ed.), *Key Concepts in Theatre/Drama Education*. Rotterdam, Netherlands: Sense Publishers, pp. 327–31 (328).

Giroux, H. (2003). *Public Time and Educated Hope: Educational Leadership and the War Against Youth*. www.ciconline.com/wo4-democracy, May 2004.

Goffman, E. (1969). *The Presentation of Self in Everyday Life*. London: Allen Lane.

Haseman, B. (2006). 'A manifesto for performative research'. *Media International Australia Incorporating Culture and Policy*, 118, 98–106.

Haseman, B. and Mafe, D. (2009). 'Acquiring know-how: Research training tor practice – led research'. In H. Smith and R. T. Dean (Eds), *Practice – Led Research, Research Led Practice in the Creative Arts*. Edinburgh: Edinburgh University Press, pp. 211–29.

Henry, M. (2000). 'Drama's ways of learning'. *Research in Drama Education: The Journal of Applied Theatre and Performance*, 5(1), 45–62 (51).

Kemmis, S. and McTaggart, R. (2005). 'Communicative action and the public sphere'. In N. K. Denzin and Y. S. Lincoln (Eds), *The Sage Handbook of Qualitative Research*, 3, 559–603.

Kovach, M. (2010). 'Conversational method in indigenous research in first people'. *Child & Family Review*, 5(1), 40.

Leavy, P. (2009). *Method Meets Art: Arts-Based Research Practice*. New York: The Guilford Press.

McNiff, S. (2007). *Art-Based Research*. London: Jessica Kingsley Publishers.

Norris, J. (2009). *Playbuilding as Qualitative Research: A Participatory Arts-Based Approach*. Walnut Creek, CA: Left Coast Press.

O'Connor, P. (2007). 'Applied theatre: Pure of heart-naively complicit'. *Caribbean Quarterly*, 53(1 and 2), 23–37.

O'Toole, J. (1992). *The Process of Drama*. London: Routledge.

Osterland, E. (2013). 'Evalution of theatre for social change: What counts and what is being counted?' In *Applied Theatre Research*, vol. 1, no. 1: Intellect Journals: United Kingdom.

Rossatto, C. (2005). *Engaging Paulo Freire's Pedagogy of Possibility*. Toronto: Rowan and Littlefield Publishers, p. 81.

Saldana, J. (2011). *Ethnotheatre: Research From Page to Stage*. Walnut Creek, CA: Left Coast Press.

Sardar, Z. (June 2010). 'Welcome to postnormal times'. *Futures*, 42(5), 435–44 (436).

Smith, L. (1999). *Decolonizing Methodologies: Research and Indigenous Peoples*, 2nd edn. London and New York: Zed Books, p. 176.

Springgay, S. and Irwin, R. L. (Eds) (2008). *Being with a/r/tography*. Rotterdam: Sense Publishers.

Thompson, J. (2008). 'The ends of Applied Theatre'. In Sheila Preston and Tim Prentki (Eds), *The Applied Theatre Reader*. London: Routledge, pp. 116–24.

—(2009). *Performance Affects*. London: Palgrave Macmillan, p. 2.

Winston, J. (2011). *Beauty and Education*. London: Routledge.

Author Index

Subject Index